Writing the Field Recording

Writing the Field Recording

Sound, Word, Environment

Edited by Stephen Benson and
Will Montgomery

EDINBURGH
University Press

Edinburgh University Press is one of the leading university presses in the UK. We publish academic books and journals in our selected subject areas across the humanities and social sciences, combining cutting-edge scholarship with high editorial and production values to produce academic works of lasting importance. For more information visit our website: edinburghuniversitypress.com

Edinburgh University Press Ltd
The Tun – Holyrood Road,
12(2f) Jackson's Entry,
Edinburgh EH8 8PJ

First published in hardback by Edinburgh University Press 2018

Typeset in 11/13 Adobe Sabon by
IDSUK (DataConnection) Ltd, and
printed and bound in Great Britain
by CPI Group (UK) Ltd, Croydon, CR0 4YY

A CIP record for this book is available from the British Library
ISBN 978 1 4744 0669 7(hardback)
ISBN 978 1 4744 5480 3(paperback)
ISBN 978 1 4744 0670 3 (webready PDF)
ISBN 978 1 4744 0671 0 (epub)

Contents

Acknowledgements

The editors gratefully acknowledge permission received from the following institutions and individuals to use copyrighted material.

'Field' from *About Looking* by John Berger, © 1980 by John Berger. Photograph © Jean Mohr. Used by permission of Pantheon Books, an imprint of Knopf Doubleday Publishing Group, a division of Penguin Random House LLC, and of Bloomsbury Publishing PLC. All rights reserved.

Permission to reprint examples from Manfred Werder's scores has been kindly granted by the composer and their publishers as follows: Werder, Manfred, 2005[1]. © 2005 Manfred Werder and Edition Wandelweiser GMbH. Reproduced by permission. All rights reserved.

In addition, the editors would like to thank Manfred Werder for permission to quote from unpublished correspondence.

'Description without Place' from *The Collected Poems of Wallace Stevens* by Wallace Stevens, copyright © 1954 by Wallace Stevens and copyright renewed 1982 by Holly Stevens. Used by permission of Alfred A. Knopf, an imprint of the Knopf Doubleday Publishing Group, a division of Penguin Random House LLC. All rights reserved.

'July Mountain' from *Opus Posthumous: Poems, Plays, Prose* by Wallace Stevens, copyright © 1989 by Holly Stevens. Copyright © 1957 by Elsie Stevens and Holly Stevens, copyright renewed 1985 by Holly Stevens. Used by permission of Alfred A. Knopf, an imprint of the Knopf Doubleday Publishing Group, a division of Penguin Random House LLC. All rights reserved.

'Further in the summer than the birds' J 1068/F 895; and 'I've heard an organ talk sometimes' J 183/F 211 by Emily Dickinson, from *The Poems Of Emily Dickinson: Reading Edition*, edited by Ralph W. Franklin (Cambridge, MA: The Belknap Press of Harvard University Press), Copyright © 1998, 1999 by the President and Fellows of

Harvard College. Copyright © 1951, 1955 by the President and Fellows of Harvard College. Copyright © renewed 1979, 1983 by the President and Fellows of Harvard College. Copyright © 1914, 1918, 1919, 1924, 1929, 1930, 1932, 1935, 1937, 1942 by Martha Dickinson Bianchi. Copyright © 1952, 1957, 1958, 1963, 1965 by Mary L. Hampson.

'Disquiet' text © Lisa Robertson, published in *Nilling* (Toronto: BookThug, 2012). Reprinted with permission. Prior to its publication in *Nilling*, 'Disquiet' had appeared in *Anglophonia Caliban* and *dANDelion Magazine*.

Audio material available at https://edinburghuniversitypress.com/ book-writing-the-field-recording-hb.html [click on the 'resources' tab]. comprises illustrative excerpts from Eva-Maria Houben's *druids and questions*, CD (Wandelweiser, EWR 1104, 2011); Michael Pisaro and Greg Stuart's *July Mountain* (Gravity Wave, gw 002, 2010); and Graham Lambkin and Jason Lescalleet's *The Breadwinner* (Erstwhile 052, 2008) and *Air Supply* (Erstwhile 059, 2010) (both used with the permission of the musicians and Jon Abbey of Erstwhile Records). Lisa Robertson and Jonathan Skinner's contributions to this book are designed to be read alongside field recordings made by the authors. All rights reserved.

The editors wish to thank Jackie Jones, James Dale and Adela Rauchova of Edinburgh University Press.

Introduction: Writing the Field Recording

Stephen Benson and Will Montgomery

A hen's cackle has a 'distinct, sharp-edged existence' for John Berger, on the first page of his brief and enigmatic essay 'Field', which closes his 1980 book *About Looking*.[1] The book collects essay from the 1960s and 1970s on topics as diverse as Don McCullin's war photography, the cartoonishness of Francis Bacon and René Magritte's predilection for figures of the impossible. In the suggestive final essay, which is unlike any of the others, the writer becomes aware of an 'intense experience of freedom' as the acoustic event of the hen's cackle interrupts the 'roar' of undifferentiated experience, the more or less congested inward reverie in which we all subsist. The essays in the present collection exist in a clearing made possible by Berger's essay. None is a direct response to it, but they are all, in ways that are more or less direct, engaged with its workings and its provocations.[2]

'Field' primarily concerns visual experience: after the opening, Berger outlines a demarcated space of possibility, a field that both hosts significant events, and, as the essay progresses, becomes an event itself (a paradox Berger acknowledges). In editing this book, our concern has been to turn our attention back towards the acoustic origins of Berger's definition of the field.

At the opening of his essay, Berger attributes contradictory qualities to the experience he is describing: a silence that becomes a roar, and a 'tiny hub of dense, silent noise'. The terms of the argument seem Cagean, both through their complication of silence and their refusal to demarcate aesthetic and everyday events: 'I knew that in that field I could listen to all sounds, all music'.[3] The experience that Berger is describing involves a particular framing of experience – a focusing of attention within determinate spatial and temporal parameters.

The 'field' is both a two-dimensional space akin to a canvas and a three-dimensional space that is open, like a stage, to 'exits and entrances'. However, Berger promptly dismisses these analogies 'because they invoke a cultural context which, if it has anything what-soever to do with the experience in question, can only refer *back* to it rather than precede it'.[4] The experience of 'field', then, is a founda-tional one that may inform subsequent cultural constructions of field but is not exhausted by them. In other words, Berger is describing a non-verbal, pre-aesthetic experience that may be re-encountered in a 'cultural context' through verbal or visual stimuli.

Berger is not writing about experience per se, but about a particular kind of experience that disrupts the unreflective lived narratives of self-hood. This experience is 'illogical' and it has the potential to generate both happiness and freedom. The delimitation of the field of opera-tion is a precondition for the experience. An event, which must not be too pronounced or dramatic, precipitates a distinct kind of aware-ness, a highly attuned perception of the world unfolding in time. One thing leads to another: 'Having noticed the dog, you notice a butterfly. Having noticed the horses, you hear a woodpecker and then see it fly across a corner of the field. You watch a child walking and when he has left the field deserted and eventless, you notice a cat jump down into it from the top of a wall.'[5] All of these miniature occurrences are insignificant in themselves, and there is no need to relate one event to another, but Berger is interested in a distinct perceptual attitude in which the stream of internal thought is quietened and the rich contin-gency of the world is made available to the perceiver.

Berger is reluctant to present his argument in any particular theoretical idiom. While he acknowledges that psychoanalysis may locate the origins of this experience in infancy – 'Remember what it was like to be sung to sleep', he writes – he rejects this way of theorising his notion of field because it might 'systematise' what he is addressing.[6] Yet, to take one example, psychoanalytic writer Christopher Bollas in his book *Being a Character* provides a use-fully a-systemic description of the kinds of non-verbal triggers from one's lived personal history that may give a particular experience its intensity: 'the experience is more a dense condensation of instinctual urges, somatic states, body positions, proprioceptive organisings, images, part sentences, abstract thoughts, sensed memories, recol-lections and felt affinities, all of a piece. It is impossible to put this complexity into words'.[7] Bollas's terms are helpful, as they link the somatic and linguistic traces of unconscious content to the narra-tive unfolding of experience that Berger describes. While the factors that confer distinctive qualities upon a particular experience will vary enormously from perceiver to perceiver, what is most enlivening in Berger's essay is the liberatory potential of delimitation. Berger's

<u>field is a space of framed potential, a scene that disrupts ordinary experience.</u> However lacking in combative rhetoric, this field is a reframing of the disruptive potential of avant-garde art. <u>His event is external to the perceiver but it makes that perceiver aware of the multifarious happening of the world.</u> There is a 'minimum of order' in this arrangement, and the intensity of the perceiver's experience is dependent on non-intentional factors. The world that is other to the self is encountered in ways that pleasurably exceed the parameters of everyday experience. Indeed, the framing action of the field is encountered as generative.

We are drawn to the suggestive potential of Berger's concept of field for artists. As several of our contributors note, the term 'field' has many meanings. We wish to explore the affinities between two activities that lie to one side of the visual arts, but seem especially responsive to Berger's essay: field recording and literature. For some of our contributors, an understanding of 'field' is relevant to the relatively under-theorised practice of field recording, while for others the field recording becomes a means of figuring acoustic attention. Some contributors take concepts of 'field' and 'field recording' as the points of departure for a kind of writing that attends to the peculiar combination of materiality and elusiveness that characterises sound. Poetry and text scores are explored as points at which the friction between text and sound is offered to the reader and listener's attention. None of these essays seeks to outline a specifically Berger-esque aesthetic. Rather, Berger's essay is taken as a catalyst, a clearing of space for thought; an event such as the hen's cackle that so provoked Berger himself.

Our book is divided into three sections, each of which opens a different perspective on the field: 'Opening the Field', 'The Poetics of the Field' and 'The Field in Practice'. In the first of these sections, the title of which echoes Robert Duncan's clearing of textual space for open-field poetics, the book explores some of the key relationships between literature and music in recent practice. We argue for rich affinities between literature and field recording, and our second section addresses the presence of poetry in various field-recording-related works. Our third section comprises creative-critical essays that respond to the uncertain relationship between words and sounds by innovating with the essay format.

With felicitous synchronicity, 1971, the year of Berger's 'Field', also saw the publication of Ponge's *La Fabrique du Pré – The Making of the* Pré – the journal-essay that is a prepositional accompaniment for Ponge's 1964 poem 'Le Pré'. The notes begin in 1960: 'What I feel like writing is "The Pré": a 'meadow', a *pré* between woods (and rocks) and stream (and rocks)'.[8] Ponge, like Berger, has in mind a specific location in France, in this case, 'at Chambon-sur-Lignon . . . not far from Chantegrenouille' (p. 21). The published volume includes a photograph of 'the spot where we were, the spot where we happened to be', one of a number of related images – paintings, music manuscript, maps – presented in the text as another set of parallel elements, each its own spot, now, for the reader. Ponge's location is different from that of Berger. He overlooks a scene from 'among the rocks', whereas Berger is adjacent to his field, parked alongside (although Berger's *'ideal* field' can be 'seen either from above . . . or from below'); and Ponge's spot, in being a *pré*, is more eventful than Berger's, and differently, a site of water, trees and rocks. The differences are manifold; and yet as a contemporaneous instance of what we might call field thinking, the Ponge bears an extraordinarily rich relation to the Berger, and to the matter, conceived in the broadest sense, of a field and of recording.

Ponge's meadow is an occasion happened across, what Berger calls 'the experience'. It is an event marked in the poem as 'propose[d]' to us by Nature' (p. 225). But it is also, as happening, 'The very thing to which we were disposed'. It becomes in this double-sided relation a 'proposition' akin to the ground/event of Berger's field, the latter of which works, conceptually, the 'prefix of prefixes' that is given by and discovered via the *pré* (p. 227). The site, in being 'limited', precedes its framing by an act of attention, but once framed it is also a location generative of the matter newly to hand. Where Berger's brief but concentrated prose essays the possibility of what he intuits and wishes to articulate – we feel the thinking of the sentences as happening unobstrusively in the language – Ponge's hybrid work, a field open unto itself, is laid out in a gradually expanding surface of associations: etymological, topographical, spatial, historical, tropological, philosophical and lyrical. These associations are both the material of the present work and the workings towards its becoming present ('Prefix, already, in prefix, present indeed in present' (p. 227)). Ponge is the more materialist of the two, here at least, in making bountifully apparent language's own field records. Hence the notion of a field recording as both a marking of certain of the specificities of a site and the siting of a series of idiomatic marks. Again, the *pré*, in its fullest resonance, is at once the spot in which something has happened, in which something is happening and in which, now and processually, something will be made to happen. As such, it is the spot in which something will be found to have happened.

Berger's field, described initially as having 'interrupted' conscious self-making, comes to be acknowledged in the closing lines as manifestly of 'the same proportions as your own life'. Hence, 'Suddenly', not to say movingly, 'a happiness which is instantly recognizable as your own', a sentiment the inflection of which is echoed in Ponge's realisation, made on a November night in 1962, that his is to be a praise poem, to the 'Nature' of the world and of its human selves (p. 89). Both notes, of happiness and of praise, are far from incidental. The field recording, as conceived and performed in these two exploratory texts, is an act of acknowledgement as well as a 'proposition'. Both Berger and Ponge are concerned with the field in the broadest sense of an openness of orientation, what the latter calls a 'way of being'. The orientation is ecological, an imbrication of site and siting, of field and recording.

* * *

While the practice of field recording simply means recording outside the studio, the term has taken on different meanings in recent decades. It was once used to describe recordings of, say, folk music made by ethnomusicologists 'in the field', but it now embraces the recording of everything from rural soundscapes to contact-mic'd domestic appliances, industrial machinery to the sounds of pondweed, prawns or herring, distant thunderstorms detected with a VLF (very low frequency) recorder to the footsteps of ants. Ecologists such as Bernie Krause document the impoverishment of natural environments through the thinning-out of acoustic ambiences. Sound can be aestheticised and weaponised: the devastating march of the bark beetle through North American forestry is documented by David Dunn through quasi-musical field-recording collages on one hand, while, on the other, he uses sound recordings to disrupt the reproductive cycle of the pest.[9] Outside academia, inexpensive digital audio recorders have offered opportunities to amateur and semi-professional recordists, from weekend nature recordists to bedroom bricoleurs. In the world of experimental music, a disenchantment with both free improvisation and electronica created the climate for a turn towards sounds that were sourced from neither musical instruments nor computers. The term 'field recording' has passed from a description of a non-studio recording to an uneven and hazily defined subgenre. Field recordings, processed and unprocessed, are used in soundscape composition, musique concrète and sound art. Many labels issue such work in CD format. Netlabels and audio-streaming platforms such as SoundCloud provide a forum for the sharing of audio that bypasses the old channels of distribution. Online mailing lists are dedicated to topics as diverse as Sound Studies, species recording and DIY microphone manufacture. A number of sound maps (including one based on field-recording realisations of John Cage's *4'33"*) allow listeners both to hear and upload recordings made almost anywhere in the world.

For the influential soundscape theorist R. Murray Schafer, the world can be treated as a 'macrocosmic musical composition'.[10] While Schafer's concept of sound is somewhat atavistic – grounded in a celebration of pre-industrial listening environments – his commitment to a renovation of listening habits provided a powerful impulse, particularly for those who sought to capture the richness of the natural world, and to document vanishing environments. Acoustic ecology and the emerging discipline of soundscape studies offered a framework for recordists such as Hildegard Westerkamp, Douglas Dunn, Barry Truax, Peter Cusack and Douglas Quin. Chris Watson's releases on the Touch label took soundscape-composition into territory influenced by electronic and industrial music (Watson is a former member of Cabaret Voltaire).[11] Watson's example notwithstanding, field recording did not really become a generalised activity until the latter part of the 2000s. Francisco López, Jacob Kirkegaard, Lee Patterson, Robert Curgenven, Olivia Block, Toshiya Tsunoda and Jana Winderen each found highly distinctive ways of working with non-studio sound.

In our book, the strand of field recording that has most interested us has been related to music, though the relationship between the two has taken many different forms. In particular, we seek to explore the ways in which this music-oriented practice encounters literary language, whether (to take just three examples) through musical responses to poetry, the para-poetic qualities of text scores, or creative-critical texts that explore concepts of listening by other means than the microphone.

In his influential book *The Soundscape*, Schafer points to Cage's influence, and, beyond Cage, the nineteenth-century author and naturalist Henry David Thoreau.[12] Acute descriptions of sound abound in Thoreau's *Journal*, where the telegraph wire is read as an Aeolian harp, and where, in July 1851, he writes, 'This earth was the most glorious musical instrument'.[13] In a beautiful passage from the 'Sounds' chapter of *Walden*, the sound of a church bell is enriched by the natural environment through which it echoes and resonates. Thoreau was crucial to Cage's late work. He mined the *Journal* for sound-related words in his monumental *Empty Words* multimedia performance piece. The language of the journal, especially its 'references to sounds or silence', is treated by Cage after the ecological manner of a de- or re-composition, as 'material' turned over in four increments.[14] The result, *Empty Words*, is a newly sounding work, resolutely Cagean in its singular acoustemology: a field recording of a field recording. *Mureau*, another version of Thoreau, is no less impressive. Cage listens to Thoreau's listening and translates it into another thing altogether. Cage's other literary lodestone was James Joyce's *Finnegans Wake*, from which he generated several series of mesostics, culminating in the colossal *Roaratorio, an Irish Circus on Finnegans Wake*. This piece combines a reading of the second writing-through of *Finnegans Wake* with field recordings made at places and with sounds mentioned in Joyce's novel, and with Irish traditional music.

Such historical confluences of text and sound are important to this volume. We wish to explore some of the ways in which contemporary writers, composers and artists tackle this confluence, which, in the words of composer Michael Pisaro, might open up an 'alternate kind of reading'.[15] In an era in which recorded sound is of an unprecedented ubiquity, what is its relation to that other form of encrypted sound, writing? Can a sound-oriented sensibility lead to a new kind of writing? And can sound recordings lead us to new readings of old texts? How useful, or even possible, is the description of sound? Can a field recording be written down?

Pisaro's chapter is an important statement on the roles that field recording and poetry play in his work. The chapter begins with a differentiation of what, for Pisaro, are key compositional categories: location, space and place. He discusses his collaboration with Japanese sound artist Toshiya Tsunoda, and, in more detail, his work *July Mountain*, a composition based on field recordings and percussion that is catalysed by Wallace Stevens's late poem of the same name. A great number of Pisaro's compositions engage poetry in one way or another, and this essay opens up the potential for encounters between environmental sound, musical sound and literary texts.

Dominic Lash's chapter also reflects on the relationship between text and music. Lash focuses on a composition that exists in a post-Cagean space of listening. Eva-Maria Houben's electroacoustic work *druids and questions* attends to a nineteenth-century author with an acute ear, Emily Dickinson, and places her writing alongside the work of another American nonconformist, Charles Ives. Lash's essay considers the ways in which materials by Dickinson and Ives are filtered through Houben's organ recordings, arriving at a dynamic concept of field. Lash notes a preoccupation with temporality in Houben, Dickinson and Ives, arguing moreover that all three 'confront wildly disjunctive phenomena with one another: extremes of scale, of time, of resemblance, of origin'.

Lash has worked closely with Compost & Height, initially a label but then a web-based nexus of activity that seeks to establish connections between field recording, composition and writing. The organisers, Sarah Hughes and Patrick Farmer (the latter of whom also contributes to this volume), form part of an international network in which post-Cagean text scores (often aligned with the Wandelweiser composers' collective), free improvisation, field recording and literature overlap.[16] What we observe, then, is a cluster of activity that spans disciplines, but that is still usually confined to the musical sphere and to a musical audience. Our aim with this book is to broaden the purchase of this fascinating set of sound-motivated investigations. Schafer's concept of macrocosmic composition seems anachronistic now, in our time of environmental blight, but the literary sensibility that runs through *The Soundscape* is worth recovering. We believe that the relationship between two forms of recording – words and sounds – is yielding art that has largely escaped attention outside the networks that generate it.

* * *

The radical ideas advanced by composer, writer and artist John Cage are close to those of Berger's short essay, and these form a key reference point for many of the artists and practices discussed in this book. However, we want to argue that Cage be encountered as an index of circumscribed potential rather than a figure of unlimited openness. One of the cornerstones of Cage's thought, derived from his reading of Ananda K. Coomaraswamy, is the contention that art should 'imitate nature in its manner of operation', rather than seeking somehow to represent nature.[17] The extent and quality of that imitation was more far-reaching than a loose commitment to, for example, the random patterning of rainfall or snowflakes. In his 1963 text 'Happy New Ears', Cage brings a historical perspective to his understanding of nature: 'Our understanding of "her manner of operation" changes according to advances in the sciences. These advances in this century have brought the term "space-time" into our vocabulary. Thus, the distinctions made between the space and the time arts are at present an oversimplification.' In the essay, Cage aligns space and time, respectively, with the printed text, which had the 'characteristics of objects in space', and performance, which contained 'aspects of processes in time'.[18] Now he wanted to complicate that relationship. It is our view that the text score encompasses both the spatial and processual aspects of Cage's attitude towards the contemporary artwork.

In common with Berger, Cage directs attention away from the organising demands of subjectivity, and towards the destabilising potential of the aleatory. In 'Happy New Ears', he indicates the potential freedom that can be attained by groups of performers:

> [M]usicians, since they are several people rather than one person as a painter or sculptor is, are now able to be independent each from another. A composer writes at this moment indeterminately. The performers are no longer his servants but are freemen. A composer writes parts but, leaving their relationship unfixed, he writes no scores. Sound sources are at a multiplicity of points in space with respect to the audience so that each listener's experience is his own.[19]

While the liberatory rhetoric of 'freemen' is, viewed from our own perspective, over-optimistic, the qualified autonomy of Cage's notion of performance is enhanced in the context of group practice. Several independent lines may be pursued at the same time. With 'multiplicity of points in space', Cage may be thinking not only of the importance of placement to an acoustic experience, but of happenings and the potential for spatialised performance. The coincident occurrence of discrete systems was something he encouraged in his work: the simultaneous performance of distinct compositions, for example, or the parallel unfolding of his music and the choreography of Merce Cunningham, the dancers operating independently of the music. A different kind of simultaneity is ventured in the late 'Numbers' pieces, where the number assigned to the composition corresponds to the number of performers. The pieces are divided into time-brackets in which fixed and unfixed events may take place. What emerges is a constantly changing, multi-voiced panorama of sound in which compositional frame and the distinct choices of the performer interact in ways that will vary from realisation to realisation. The 'Numbers' pieces are a good example of the interplay between determinate rigour and freedom, which the composer explored throughout his career. In some compositions, Cage worked with graphic materials in order to find richer means of providing guidance for the performer. In *Variations II*, for example, up to eleven transparent sheets containing lines and dots are superimposed at random and the performer is invited to use the resulting visual information to determine sonic characteristics such as frequency or amplitude. *Variations III* requires the interpretation of randomised visual material according to complex instructions, and is 'for one or any number of people performing any actions'.

A 'multiplicity of points in space' is a means of thinking about the field that finds expression in the work of Michael Pisaro, discussed later in this book (see Pisaro's remarks on points in his first experience of experimental music, Cage's *Winter Music*, and such of his compositions as *A Mist is a Collection of Points*).[20] Here, to one side of the concept of performance, one can encounter the possibility of spatial overdetermination: the field as overloaded environment in which it is hard to allocate significance or apprehend the full density of occurrences. It is not the responsibility of the composer to organise and apportion significance. Such work is, in Cage's view, not 'an attempt to bring order out of chaos nor to suggest improvements in creation, but simply a way of waking up to the very life we're living'.[21] As with Berger, the focus is on an awakening that is transformative but not transcendental.

In his essay 'A Music Lover's Field Companion' he writes of his own realisations, without instruments or audience, of his silent piece (often formalised as *4'33"*, and discussed below): 'I have spent many pleasant hours in the woods conducting performances of my silent transcriptions, that is, for an audience of myself, since they were much longer than the popular length which I have had published.' Cage goes on to describe three movements that are defined first by his actions (the identification of a mushroom), second by the arrival of a buck and a doe, and thirdly by a return to the first part. This performative listening, he writes, has 'all those profound, so-well-known alterations of world feeling associated by German tradition with the A-B-A.'[22] In this view, which finds an echo in the work of Swiss composer Manfred Werder (discussed in this collection by Will Montgomery and Nick Melia), musical performance is reframed as private listening in a reconfigured mode of attention to the world's unfolding.

Unlike musical manuscript, graphic and text scores are not limited to the equal tempered scale. The graphic score and the text score are each a means of arriving at a qualified indeterminacy. With a graphic score, a performer will often decide to align a feature of the score with a particular parameter of a performance – the duration or volume of a particular musical event, for example, might be connected to the length of a line, or its positioning on a page. However, the interpreter, not the composer, will usually decide how to interpret the visual information in the score. A text score has a more complicated relationship to sound than either a conventional score or a graphic score. Words convey semantic information in ways that cannot be replicated by non-verbal means. When strung together in phrases, sentences and paragraphs, words signify in clusters, placing abstract concepts in grammatical relationships that have no graphic equivalent. Text may function as the vehicle for musical information, but it cannot suppress the meaning-making potential of the text-as-text. Whatever the aim of the composer, even the most functional of instructions is likely to convey unintended meanings through sound association, metaphor or idiom in ways that cannot be predicted. Indeterminacy does not operate solely as a compositional principle. It is also a feature of textual communication – one that may be exploited for literary purposes. Some text scores, in other words, have a para-poetic quality, an indeterminacy that may, more or less knowingly, be cultivated by both composer and performer. This feature of the text score has been evident from the earliest mid-twentieth-century experiments.[23]

Cage's most famous and challenging work – possibly the defining challenge of twentieth-century composition – is his *4'33"* or, in a phrase he preferred, his 'silent piece'. As Liz Kotz and others have shown, there are various versions of the composition: *4'33"* exists as a blank staff notation score, a graphic score and a text version.[24] The title was supposed to be the duration, which could be any length, and there could be any number of performers and any instrumentation. The text score has been denigrated by some as a later formalisation of the piece.[25] Kotz argues against this, suggesting that the text score version of *4'33"* ceases to be 'a system of representation and becomes a proposal for action'.[26] She goes on to argue that this work anticipated the development of conceptual art's privileging of concept over enactment:

> by prying open the regulatory relation between sign and realisation, Cagean indeterminacy repositioned writing as a kind of productive mechanism, thereby giving notation a functional and aesthetic autonomy – an autonomy that opened the door for the scores, instructions or snippets of language to themselves *be* the work, while individual realisations occur as 'instances', 'samples', or 'examples' of it.[27]

Viewed in this way, the reduced and functional nature – the very simplicity – of *4'33"* is essential to its enormous disruptive potential.

More than this, it is significant that it has been the third version of the score – the typewritten one – that has been the most influential. The great portability of text, its transposability, means that language can bring a new kind of indeterminacy into play in musical performance. In time, the text score's relation to the performance becomes so oblique that linguistic indeterminacy itself (a phenomenon that Cage awoke to in his later literary texts) complicates the nature and function of the score.

Manfred Werder is of particular importance within the current context for his sustained concern for 'a theoretical and performative use of silence to define the ontological "field"'. Nicholas Melia provides a compact history of the concept of the field as inherited by Berger, taking Michael Faraday as starting point and tracing a passage across from the physical into the social and psychological sciences. The elements of the 'topographical imagery' are various and open to quite different inflections – bodies, events and units; conceptions of space; dynamics and relationality within space and across time – and can be felt still as present within Berger's relatively late recasting. The link with specifically acoustic activity, for Melia, is the matter of silence as reconceived spatially within twentieth-century thought, and as played out by Cage and those practitioners affiliated with the post-Cagean Wandelweiser group. As such, Melia draws the link with Berger, a link made via, not to say within, a form of field thinking. In Werder's case, and as detailed here in Will Montgomery's essay, the specific form of this thinking is in part the material of the text score, the 'plane' of which is conceived by Werder as 'a field of incidence – unassignable unpredictability'. The merest fragments from literature and philosophy, presented without framing guidance, establish a 'small textual clearing' the singular and non-pejorative insufficiency of which undoes received conventions of the relation of sound to world, and of performer to listener. The field, whether understood in terms of text score, performance, acoustic event or recording, is opened as potential – a potential that remains.

Cage taught composition in the New School for Social Research in New York for five years from 1956. The most significant consequence of this period was the emergence of the Fluxus group of artists. Dick Higgins, Alison Knowles, La Monte Young, George Brecht, Al Hansen and Jackson Mac Low all attended Cage's classes. They were influenced by Cage and were interested in working with text scores as a cross-disciplinary tool. Brecht developed what he called 'event scores' – short texts notionally designed to outline the parameters of a performance. This mode of operation was widely adopted within the evolving international Fluxus movement, and used by artists including Wolf Vostell, Milan Knizak, Nam June Paik and Mieko Shiomi.[28] Brecht's 1963 collection of event scores *Water Yam* was a set of scores printed on cards packaged in a box – the first in a short series of Fluxus boxes. Most of the cards conform to a deliberately functional formatting style: capitals for titles and bullet points for the details of the score. Many of the scores in the *Water Yam* box are clearly instructions for performance:

BED EVENT

Discover or arrange: ✻

- a white bed
- a black item on or near it[29]

For any spectator or witness to the performance, the decisions made by the interpreter(s) are likely to be as significant in their evaluation of the performance as the performance itself. Interpretation becomes an aesthetic act of equal or greater status to that of the composition of the score. The text score is thus a matrix of possibility, a field of operation that is delimited, but that nonetheless offers enormous freedom to the interpreter. Moreover, the score may also be understood as a self-sufficient textual object – a text in which interpretation entirely eclipses the performative. Read this way, the score merely gestures at performance. Indeed, Fluxus event scores have their most productive afterlife in this way, contemplated as potential rather than actualisation. Some of Brecht's scores stretch the notion of potential performance to an interpretative limit, implicitly proposing textuality rather than performance as their primary sphere of operation:

WORD EVENT

- EXIT[30]

Three words and a bullet point are all that the interpreter is given to work with in this exemplary event score.[31] Such texts, poised between the information-bearing convention of the score, and the suggestive potential of a literary text, have a para-poetic function. They require interpretation, and that interpretation falls between the physical, performative enactment of the text and the kind of internal readerly interpretation that a literary text might elicit. They inhabit, in other words, a terrain that lies between Cage's distinction between the literary and the performative, 'objects in space' and 'processes in time'. The extreme reduction of the score leads to an amplification of interpretative possibilities. The notion of language pregnant with performative potential is important to our collection, which reflects on the possible encounters between the sense encoded in text and the sense encoded in sound.

* * *

The field recording, wherever placed along the dual continua of sound/writing and creative/critical practice, is perhaps the emblematic form or figure for what has been an extraordinary growth and diversification of interest in matters sonic, beginning in the 1990s and blossoming in the decades that have followed. The metaphor of the turn, that trope of tropes, is overused in descriptions of art and thought, but in this case it is warranted; for there has been an acoustic turn, a series of related reorientations so wide-ranging and various that *Sounds: The Ambient Humanities*, the titular proposal made by a recent study, appears far from overstatement.[32] The dramatic increase in field recording-based activity and interest, various in type and orientation, is roughly contemporaneous with this turn; indeed, the two are fascinatingly, if complicatedly, intertwined, a fact attested by a number of the essays gathered here and by many of the recordings themselves. All the constituent parts of an institutional ecosystem thus turned are in place: the anthologies, the review essays, the book series, the keywords, the journals, the educational programmes and, emerging surreptitiously, the canon.[33] The current volume, mindful of the weight of such material, makes no self-justifying claim to outsider status. If, however, the process by which this infrastructure is established, and so quickly, has something about it of the rote, there is no need for despair or disdain; indeed, to respond as such would be to fall prey to a 'sticky sanctity' regarding creative practice that is not less mechanical than are the apparently predictable trajectories of the academic turn.[34] Default characterisations of an organic and animate art tethered and mistranslated by critics are particularly misleading in the case of the field recording, for two reasons. Firstly, the fact, common today across the acoustic, visual and verbal arts, that many practitioners and performers are themselves affiliated or involved in some manner with the academy, albeit often for reasons of exigency. This is not to downplay the tensions of such arrangements or to simplify the complex historical relations existent between an educational sector much expanded, albeit still embattled, and a resourcing of the arts sometimes scandalously depleted. The fact remains nevertheless that a binary-oriented conception of creative and critical practice, within or without the classroom, has become increasingly untenable during the decades of work considered in the present volume.[35]

The second and more immediate reason for resisting an imagined resistance to the prospect of yet one more institutionalised framing is that the act of framing is itself indigenous to the field recording. The signal invention of Cage, one that continues to resonate for musical and artistic practice today, is that of the frame; specifically, of composition, performance and reception, and of the social relations inherent in each, as matters variously of framing.[36] The field recording teaches us about the frame. Hence, for example, Michael Pisaro's 'Ten Framing Considerations of the Field', in which the 'reduction' of the cognitive and auditory field in the act of its recording, that shutting off that is also an opening out, is conceived, with an overt nod to Cage, in terms of a set of framing operations: duration, occasion, location, placement of microphone, together with a series of post-recording decisions.[37] To frame the field recording, in whatever fashion, is thus not to impose on it from an elsewhere but to continue in the spirit of its form. And to say as much is not to claim a simplifying or self-justifying parity for critical practice, rather to suggest that one of the most interesting aspects of the field recording, one of the ways in which it resonates with potential, is its putting into play of the frames by and according to which we experience and come to know the acoustic environment in all its possible and impossible significance.

Such frames are in play in Stephen Benson's chapter, 'The Nondescript', which combines a survey of recent thinking in Sound Studies with close descriptive analysis of a collaborative trilogy made by Graham Lambkin and Jason Lescalleet. Benson situates the work of Lambkin and Lescalleet in relation to their contemporaries, and argues for the significance of the specific motifs of friendship and the domestic to an acoustically inflected notion of the common.

Again, the rise to prominence of the field recording as a phenomenon can be placed alongside the acoustic turn in the humanities. The former could well serve to frame the latter, not only as an analogous repertoire of verbal texts but also acoustically: as sounds to frame and so orientate the propositions of criticism and theory. The possibility of an auditory conception of critical practice, a potentially radical reimagining, is one of the more far-reaching promises of the subject of the present collection: the field recording as a way not only of listening, and of conceiving listening, but also of reading, albeit reading slantwise, in a newly calibrated register. This is the possibility pitched in theoretical terms, and without reference to the field recording except by implication, in Jean-Luc Nancy's *Listening* (*A l'écoute*, 2002), a work of Continental philosophy that has rapidly come to stand as a key work in the acoustic reorientation within and beyond the academy, specifically, in this case, in the field of philosophy. Looking back from the Nancy book, with the benefit of hindsight, we can identify the 1970s as that decade in which the stakes and potential scope of this reorientation were sounded: in Jacques Attali's *Noise: A Political Economy of Music* (1976), *The Soundscape* by R. Murray Schafer (1977), and, to stretch the frame just a little, in several of the volumes of Cage's written oeuvre, the treasures of which are still today being discovered.[38] The resonance of these works, each *sui generis*, began fully to be felt in the 1990s, in the likes of Douglas Kahn and Gregory Whitehead's collection *Sound, Radio and the Avant-Garde* (1992) and Kahn's seminal *Noise, Water, Meat: A History of Sound in the Arts* (1999); and in Michel Chion's *Audio-Vision: Sound of Screen* (1994), Bruce R. Smith's *The Acoustic World of Early Modern England: Attending to the O-Factor* (1999) and Alain Corbin's *Village Bells: Sound and Meaning in the Nineteenth-Century French Countryside* (1998). Peter Szendy's *Listening: A History of Our Ears* (2001) and David Toop's *Ocean of Sound* (2001) marked the continuation, and continued diversification, of interest in the new millennium, since which time there has been a sustained concern for the auditory, conceived in the broadest sense, as marked in such signal works as Jonathan Sterne's *The Audible Past: Cultural Origins of Sound Reproduction* (2003), Don Ihde's *Listening and Voice* (2007), Seth Kim-Cohen's *In the Blink of an Ear: Towards Non-Cochlear Sonic Art* (2009), Salomé Voegelin's *Listening to Noise and Silence: Towards a Philosophy of Sound Art* (2010), Daniela Cascella's *En abîme: Listening, Reading, Writing: An Archival Fiction* (2012) and Brian Kane's *Sound Unseen: Acousmatic Sound in Theory and Practice* (2014), to name but a few. The appearance in 2015 of the first issue of the journal *Sound Studies*, and, most recently, of the English translation of François J. Bonnet's *The Order of Sounds: A Sonorous Archipelago*, suggests no abatement in interest.

The constituent works of sound studies are manifold in orientation, as this briefest of name-checkings indicates: from philosophy, historiography and sociology, to cultural studies, and literary and art criticism, with much hybridity and mixing of modes along the way. Indeed, the field has reached that point of maturity in its life – a further turning point? – at which matters of nomenclature and of sub-fields can be debated at length.[39] With the ready availability, now, of genealogies of the field, the question for the present volume is one of relations, both immediate and more distant, more speculative: what is the relation, beyond the facts of contemporaneity, between the field recording, as practice and as concept, and various of the strands that make up sound studies, with the latter conceived in the broadest of terms? What might each learn from the other regarding the three main constituent elements of concern – listening, sound and writing – in so far as we are able to separate them out?

To begin, the field recording would appear self-evidently to be congruent with the pronounced concentration, within the broad area of sound studies, on listening: as sensory act, as concept and as event. The latter concentration is one of the signal traits of the acoustic turn, exemplified in Nancy's short book. While clearly and variously related to contemporaneous work on the subject, it is to be distinguished both from social and cultural histories of listening and from physiological and analytical accounts. Listening is conceived here ontologically – listening *as such* – in the light of phenomenology, aesthetics and psychoanalysis. The relatively identifiable turn in orientation – to speak in the broadest of introductory registers – involves a move away from and against an 'ocular-centric' philosophy, perceived as dominant in the Western tradition, for which sight is the presiding and defining sense, never more resolutely than in its underpinning presence in conceptions and figurings of sense itself, and of the self that senses: in the primal subject–object scenario of seeing and seen and the various binary fundamentals that follow; in sense conceived first and foremost as a subject's understanding, hence as self-constituting meaning-making; and of sense in this dispensation as disavowing and repressing the sensory as a matter of the body as matter. Against this discursive backdrop, Nancy begins by wondering whether 'listening is something of which philosophy is capable', a question to which his own thought is resonating response, as is that of others writing contemporaneously on and around the subject: Jean-François Lyotard, Peter Szendy, Adriana Cavarero and François J. Bonnet (and, before them, Jacques Attali), together with those commentators concerned to develop the field, including Christoph Cox, Anthony Gritten and Adrienne Janus.

Nancy's listening subject – 'The subject of listening or the subject who is listening' – is avowedly not phenomenological or philosophical: 'he [*sic*] is perhaps no subject at all, expect as the place of resonance, of its infinite tension and rebound, the amplitude of sonorous deployment and the slightness of its simultaneous redeployment'.[40] Listening, as figure and site, is both prior to and other than sense conceived as meaning and to the subject understood as that which senses; and articulate listening thus conceived involves the performative playing of a repertoire of acoustically inflected motifs: 'accent, tone, timbre, resonance, and sound' (p. 3). Where hearing is a teleological 'straining towards a possible meaning', 'To be listening is always to be on the edge of meaning' (pp. 6–7), hence the invention of the sense of listening as 'a fundamental resonance . . . resonance as a foundation, as a first or last profundity of "sense" itself' (p. 6). The figure of resonance gives a founding relationality, not externally, as a resonance of subject and object – the subject is a quasi-tympanic 'place of resonance' – but within, and returning ever anew: 'To be listening is thus to enter into tension and to be on the lookout for a relation to self: *not*, it should be emphasized, a relationship to "me" . . . or to the "self" of the other . . . but to the *relationship in self*' (p. 12). Resonance, an internal relationality, is the form of the body reconceived as a 'resonance chamber' (p. 31), a reverberation 'hollowed out' by a rhythm that is timbre. As such, 'listening opens up in timbre'; timbre that is 'the resonance of sound' (p. 40).

Nancy, as mentioned, is not alone in pursuing lines of thought in this register; and, as he makes clear, his exploratory account is itself a development and revision of lines suggested by various precursor thinkers.[41] But his work serves well as an example, perhaps *the* example (given its emblematic status), of what Brian Kane calls the 'ontological turn' within sound studies; albeit Nancy is unknowing, here at least, of the existence of such a field, unlike several others of those writing self-consciously from within this location.[42] In as much as any ontology of listening is by definition transcendental, or quasi-transcendental, in the Kantian sense, and thus a priori, the question of the relation between such theorising and the field recording is beside the point. This is not to say, of course, that critical accounts of soundworks that use field recordings do not draw frequently on contemporaneous theorising in this vein, both overtly, to foster or bolster an interpretation, and tacitly, by invoking a shared 'sonotropic' register, a 'rich metaphorology' of acoustically inflected figures – resonance, most obviously.[43] Several of the essays collected here are thus oriented, especially when seeking to valorise in ethical terms the event of and worldly attitude towards sound and audition, a move familiar as a development of those idealising philosophical accounts of music common in the second half of the nineteenth century – in Schopenhauer, most influentially. Forms of phonocentrism – or, alternatively, of 'acousmania' – are certainly evident in the acoustic turn.[44]

The encounter of theory and criticism can yield rich readings, whether the auditory field is recorded, transcribed or imagined.[45] The direction of traffic tends, however, and as so often, to be one way, from theory to criticism (or practice). Nancy's study is ontological in orientation and yet its frame of reference, both by implication and in those moments when it does reach down to traditions of practice, is usually conventional in its taking of music, especially the music of the Western art canon, as exemplar and norm: music's materials, its works, its genres and its customary listening practices and forms of sociality.[46] The same situation is evident in philosophical encounters with poetry and poetics, with the same resulting question: in what ways might wide-reaching developments in practice extend or even challenge those theoretical accounts which allude to or implicate specific art forms and aesthetic experiences? Not that possibilities of this orientation remain entirely untapped; they are, however, still strikingly underexplored.[47]

One example of the challenge practice poses to theory can be found in Jonathan Skinner's essay, in which a writer identified with ecopoetics discusses the relationship between his poetry and his field-recording practice. This he does with specific reference to his *Directions for the Ear*, a boxed sequence of 40 nine-line poems printed on index cards and accompanied by 40 short recordings. Shifting genres nimbly, Skinner blends poetry with reflections on sound and the natural world and spectrograms of some of the sounds he recorded. The sonic preoccupations of the text are more than merely thematic. Rather, they lead Skinner to a mode of expression in which the experience of the acoustic crosses between literary and theoretical paradigms.

A very different example of an approach to theory that is conditioned by practice is found in the essay by the poet-critic Dell Olsen, a pioneer of practice-based pedagogy in the UK. At the heart of Olsen's essay is a discussion of the recent work of two contemporary American poets, Peter Gizzi and Juliana Spahr. Olsen considers the ethical and acoustic commitments of each poet in the context of Berger's essay, and broadens her discussion to include the writing of Nancy, Roland Barthes and Rosalind Krauss on one hand, and the art of Pauline Oliveros, Hildegard Westerkamp and Bernie Krause on the other.

In terms of sound – to shift to the second constituent element of the acoustic turn – the field recording in its more archival and socially minded modes might be said benignly to confirm rather than extend or revise contemporaneous philosophies of listening, however radically different such sounds might be from those of music in establishing scenarios of acoustic attention. Caleb Kelly identifies a 'reactionary return to realism' in field-recording practice, a result, so he suggests, of 'a naïve belief in the non-mediation of sound'.[48] There may well be an 'anti-intellectual' tendency in certain strains of the subculture of the field recordist, but this should not lead to a disavowal of that rich line of practice rooted in the Schaferian soundscape and sound-walk, and in the acoustic ecology movement in all its guises and forms of activity, including those with documentary intentions. The most accomplished work in this vein, certainly as conceived in relation to the present volume – work on the Gruenrekorder and winds measure imprints, for example, and by David Dunn, Annea Lockwood, Hilde-gaard Westerkamp and Chris Watson, among many others – straddles the borders of environmental sound, music and sound art, conscious simultaneously of the state and status of specific places, of the many framing acts of recording and editing by which a location is made and marked, and of those aesthetic properties of sound – quasi-musical if the listener is so inclined – freed up by the Cagean angle of contem-plation. This is a committedly acoustic ecology 'not [of] the world but [of] the relationship between the world and its representation'; an ecology evident in soundworks themselves, certainly, but also in allied textual descriptions, both creative and critical.[49] Hence a work such as Brandon Labelle's *Acoustic Territories: Sound Culture and Everyday Life*, Schaferian in spirit, in which specific 'sonic figure[s]' are proposed as forms of experiencing and participating in everyday fields of 'auditory life' – the echo of the underground, the vibration of the street and the transmissive in the air.[50] Labelle's method is partly transcriptive, a self-conscious recording of local environments, and, as such, stages questions of coercion, co-option and intervention in ways correspondent entirely with those of field recordings: 'unfolding auditory experience as locational and poignantly embedded within processes of social exchange'.[51]

Labelle's deployment and foregrounding of a repertoire of figures as a means 'creatively [to] engage' auditory life brings us back to the metaphorology of the acoustic turn.[52] Janus suggests several ways in which Nancy relies in the theorising of listening on a 'relative sup-pression of noise', a mark, again, of the often-tacit influence, in philo-sophical accounts, of music and listening as conceived by and within the Western art canon. A 'noisier' thinking, differently informed – Labelle's would be one instance of such – might lead to a counter-metaphorology, less familiar than that of airy resonance; one, say, of 'turbulence' and 'infection', to borrow Janus's own suggestions.[53] As Labelle's work demonstrates, noisier thinking thus conceived is an effect of an admittance to thought of the sound effects of modernity, rather than what is an often unconscious filtering out: the matter and effect of technology, transport, media, architecture and artefactual life in all its ambient influence. There is of course nothing new in such a notion, whether understood in terms of a modernity experienced, for better or worse, as significantly acoustic in character or of that character as potentially artistically noteworthy. And yet the extraordinary soundworlds of contemporary phonography, those worlds that have followed variously in the wake of Schaeffer, Schafer, Cage, Luc Ferrari, Alvin Curran and their company, have effected a paradigm shift in the experience and understanding of what a sounded field is, and of what such a field could or should be.

Two aspects in particular mark this effect. The field recording as conceived within the frame of acoustic ecology has been and continues to be hugely significant, both archivally, as a means of drawing attention to the characteristics of particular sound environments, especially those unnoticed or overlooked, and ecologically, within a specifically bioacoustic and biophonous orientation towards preservation and the marking in sound of forms of endangerment. The more overtly or confessedly interventionist of such recordings (the use of montage in Chris Watson's *Weather Report*, for example) work to acknowledge mediation, both in the act of recording and in post-recording editing, each as related in the manner of synecdoche with human intervention in the physical and animal environment. And yet the scalic relation thus predicated – micro to macro – and the tacit valorising of an ethics of interrelation and coexistence, the human and the nonhuman, remain still within an essentially anthropocentric framing. Field recording-oriented practice, like any other art form, is subject potentially to an imperative to be, somehow or other, interesting. The interesting is what provokes and sustains attention, at whatever level of intensity; but the problem of such a seemingly benign requirement, from the point of view of a thinking of the Anthropocene, is that it is precisely 'those topics and psychological and cognitive structures that constitute the "interesting" – not just for a small number of critical specialists, but for most human beings' – that are 'at odds with the scale, complexity and the multiple and nonhuman contexts involved' in conceiving climate change and the environment.[54]

Environmental crisis, in being a crisis in the thinking of scales of time and space, is inconceivable, unlocatable and ungraspable. As such, it is, or can be felt as, boring. Art works to make it interesting, but, again, that work often involves the imposition of forms of interestingness that are themselves implicated in the problem at hand.

challenging the 'interesting'.

Phonography as it has developed is in many ways uniquely suited to the times, in its focused sounding of a real so vast or microscopic as to be overwhelming of human empathy or cognition, an effect specifically of the singular relationship, both intimate and alien, of sound to real-world source. And yet could it be also that the field recording as artwork is most suited to the time of environmental crisis in being a species of the 'merely interesting' – that is, in sounding its environment in a way that does not arrest attention but rather establishes a relation over time, a kind of hovering presence that is both implicated and distanced?[55] A being-with that partly frustrates the demands of interestingness and, in so doing, places the listener in semi-relation to a sounded world that is both given and other? Carol Watts considers some of these possibilities in a performative piece of 'magpie reading' that mimics all manner of relations – between human and animal selves, materials and texts. The field, as idea and location, is here expanded so as to acknowledge the current ecological context and a 'bio-imbrication' of occupants and events. Watts articulates a series of acts of 'imagined shared poiesis or making' – of field making, whether recorded in sound or word or concept, by bird or by human. There is no single space but rather a 'constellatory world' the excesses of which – the manifold happenings and interactions – result in and produce in turn a series of benign part-recognitions that are themselves fields of action.

We might say that the field recording, in practice, as sounded and as written, resonates most potently with its moment not only in its marking of the givenness of a sounding world, with whatever degree of explicitness and staged mediation, but in the orientation it implies or requires of its auditors. Herein lies the second of the ways in which the extraordinary blossoming of practice in recent decades has offered rich possibilities for theorisation; for thought, that is, rather than vice versa, as that relation is more commonly conceived. One exemplary line of thinking here concerns a queering, in the most far-reaching sense, of the being-oriented that is central to the phenomenologically inclined approach of so much writing about sound and acoustic experience; and of the relatively seamless matching of these approaches with detailed histories of subcultures of listening.[56] The insights of such writing are many and various, but there is a parallel mode that works otherwise, with the proposition that sound holds in itself – note the ontological register – an inherent and variously operative queerness: in the constitutive disjunction of sound and sounding thing, and the resultant 'quasi-object which is neither a material object nor fully human, but somehow expressive and thing-like at the same time'.

The effect is thus of 'a certain self-estranging quality of shock, difference or resistance to normative meanings', a 'recalcitrance' in sound's 'universal and inhuman force'. And therein resides sound's queerness. This is a universalising proposition concerning sound as such and as conceived on an extra-human ecological scale; and yet it is in the expanded and reoriented site-specificity of certain strains of phonographic practice that sound as queer is most forcefully and tactically encountered, and via the experience of which acoustic ambience itself is turned. As a development of, or counterpart to, field recording as an essentially archival or documentary practice, however self-reflexive, this is a challenging and exciting proposition.

Turning finally to writing, we might say that hovering over these summary accounts of listening and sound as fashioned variously by the interested commentary of recent decades is the matter of script, in all its modellings: as ascription, inscription, transcription and description, with those cognate practices of notation, annotation and translation. The rich resonance of the field recording, as idea, is a result of its being linked, historically and conceptually, to both a mimetic ideal and ethics of ethnographic transcription and archiving, and, conversely, a non-mimetic, medium-aware conception for which the trans- of transcription is a form always of othering. As Drew Daniel attests,

> the very act of digitally recording audio is itself already a kind of inscription, for the smooth analogue waves of sound as vibrations are themselves being attenuated and rendered into a digital approximation, a string of encoded zeros and ones which are also, themselves, already lossy with respect to the originals they store and preserve. So the distinction between the two transcripts can itself be made to soften and blur.[57]

The idea of 'originals' is moot, but the point remains. The field recording, as recording, is caught up in ideas of script and scripting – not after the manner of practice and theory or act and rationalisation, but indigenously and at every point of engagement: from conception, through act and edit, to the afterlife of reception. Therein lies its rich promise, to which the present volume hopes variously to testify.

Beyond the important and increasingly rich literature by recordists, poets, musicians and composers, there are perhaps three ways in which the field of the field recording can be considered in terms specifically of practices of writing.[58] The first two of these are in effect flip sides of the same idea: the idea, that is, of literature *as* field recording. Hence, most conventionally, literature read as an archive, however inventive, of the sounded fields of the past and of the past's hearings and understandings of such. Historicist readings of specific subcultural soundscapes, as these soundscapes are recorded in literature, are now a recognised genre of literary and cultural history, the most ambitious examples of which acknowledge the challenges and possibilities of tuning-in to the past – the challenges and possibilities, that is, of what Steven Feld, marking a slight distance from received ideas of acoustic ecology (hence of literature as Schaferian 'earwitness') and, indeed, of the soundscape, calls 'acoustemology': 'relational listening histories . . . methods of listening to histories of listening – always with an ear to agency and positionalities'.[59]

The other, related conception of literature as field recording originates with Cage and Fluxus, and has been explored most inventively in the text score as that medium of notation has developed since the 1950s. The performative act inherent in any reading of a verbal text, acoustemological or otherwise, is here made explicit; but rather than the performance of reading being conceived as explanatory or interpretative in the conventional sense, the verbal text becomes a merely provisionally silent prompt to action – the action, in particular, of sounding.

This leaves the third and perhaps most fascinating resonance of the field recording conceived as itself a form of de-, in- or tran(s)-scription. The challenge of Feld's acoustemology includes an acknowledgement of the extent to which listening, and so sound, has tended to be translated in an occluding and erasing fashion by writing; not only in the precedence accorded to material traces of sight and touch in the archive, but also by writing's tendency to operate with a set of variously explicit and covert figures oriented towards cognition as a scenario primarily of seeing and seen. Thinking otherwise, with sound in mind and mind in sound, involves therefore attending to a new figurative repertoire such as has been touched on already in relation to Nancy and others. The field recording, in being itself transcriptive, adds another layer of complexity. It is at once creative, in the sense of being an act of artful imagining or intervention, however conceptually oriented, and critical, as a form of scripting of those events to which it attends. As such, writing that results from it, directly or indirectly – the latter in the sense of writing conceived as it were in the shadow of the field recording – might itself testify imaginatively to possibilities of this doubleness or hybridity. Cage's prose works are again exemplary in this regard, and we can identify an increasing number of analogous texts, artfully hybrid in conception, for which the field recording as an idea of a relation to sound both creative and critical might be said to have served as prompt.

Lisa Robertson's 'Disquiet' is one such; a work accompanied by field recordings that are themselves responses to photographs. The hybrid piece is a collection of discrete blocks of text that in its grammar and its figures articulates an 'enmeshed' 'prosody of noise' in the city, policed by the corporate spectacle of the modern metropolis and yet carrying still an 'unwilled surplus' resistant to normative requirements of meaning and communication – even when, as in the case of the Schafer's World Soundscape Project, such requirements appear benignly preservationist in intention. Disquiet thus conceived can 'bathe the listener in potential', and the writing itself, in its soundful moving and shaping, voices the possibility.

The creative-critical relation of field to sound is worked affectingly in Daniela Cascella's essay for the present volume, in which the possibilities of a field writing are played out like a set of variations, edge to edge – or hedge to hedge. The field recording, conceived here in the most expansive sense, is a contingent gathering of manner of transcriptions, including those closest to the heart and to memory. But it is always and necessarily 'a text on edge', mindful – now more than ever – of the workings of inclusion and exclusion, and of the rabbit holes that mark hidden or obscured, or simply other, territories.

In a related vein, Patrick Farmer has in recent years extended his field recording practice to include the production of texts, notably a trilogy of poetic texts that reflect obliquely on the process of writing about sound or, more precisely, writing sound. His 'Bittern Space' reflects on these texts, seeking to gather together and re-present the attention to the acoustic the three books enabled. Woven into his episodic contribution to this volume are references to numerous other authors, citations from his own work, and drawings. The chapter is *sui generis*.

These are literatures of the field recording in the most expansive sense of the phrase. Daniela Cascella's 'Archival Fiction', *En abîme: Listening, Reading, Writing*, is another example, lighter in texture and more introspective in orientation, but equally attentive to the creative-critical possibilities of 'writ[ing] from the side of somebody who listens'.[60] It is an avowedly 'hybrid operation', 'layered' where the Robertson is 'enmeshed', a fluid and variously site-specific mix of autobiography, reading diary, description and memorial, moving always around and about the matter of sound and listening: 'in constant motion between feeling, knowing, understanding: to shape, report or recall an act of listening in words is an inclusive gesture, not an abstraction' (p. 102; p. 80). Again, this inclusivity, a 'cohabitation of worlds', is writing that comes after the field recording in the fullest sense: in the wake of the field recording, in allusion to it, in imitation of it and in pursuit of it (p. 73). The field recording makes such writing possible, even as it implies a blurring of a distinction between the two forms; and the writing in its turn maintains the possibilities of its sounding partner.[61] Each is to the other both ground and event, a scenario that offers, however indirectly, fitting testimony to the continued resonance of Berger's essay.

Note on audio: a number of mp3s that support the essays in this volume can be found at the following url: https://edinburghuniversitypress.com/book-writing-the-field-recording-hb.html [click on the 'resources' tab].

Notes

1. John Berger, 'Field' [1971], p. 31. References to 'Field' are to the text as reprinted in the current book.
2. Our authors, with the exception of Lisa Robertson, were asked to consider Berger's essay when preparing their contribution. Robertson's field-recording essay is reprinted from her collection *Nilling* (Toronto: BookThug, 2012).
3. Berger, 'Field', p. 31.
4. Ibid., p. 33.
5. Ibid., p. 34.
6. Ibid., p. 32.
7. Christopher Bollas, *Being a Character: Psychoanalysis and Self Experience* (London: Routledge, 1993), p. 29.
8. Francis Ponge, *The Making of the* Pré, trans. Lee Fahnestock (Columbia and London: University of Missouri Press, 1979), p. 21. This volume includes the poem 'Le Pré'. Further references are included in the text.
9. David Dunn's bark-beetle recordings are issued as *Sound of Light in Trees* (Earthear, 2006). For his work on curbing the spread of the beetles, see http://news.nau.edu/sonic-weapon-successful-in-bark-beetle-battle/#.WDHrVHd0eHo (last accessed 6 April 2017).
10. R. Murray Schafer, *The Soundscape: Our Sonic Environment and the Tuning of the World* [1977] (Rochester, VT: Destiny, 1994), p. 5.
11. Key releases by Watson are *Stepping into the Dark* (Touch, 1996), *Outside the Circle of Fire* (Touch, 2000) and *Weather Report* (Touch, 2003).
12. Schafer, *The Soundscape*, p. 5.
13. Henry David Thoreau, *Selections from the Journals* (New York: Dover, 1995), p. 8.
14. John Cage, *Empty Words*, in *Empty Words: Writings,'73–'78* (Middletown, CT: Wesleyan University Press, 1981), pp. 1–77, p. 11.
15. Michael Pisaro, 'Writing, Music' in *The Ashgate Research Companion to Experimental Music*, ed. James Saunders (Farnham: Ashgate, 2009).
16. The six-CD set *Wandelweiser und so weiter* (Another Timbre, 2013) captures some of the energies at play. The Brussels-based Q02 organisation has been an important nexus of activity.

17. See, for example, John Cage, 'Happy New Ears!', *A Year from Monday* (Middletown, CT: Wesleyan, 1963), p. 31.
18. Ibid., pp. 30–1.
19. Ibid., pp. 32–3.
20. Michael Pisaro, 'Writing, Music', p. 27. See also pp. 32–5 for discussion of the 'point'. *A Mist is a Collection of Points*, audio CD (New World Records, 2015). As Jenny Gottschalk observes in her liner note, many of Pisaro's recent compositions have used grains as percussive tools because of the unpredictability and density of the sounds they make.
21. John Cage, 'The Future of Music: Credo' in *Silence: Lectures and Writings* (Middletown, CT: Wesleyan, 1961), p. 12.
22. Cage, 'Music Lovers' Field Companion' in *Silence*, op. cit., p. 276.
23. David Grubbs's book *Records Ruin the Landscape* (Durham, NC and London: Duke University Press, 2014) explores the insight that the Cagean epoch in music initiated experiments in duration, performance and notation ('open-ended poetic instructions and descriptions') that were unsuited to recording or to dissemination via long-playing record (pp. 2–3).
24. Liz Kotz, *Words to be Looked At: Language in 1960s Art* (Cambridge, MA: MIT Press, 2010), chapter 1, pp. 13–58.
25. Ibid., p. 24.
26. Ibid., p. 17.
27. Ibid., p. 36.
28. See the *Fluxus Performance Workbook*, ed. Ken Friedman, Owen Smith and Lauren Sachwyn (Performance Research e-publications, 2002), a freely circulated e-book available from websites including http://www.deluxxe.com/beat/fluxusworkbook.pdf
29. George Brecht, *Water Yam* (London: John Gosling, 1973), n.p.
30. Ibid.
31. George Maciunas remarked in a 1964 letter to Tomas Schmit, 'The best Fluxus "composition" is the most strongly impersonal, ready-made sort, rather like Brecht's "Exit" it does not demand that any one of us perform it, but it happens every day.' In *Fluxus etc./Addenda II*, ed. Jon Hendricks (Pasadena: Baxter Art Gallery, California Institute of Technology, 1983), p. 166.
32. John Mowitt, *Sounds: The Ambient Humanities* (Oakland: University of California Press, 2015).
33. The first volume in the Sound Studies series published by Bloomsbury appeared in 2004. The *Journal of Sonic Studies* first appeared in 2011, while *Sound Studies*, the journal, was launched in 2015. Representative anthologies and overviews include: *The Auditory Culture Reader*, ed. Michael Bull and Les Back (London: Berg, 2003; 2nd edn published by Bloomsbury, 2015); *The Sound Studies Reader*, ed. Jonathan Sterne (London: Routledge, 2012); *Sound*, ed. Caleb Kelly (London and Cambridge, MA: Whitechapel Gallery and MIT Press, 2011); *Keywords in Sound*, ed. David Novak and Matt Sakakeeny (Durham, NC and London: Duke University Press, 2015).

34. Denise Riley, *The Words of Selves: Identification, Solidarity, Irony* (Stanford: Stanford University Press, 2000), p. 93. Riley is discussing the relation between the 'poetic' and the 'analytic' in creative and critical writing.

35. Relations across different communities of practice, most obviously those allied primarily with creative and the critical practice, are of course fragile and sensitive.

36. See, for example, Kyle Gann, writing about *4'33"*: 'To Cage it seemed, at least from what he wrote about it, to have been an act of *framing* . . . It begged for a new approach to listening, perhaps even a new understanding of music itself, a blurring of the conventional boundaries between art and life'. *No Such Thing as Silence: John Cage's 4'33"* (New Haven and London: Yale University Press, 2010), p. 11.

37. Michael Pisaro, 'Ten Framing Considerations of the Field', *Experimental Music Yearbook* (2010) – http://experimentalmusicyearbook.com/ten-framing-considerations-of-the-field

38. John Cage's *Silence: Lectures and Writing*, the first of what became a quintet of volumes of writing, was published in 1961.

39. See, for example, Melle Kromhout, 'Sound Studies: A Discipline?' (https://soundstudiesblog.com/2014/08/11/sound-studies-a-discipline-afterthoughts-on-the-sound-signatures-winter-school-amsterdam-january-2014/), and the discussion in the opening pages of Brian Kane, 'Sound Studies without Auditory Culture: A Critique of the Ontological Turn', *Sound Studies* 1.1 (2015): 2–21.

40. Jean-Luc Nancy, *Listening*, trans. Charlotte Mandell (New York: Fordham University Press, 2007), pp. 21–2. Further references are included in the text.

41. Adrienne Janus and Anthony Gritten each offer detailed expositions of Nancy's thinking on the subject of listening, situating it within a philosophical tradition (Janus) and a range of theorizations of music (Gritten). See Janus, 'Listening: Jean-Luc Nancy and the "Anti-Ocular" Turn in Continental Philosophy and Critical Theory', *Comparative Literature* 63 (2011): 182–202; and Gritten, 'The Subject (of) Listening', *Journal of the British Society of Phenomenology* 45 (2014): 203–19.

42. Kane, 'Sound Studies without Auditory Culture'. Kane focuses here on three writers on sound whose work he identifies as broadly ontological in orientation and ambition: Steve Goodman, Christoph Cox and Greg Hainge.

43. Martin Scherzinger, 'On Sonotropism', *Contemporary Music Review* 31 (2013): 345–51. Veit Erlmann, author of an exhaustive history of the idea of resonance, refers to the 'rich metaphorology', evident across the humanities, 'that seeks to replace the binaries of structuralist thought with a notion of discourse that is diametrically opposed to a distancing and objectifying form of knowledge' ('Resonance' in *Keywords in Sound*, ed. Novak and Sakakeeny, pp. 175–82, p. 175.)

44. Steven Connor, 'Acousmania' (http://stevenconnor.com/acousmania.
html). Suffice to say, Connor, while interested in such developments, is
sceptical of their argument.

45. Continental philosophy's influence on work in sound is manifest also,
as prompt or instruction, in the compositional activity of several of
the members of the Wandelweiser group, especially Manfred Werder
and Antoine Beuger. See the essays by Will Montgomery and Nicholas
Melia in the present collection.

46. 'How much . . . does his [Nancy's] description of philosophical listening rely on examples taken from the classical musical tradition'
(Janus, 'Listening', p. 200).

47. Bonnet, for example, in the section of his book titled 'Phonophanies',
touches on Cage, Francisco López and David Toop, among other postwar and contemporary musicians and sound artists (*The Order of
Sound*, pp. 261–327).

48. Caleb Kelly, 'Thoughts on the Representation of Sound', *Wolf Notes* 7
(July 2014): 8–10, p. 9 (PDF available at https://wolfnotes.wordpress.
com/wolf-notes/).

49. Will Montgomery, 'Beyond the Soundscape: Art and Nature in Contemporary Phonography' in *The Ashgate Research Companion to
Experimental Music*, ed. James Saunders (Aldershot: Ashgate, 2009),
pp. 145–61, p. 161.

50. Brandon Labelle, *Acoustic Territories: Sound Culture and Everyday
Life* (London: Bloomsbury, 2010), p. xxv. Labelle's book, in being
sociologically and historically inflected but also conceptually ambitious,
is similar in orientation to a number of studies of specific soundscapes
published over the past twenty years.

51. Ibid., p. xix.

52. Ibid., p. xviii.

53. Janus, 'Listening', p. 199.

54. Timothy Clark, *Ecocriticism on the Edge: The Anthropocene as a
Threshold Concept* (London: Bloomsbury, 2015), pp. 176, 181.

55. On the 'merely interesting' as a specific type of aesthetic or affective
response, see Sianne Ngai, *Our Aesthetic Categories: Zany, Cute,
Interesting* (Cambridge, MA: Harvard University Press, 2012), p. 112.

56. The particular line of thinking summarised here is that suggested by
Drew Daniel. See 'All Sound is Queer', *The Wire* 333 (November 2011):
43–6, and 'Transcripts: Towards a Queer Phenomenology of the Field
Recording' (http://www.catherinepancake.com/QUEERINGDANIEL.
pdf). Daniel describes in the latter the influence in particular of Sara
Ahmed's *Queer Phenomenology: Orientations, Objects, Others* and,
from contemporaneous work on sound, the likes of Steve Goodman's
Sonic Warfare: Sound, Affect, and the Ecology of Fear (Cambridge,
MA: MIT Press, 2012).

57. Daniel, 'Transcripts', p. 11.

58. See, for example, *In the Field: The Art of Field Recording*, ed. Cathy Lane and Angus Carlyle (Devon: Uniformbooks, 2013), and a number of the short contributions to *Autumn Leaves: Sound and the Environment in Artistic Practice*, ed. Angus Carlyle (Paris: Double Entendre, 2007).
59. Steven Feld, 'Acoustemology' in *Keywords in Sound*, ed. Novak and Sakakeeny, pp. 12–21, p. 15. Feld coined the term in 1992. See also, for example, Justin Patch, 'Caught in the Current: Writing Ethnography That Listens', *Journal of Sonic Studies* 4.1 (2013), http://journal.sonicstudies.org/vol04/nr01/a09.
60. Daniela Cascella, *En abîme: Listening, Reading, Writing* (Winchester, UK; Washington: Zero Books, 2012), p. 86.
61. Another recent example of writing-as-field-recording is Patrick Farmer's *try i bark* (Oxford: Compost & Height and Organized Music from Thessaloniki, 2012).

Field

John Berger

'Life is not a walk across an open field'
Russian proverb

Shelf of a field, green, within easy reach, the grass on it not yet high, papered with blue sky through which yellow has grown to make pure green, the surface colour of what the basin of the world contains, attendant field, shelf between sky and sea, fronted with a curtain of printed trees, friable at its edges, the corners of it rounded, answering the sun with heat, shelf on a wall through which from time to time a cuckoo is audible, shelf on which she keeps the invisible and intangible jars of her pleasure, field that I have always known, I am lying raised up on one elbow wondering whether in any direction I can see beyond where you stop. The wire around you is the horizon.

Remember what it was like to be sung to sleep. If you are fortunate, the memory will be more recent than childhood. The repeated lines of words and music are like paths. These paths are circular and the rings they make are linked together like those of a chain. You walk along these paths and are led by them in circles which lead from one to the other, further and further away. The field upon which you walk and upon which the chain is laid is the song.

Into the silence, which was also at times a roar, of my thoughts and questions forever returning to myself to search there for an explanation of my life and its purpose, into this concentrated tiny hub of dense silent noise came the cackle of a hen from a nearby back garden, and at that moment that cackle, its distinct sharp-edged existence beneath a blue sky with white clouds, induced in me an intense awareness of freedom. The noise of the hen, which I could not even see, was an event (like a dog running or an artichoke flowering) in a field which until then had been awaiting a first event in order to become itself realisable. I knew that in that field I could listen to all sounds, all music.

From the city centre there are two ways back to the satellite city in which I live: the main road with a lot of traffic, and a side road which goes over a level crossing. The second is quicker unless you have to wait for a train at the crossing. During the spring and early summer I invariably take the side road, and I find myself hoping that the level crossing will be shut. In the angle between the railway lines and the road there is field, surrounded on its other two sides by trees. The grass is tall in the field and in the evening when the sun is low, the green of the grass divides into light and dark grains of colour – as might happen to a bunch of parsley if lit up by the beam of a powerful lamp at night. Blackbirds hide in the grass and rise up from it. Their coming and going remains quite unaffected by the trains.

This field affords me considerable pleasure. Why then do I not sometimes walk there – it is quite near my flat – instead of relying on being stopped there by the closed level crossing? It is a question of contingencies overlapping. The events which take place in the field – two birds chasing one another, a cloud crossing the sun and changing the colour of the green – acquire a special significance because they occur during the minute or two during which I am obliged to wait. It is as though these minutes fill a certain area of time which exactly fits the spatial area of the field. Time and space conjoin.

The experience which I am attempting to describe by one tentative approach after another is very precise and is immediately recognizable. But it exists at a level of perception and feeling which is probably preverbal – hence, very much, the difficulty of writing about it.

Undoubtedly this experience must have a psychological history, beginning in infancy, which might be explained in psychoanalytic terms. But such explanations do not generalise the experience, they merely systematise it. The experience in one form or another is, I believe, a common one. It is seldom referred to only because it is nameless.

Let me now try to describe this experience diagrammatically in its ideal mode. What are the simplest things that can be said about it? The experience concerns a field. Not necessarily the same one. Any field, if perceived in a certain way, may offer it. But the *ideal* field, the field most likely to generate the experience, is:

1. A grass field. Why? It must be an area with boundaries which are visible – though not necessarily regular; it cannot be an unbounded segment of nature the limits to which are only set by the natural focus of your eyes. Yet within the area there should be a minimum of order, a minimum of planned events. Neither crops nor regularly planted lines of fruit trees are ideal.
2. A field on a hillside, seen either from above like a table top, or from below when the incline of the hill appears to tilt the field

towards you – like music on a music stand. Again, why? Because then the effects of perspective are reduced to a minimum and the relation between what is distant and near is a more equal one.

3. Not a field in winter. Winter is a season of inaction when the range of what is likely to happen is reduced.
4. A field which is not hedged on all sides; ideally, therefore, a continental rather than an English field. A completely hedged field with only a couple of gates leading into it limits the number of possible exits or entrances (except for birds).

Two things might be suggested by the above prescriptions. The ideal field would apparently have certain qualities in common with (a) a painting – defined edges, an accessible distance, and so on; and (b) a theatre-in-the-round stage – an attendant openness to events, with a maximum possibility for exits and entrances.

I believe, however, that suggestions like this are misleading, because they invoke a cultural context which, if it has anything whatsoever to do with the experience in question, can only refer *back* to it rather than precede it.

Figure I.1   Berger's field

© Jean Mohr, 'About Looking', Bloomsbury Publishing Plc. Used with permission.

Given the ideal field now suggested, what are the further constitutive elements of the experience? It is here that the difficulties begin. You are before the field, although it seldom happens that your attention is drawn to the field before you have noticed an event within it. Usually the event draws your attention to the field, and, almost instantaneously, your own awareness of the field then gives a special significance to the event.

The first event – since every event is part of a process – invariably leads to other, or, more precisely, invariably leads you to observe others in the field. The first event may be almost anything, provided that it is not in itself overdramatic.

If you saw a man cry out and fall down, the implications of the event would immediately break the self-sufficiency of the field. You would run into it from the outside. You would try to take him out of it. Even if no physical action is demanded, any over-dramatic event will have the same disadvantage.

If you saw a tree being struck by lightning, the dramatic force of the event would inevitably lead you to interpret it in terms which at that moment would seem larger than the field before you. So, the first event should not be over-dramatic but otherwise it can be almost anything:

Two horses grazing.
A dog running in narrowing circles.
An old woman looking for mushrooms.
A hawk hovering above.
Finches chasing each other from bush to bush.
Chickens pottering.
Two men talking.
A flock of sheep moving exceedingly slowly from one corner to
    the centre.
A voice calling.
A child walking.

The first event leads you to notice further events which may be consequences of the first, or which may be entirely unconnected with it except that they take place in the same field. Often the first event which fixes your attention is more obvious than the subsequent ones. Having noticed the dog, you notice a butterfly. Having noticed the horses, you hear a woodpecker and then see it fly across a corner of the field. You watch a child walking and when he has left the field deserted and eventless, you notice a cat jump down into it from the top of a wall.

By this time you are within the experience. Yet saying this implies narrative time and the essence of the experience is that it takes place outside such time. The experience does not enter into the narrative of your life – that narrative which, at one level or another of your consciousness, you are continually retelling and developing to yourself. On the contrary, this narrative is interrupted. The visible extension of the field in space displaces awareness of your own lived time. By what precise mechanism does it do this?

You relate the events which you have seen and are still seeing to the field. It is not only that the field frames them, it also *contains* them. The existence of the field is the precondition for their occurring in the way that they have done and for the way in which others are still occurring. All events exist as definable events by virtue of their relation to other events. You have defined the events you have seen primarily (but not necessarily exclusively) by relating them to the event of the field, which at the same time is literally and symbolically the *ground* of the events which are taking place within it.

You may complain that I have now suddenly changed my use of the word 'event'. At first I referred to the field as a space awaiting events; now I refer to it as an event in itself. But this inconsistency parallels exactly the apparently illogical nature of the experience. Suddenly an experience of disinterested observation opens in its centre and gives birth to a happiness which is instantly recognisable as your own.

The field that you are standing before appears to have the same proportions as your own life.

1971

Part One

Opening the Field

Chapter 1

Fields, Theory, Field Theory: John Berger and Manfred Werder Define a Field

Nicholas Melia

1. 'John Berger defines a field'[1]

What is John Berger's *field*?

Is this the field of chains, rings and soft canons? Of murmured and half-remembered songs and circles? Might we here follow the meandering, *ritornello* weave of childhood, traversing 'repeated lines of words and music' through 'grass not yet high'? Or is this a field of seductive – and gendered – ripenings, of 'intangible jars of her pleasure', within 'easy reach' upon a 'shelf', at once offering terrestrial and celestial plenitudes?

Perhaps it is the field of geometry and measure: of 'surface', 'corner', 'edge', field of wire horizons.[2] Or perhaps Berger's movement through the field follows a different call, tracing the faint contour of an older trail, adjacent, 'seldom referred to'; a winding, fading field path, beyond the idle chatter of hens, beyond even the 'intense awareness of freedom' it invokes; quite far now from our point of departure, and darkening where the grass has grown 'tall in the field'; quite far, where 'time and space conjoin', opening on to a call more 'immediately recognizable' to the philosopher, 'preverbal', 'nameless' –[3]

Or perhaps we might scrape away a little of the fertile topsoil, and heed Berger's epigraphic warning: *Life*, after all, *is not a walk across an open field.*

2. 'break the self-sufficiency of the field'[4]

'Field' is not Berger's first foray into the field – nor, indeed, into the *field* of fields: this is to be found in the 1969 essay 'The Moment of Cubism', in which Berger traces the changing spatial relationships between man and nature in art across a series of five epistemological breaks, from the applied geometrics of the Renaissance to the dynamic reconfiguration of empty space characteristic of post-Newtonian metaphysics. Here, the functional unity of nature and geometry characterised by the multidisciplinary logics of Leonardo and Alberti is fractured by the eruption of Copernican subjectivity, cleaving science and art, and turning the latter towards the artifice of the theatre stage. In this new space, upon which appearances conspire to engender a 'metaphorical model' for art as constructive reality, Berger asserts that the artist 'becomes primarily concerned with creation', tracing a new 'schematic' relationship to nature.[5] By the end of the eighteenth century, Kant's own Copernican turn necessitates the abandonment of the study of impenetrable and unknowable reality-in-itself, demanding a new metaphorical model for an art in which '[n]ature no longer confirms or enhances the artist as he investigates it'. Man is suddenly 'alone, surrounded by nature', with only the prism of the 'personal account' as testimony to an estrangement from the noumenal world.[6] By the nineteenth century, Berger asserts, this anxiety is sublimated in a series of surfeits and deficits describing the territorial confrontation between nature and experience, symptomatised in the 'pathetic fallacy' of romantic vitalism and the rendering 'powerless' of Impressionism before nature's 'overwhelming force'.

Ultimately, Berger situates art's modern revolutionary capacity in the 'shock' and 'incongruity' of a Cubism whose force of interjection is such that it functions at once to shatter the 'concept of nature as a projection of the desired', and to overturn any traces of determinism in the 'distinction between the actual and the desirable'.[7] Cubism, Berger argues, is 'strangely placed', 'curiously unfinished', its coordinates irreducible to the metrics of historical determination. Art, after Heisenberg, can no longer 'describe and explain nature', since it constitutes 'part of the interplay between nature and ourselves'.[8] Indeed, for Berger, the very function of contemporary art is not to reflect or *mirror* an underlying truth, but to dismantle and construct anew a 'diagram' of the 'invisible processes, forces, structures' that constitute modern life.

The power of Cubism, Berger argues, thus resides in the force of its 'unnatural' eruption at the convergence of a technological, political, social and scientific escalation, overturning 'the meaning of both time and space'[9]. Cubism not only shatters the continuity of 'illusionist three-dimensional space', but brings with it a new 'totality' of surface: everything in the pictorial plane is henceforth defined by the 'interaction between objects', rather than by recourse to the silent authority of Renaissance perspective: gone is the mediating agent determining a causal relation between depicted agents from a privileged viewpoint beyond the frame; vanquished the regulation of empty space between viewer and canvas.[10] No longer delimited thus by the Aristotelian hylomorphic properties of substance and form, the modern subject is released from the bondage of a strict causality played out between substantial bodies across three-dimensional Euclidean space. That which Berger calls a 'rigid distinction between absence and presence' becomes at once 'part of the world and indivisible from it',[11] entering into a new, dynamic, relational geometric in which the 'invisible . . . no longer intervened'.[12] Berger locates the genesis of this Gestalt redefinition of agency in Michael Faraday's concept of the field.

3. 'The wire around you is the horizon'[13]

For Berger, Faraday's attempt to wrestle with the problem of 'action at a distance' marks not only the genesis of an emergent modern subjectivity, but a new alignment of art with the physical sciences.[14] This quest for a redefinition of the geometry of causal relation, however, precedes Faraday's response to the shortcomings of Newtonian gravitational theory.[15] Newton's understanding of a universe consisting of unalterable corpuscles, forces and empty space remained fundamentally atomistic, posing the question of the movement of gravitational force *between* objects across an interstitial area: here, 'action at a distance' describes the motion of bodies produced without mechanical mediation or contact through an empty space that Newton, after Aristotle, describes as 'uniform and everywhere' identical.[16] Since such a void presents no differentiation through which change of circumstance can be evaluated, the idea of motion without mediation through the void is, for Newton, 'so great an absurdity that I believe no man who has in philosophical matters a competent Faculty of thinking, can ever fall into it'.[17] Newton's unwillingness to publicly affirm or refute the 'material or immaterial' nature of this unmediated space (arguably in order to reserve jurisdiction over the undesignated void to a higher Cause) aroused a body of speculation on the discreet function of ether as an invisible and frictionless transitional surrogate.

Until Faraday developed a method of reassessing the behaviour of charged particles in response to the problem of the action of an electrical current upon a nearby magnet, the physical sciences remained preoccupied with the problem of the influence of forces on the behaviour of distant bodies. Finally, in 1821, Faraday recognised in Hans Christian Ørsted's positing of subtle fluids as the connective medium acting between current and magnetic effect a thinking of action at a distance 'not confined to the conductor', but 'considerably extended through the circumjacent space'.[18] Faraday acknowledged Ørsted's method of explaining otherwise obscure chemical combinations as a precursor to his own assertion, following Roger Boscovitch, that not only could forces themselves be considered a sole physical actor, but that such forces retain the propensity to act upon other forces. In 1845 Faraday coined the phrase 'magnetic field' in addresses to the Royal Society (published the following year), and later asserted that 'any portion of space traversed by a line of magnetic power, may be taken as . . . a field, and there is probably no space without them'.[19] When William Thomson subsequently proposed that any space at 'every point of which there is a finite magnetic force' is called 'a field of magnetic force', the notion of the field as an expression of space saturated and governed by the behaviour of (non-substantial) forces, rather than a Euclidean space delimited by the direct, causal interaction of substantial bodies, began to accrue scientific currency.[20]

By 1865 James Clerk Maxwell had systematised Faraday's ideas in a series of mathematical equations, articulating the failure of previous mathematical theories to offer 'any express consideration of the surrounding medium' and remapping the discursive logic of space and time in the physical sciences around the concept of field.[21] In his accompanying prose, Maxwell addressed the contingency, temporality and dynamism of the 'field', describing it as '[having] to do with the space in the neighbourhood of the electric or magnetic bodies', as 'that part of space which contains and surrounds bodies in electric or magnetic *conditions*' (my emphases), and as 'that space' in which 'there is matter in motion'.[22]

Maxwell nonetheless insisted on a philosophical logic that remained indebted in textual justification, if not equation, to the inheritance of substantialism, retaining the possibility of an 'aetherial medium filling space and permeating bodies' displaced only by Einstein's theory of general relativity in 1915. Maxwell's achievement, however, lay in mathematising the field as consistent with the complete diagram of non-substantial acting forces proposed between Faraday and Thompson. Maxwell introduced the explicit temporal contingencies of energy flow and momentum to the understanding of post-Newtonian space, positing a succinct reimagining of a relational field in which, as Einstein and Infeld later ceded, 'there are no material actors. The mathematical equations of this theory . . . do not, as in Newton's laws, connect two widely separated events; they do not connect the happenings here with the conditions there', but rather create an entirely new, unified set of understandings of the dynamic extension of space and time.[23]

4. 'All events exist as definable events by virtue of their relation to other events'[24]

If field theory remained the province of post-Newtonian theoretical physics at the turn of the twentieth century, it is not difficult to see how the promise of a predictable theoretical framework supporting an actor indivisible from and charged within an entirely reorganised spatio-temporal field, freed from an invisible and intangible mediatory aetherial agent, and constituted across a differential play of forces, ignited the interest of the emergent social sciences. Indeed, Berger notes that Faraday's engagement with the problem of action-at-a-distance 'entered now, unacknowledged, into all modes of planning and calculation and even into many modes of feeling', engendering a 'startling extension through time and space of human power and knowledge'.[25] This extension was felt not only across the physical topology and compressed temporalities of a fully industrialised and increasingly mechanised Occident, but, Berger explains, in the collapse of the theological edifice historically mediating *between man and world*: the eradication of 'invisible' discontinuities 'between the individual and the general' and the renunciation of the deferred temporality of theological time offered the tantalising promise of a new, tangible form of social relation – an unmediated 'unity of the world' in which discrete actors might bear direct influence upon each other in order to constitute their territory, without necessitating a return to the unfashionable positivisms of the nineteenth century. In the newly secularised world, 'man *was* the world which he inherited'.

The subsequent development of field theory in the psychological and social sciences drank deeply from the wellsprings of post-Newtonian field theory. Central to the project was an attempt to circumscribe a unified and comprehensive theory of social being that extended beyond the causal limits of a restrictive atomism, most notably in the work of Kurt Lewin, a German Marxist of Jewish extraction whose Einstein-derived work became the most widely championed and disseminated field theory of this generation. Lewin's field theory is predicated on two assertions: firstly, that the behaviour of bodies is derived from a 'totality of coexisting facts';[26] and secondly, that these 'facts' retain the character of a dynamic field insofar as the determination of a field is dependent on 'every other part of the field'.[27] Given this mutually determining interrelation, the space in which psychology operates is thus a 'manifold', the interrelations of which cannot be properly thought 'without the concept of space'. Lewin appealed to the physical sciences in order to elucidate the multiple factors influencing an event in social space. In physics, he contended, the coordination of dimensions ('temperature, pressure, time, spatial position') constituted an abstract 'phase space' distinct from the three-dimensional 'physical space' determining the territory traversed by physical objects. Likewise, the 'life space or psychological field' in which 'psychological locomotion' or 'structural changes' unfold must be differentiated from the diagrammatic representation of 'gradations of properties'. Hence, Lewin constructed social space as a dynamic, inclusive series of *fields* or *life-worlds* described by a mutual interdependence of facts borrowing its orientation from the physical sciences, where 'facts' are understood as a dynamic system of needs and goals related by positive or negative attraction, and constitute a system of 'valences'.[28] This affective field – a conception of space in which beings and bodies are understood as permeated by valences – determines behaviour. Relations in the field are not formally causal, but are outcomes of relations and interactions between variable forces.

The relative freedom of a body to move within this field, however, necessitated the introduction of an additional, temporal dimension. Lewin, eager to distance his work from Freudian psychoanalysis, rejected the concept of *anamnesis* (a temporally determined causal distance between, for example, childhood experience and adult behaviour), and developed the 'principle of contemporaneity', consisting of 'situational units' derived from 'the problem of space-time-quanta, which is so important for modern quantum theory in physics', with extension 'in regard to their field dimensions and time dimensions'[29]. Instead of referring to a series of moments without dynamic temporal extension, Lewin's units instead describe 'a certain time period', in which the effects of past (or future) remained entirely grounded in a current situation.

Earlier Gestalt theorists Kurt Koffka, Wolfgang Köhler and Max Wertheimer similarly borrowed spatial concepts and ideas directly from post-Newtonian physics; Wertheimer, who enjoyed a close friendship with Einstein, was 'fortunate enough to . . . hear from [Einstein] the dramatic developments which culminated in the theory of relativity'.[30] Einstein's influence did not go unnoticed: in 1924

George Humphrey wrote a short parallel study on the 'Theory of Einstein and the "Gestalt-Psychologie"', discerning a mutual concern for the 'relative rather than . . . absolute treatment' of independent data, and 'the insistence upon whole processes rather than parts'.[31]

Koffka and Köhler, meanwhile, both received training in the physical sciences at the University of Berlin, before moving, like Wertheimer, to the Institut für Psychologie at the University of Frankfurt. Köhler's work is concerned with an effective and transformative interaction between 'percepts at a distance' and the subsequent positing of the field. Köhler's theoretical assertions, he explains, were only possible if, following Faraday, the 'individual percept has a field and if the "field"', which surrounds the percept, does not merely reveal the presence of this percept but also presents its specific properties'.[32] Here, properties of neural functions and processes determining perception are thus also evident properties of the field, and 'located in a continuous medium' in which 'events in one part of this medium influence events in the other regions in a way that depends directly on the properties of both in their relation to each other'.[33] To the extent that Köhler *makes the field coextensive with the relation between its percepts*, his theory of perception 'must be a field theory'.[34]

Koffka discerned in Lewin's work an application of ideas about 'force [and] field' with a 'much wider significance than the one assigned to them in physics'.[35] Attracted by the philosophical problems posed by field theory for perception, Koffka nonetheless drew explicitly on Faraday, Maxwell and Einstein, acknowledging the substitution in physics of 'empty space as mere geometric nothingness' for a 'definitively distributed system of strains and stresses, gravitational and electromagnetic', serving to determine 'the very geometry of space'.[36] The problem of 'smuggling' concepts from the physical sciences 'into the behavioral world' in order to satisfy the demand for a verifiable scientific model of human activity, is, however, presciently acknowledged. If the logics of the physical sciences are, Koffka suggests, too rigidly upheld, an invocation of the concept of 'force', for example, risks the reintroduction of a 'new kind' of dualism in which physical motion conforms to the metrics of attraction and repulsion, while psychological behaviour is reduced to an undesirable vitalism, perpetuating an obscure interaction between the two spheres.

For Koffka, this is a problem concerning the fundamental grounding of phenomenological experience, 'where the behaviour world exists' in relation to its 'ontological locus and status'. Koffka thus proposes a psychological concept of field as a 'system of stresses and strains which will determine *real behaviour*' (my italics), rather than a reconstruction of classical dualism, resulting in an 'environmental field' that collapses the opposition between the insubstantial (or 'not things') and the substantial ('things') historically constituting the problem of action at a distance. The conceptual outcome of this procedure is 'something like a force, something that goes beyond the mere static description of a thing', which 'discursive thought has separated what to naïve experience is in many cases a unity'.[37]

This unity, however, is not at all ancillary for Koffka, whose phenomenology is grounded in an affirmation of naive experience constituting as 'full a description of direct experience as possible'. Hence, Koffka's field is located beyond the false dichotomy of thing and non-thing, the substantial and the insubstantial: things 'do not fill our environment either spatially or temporally'; rather, an 'environmental field' is 'produced' in the behavioural environment by 'forces which organize it into separate objects and events', and 'forces which exist between these different objects and events'.[38] For Koffka, a unity of the differential interrelation of forces remains ontologically prior to the bifurcation of mind and body.

The theories of Lewin, Koffka and their contemporaries were not immune from criticism. In 1943 the Soviet psychologist Pitirim Sorokin subjected the metaphorical transformations governing the movement of conceptual apparatus between sociology and the physical sciences to fierce critique, calling for a 'drastic modification' in order to 'liberate' the social sciences from a 'voluntary servitude' to the metric of the physical sciences, describing the borrowing of concepts from the 'positivistic "natural-science" sociology' as 'inapplicable', 'inadequate' and 'actually misleading'.[39] While Sorokin acknowledges the necessity for a sociological concept of spatial determination in order to describe the relative positions and motions of a subject ('no location of sociocultural phenomenon, is conceivable or can be described without a concept of space'), he also considers the borrowing of concepts of space from Euclidean geometry, Minkowski–Einstein, Lobachevsky, Riemann and Cantor inappropriate, and chooses to ignore Lewin's own work on the genealogical dynamics of disciplinary transposition.[40] Rather, Lewin is found guilty by proxy of attempting to systematically apply 'post-Riemannian topological space' to unsuitable psychological territory, and while Sorokin acknowledges that '[s]paces may be constructed of any dimensions and properties, provided they are logically consistent . . . to the field of psychology and sociology', he concludes that Lewin's 'useless transcription of [metrical] terms' to describe non-metrical phenomena renders his theory 'futile' and 'perfectly useless in the field'. Particular venom is reserved for the replacement of the term 'psychology' with 'psychological field': a Trojan horse in which a 'geometrictopicological' vernacular may gain entry to the sociologist's citadel. '"Force", "vector", "field", and the like', Sorokin insists, fail to 'add anything to our knowledge of the behaviour of a hungry rat trying to get cheese'.

5. 'silence . . . also at times a roar'[41]

While it appears to Sorokin that the 'topographical imagery' of early field theory reduces the spatial geometry of sociology to a series of coordinates inherited uncritically from the physical sciences, John Levi Martin acknowledges that 'this confounding is in the world, not in Lewin's theory': 'science', as Koffka asserted, 'is apt to forget that it has not absorbed all aspects of reality', a principle affirmed with some force by a subsequent generation of sociologists.[42] In fact, questions about substantial and insubstantial bodies, causality in empty space, and the dynamic constitution of the field are shared across the surface of a complex geology of multiple, interpenetrative epistemological strata incorporating disciplinary interests far beyond the remit of the social and natural sciences. Just as action-at-a-distance necessitated a topological reappraisal of the 'empty' space between substantial bodies, so twentieth-century philosophy has, for example, implicated the similarly evacuated spatiotemporal medium of silence in its repatriation of ontology: Heidegger's re-examination of the question of the ground of being allocates a crucial function to the silent displacements of language, voice and ear, but articulates its circumscriptions of the finite and the infinite, being and beings, *Sein* and *Dasein* within a topographical lexicon privileging field, ground, path, way, clearing and site. This confrontation institutes one of the crucial moments of contemporary thought, underlying not only Heidegger's re-invocation and questioning of onto-theology but, among many other examples, Merleau-Ponty's primordial silence beneath the chatter of words, the Blanchovian and Levinasian silent yet murmuring remainder beyond *Dasein*'s finitude, the mute 'aphonism' of deconstruction, and the violent pre-rational fount of Foucault's *folie elle-même*.

A spatial reimagining and reconfiguring of the relationships between the substantial and the insubstantial, the active and the passive, the silent and the sounding, and the embodied and the empty also finds strong formal resonance in contemporary music, forcefully exemplified, if quietly articulated, in the work of Wandelweiser, the global collective of composers, artists and performers forging a music and art practice in the wake of John Cage's 'silent piece', *4'33"* (1952). Wandelweiser co-founder and composer Antoine Beuger identifies the 'discovery of silence by Cage' as the spark igniting the shared compositional tinder of the collective, but pledges nonetheless to venture beyond this seemingly exhaustive jurisdiction, multiplying silences, promising to 'mine *different* dimensions of silence' and 'filter out those dimensions which Cage could not see'.[43] The broadly formal economy, minimal aesthetic and familiar Cagean sensibility of much of the output of Wandelweiser belies the diversity and historical depth of the conceptual architecture upon which its constituent composers draw in their thinking about silence, but the scope of reference from which such thinking arises remains itself anything but impoverished.

Wandelweiser's most formally unconventional body of work is situated at the intersection of a theoretical and performative concern for the silent and the insubstantial, and an attempt to redefine the ontological 'field' in which forces – sonorous or otherwise – interact, that which Swiss composer Manfred Werder describes in his post-2004 practice as 'letting appear the world's natural abundance'.[44] It is a practice that often takes place outdoors, often over extended periods, often without material or musical intervention of any nature on the part of the composer-performer. Furthermore, despite the occasional presence of a tape recorder during the realisation of a piece, Werder is 'not a recordist'. His scores are severe in economy, without performance instruction of any persuasion, consisting of increasingly spare textual interjection upon the page. His performance practice 'brings together . . . a score, a place and the structured presence of one or a few performers (that is, the time of a day, the duration, once or repeatedly, etc.)', a procedure elaborated succinctly across the score of a piece entitled *2005¹*:

ort
zeit

(klänge)

place
time

(sounds)

Werder's work bears resemblance to the Fluxus-related and post-Fluxus text art emerging in the wake of Cage's new school courses of 1958–60. Indeed, while acknowledging the powerful centrifugal force of George Brecht's *Water Yam* (1963), Werder's compositional concern for renegotiating the metaphysical coordinates afforded by the implosion of institutionalised boundaries between senses, spaces, logics and disciplines also drew upon Lucy Lippard's pivotal text *Six Years: The Dematerialization of the Art Object* (1973), which documented the balkanised hinterlands of art practice between 1966 and 1972.[45] Like other Wandelweiser composers, Werder engages a wealth of literary and philosophical sources of broad denomination in pursuit of a redefined compositional topography, layering quotations from Badiou, Foucault, Meillassoux, Pessoa and Ponge. Perhaps most fruitfully and formatively, Werder invokes philosopher Gilles Deleuze and sinologist François Jullien, and it is this pairing to whom we will ultimately turn in pursuit of Werder's understanding of the field.

6. 'the *ground* of the events'[46]

In October 2011 Werder contributed a piece entitled 2011^4 (2011) to 'Field Fest', a field-recording event at the Q-O2 venue in Brussels. Having provided a short introduction to his work, and made available copies of the score, which consists solely in a short quotation from Iain Hamilton Grant's monograph *Philosophies of Nature after Schelling*, Werder invited the audience to assemble on the roof of the venue. Once in position, Werder 'did not talk anymore nor announce anything, remaining in . . . position . . . without producing any intentional sounds, for about 25–30 minutes'.[47] In support of the event, the composer contributed a further short text entitled 'The field', in which he elaborated the latest version of his compositional and performance strategy. The text takes the form of two short epigraphs, material from which recurs across a series of subsequent assertions, which together conspire to offer a short exposition on the notion of 'field'.

In 'The field', Werder's frame of philosophical reference shifts from an explicit invocation of French (post-)structuralism and its interlocutors found in many previous works, instead gesturing towards the curious trinity of Ponge, Schelling and Kant. The text nonetheless reveals Werder's sustained concern for a deep-ecology Deleuzism that chooses Ponge's natural vitalism and Iain Hamilton Grant's speculative realist refashioning of German idealist *Naturphilosophie* as its agents. The text commences with a quotation from Ponge's constellation of drafts published alongside the late poem 'Le Pré' (1967), reproduced here in the original French, and in Werder's own English translation: 'Le pré, aussi, est un *façon d'être*' / 'The field, as well, is a way of being'.[48] 'The field' thus commences in a doubled sense, in the form of a hanging conjunctive adverb, already 'aussi' ('as well', or also), at once presenting a commitment to a project of ongoing ontological explication already underway, and an assertion that onto-logical explication is but one among many potential permutations of the field.

If field theory notionally describes its field in the form of a rela-tion acting between forces *upon* bodies, Werder rejects the central-ity of the transcendental, self-sufficient 'human subject' (nominally a *body*) to the processes of composition, performance or, indeed, world. This refutation is furthermore doubled: firstly, Werder refutes from the position of an ostensibly Cartesian *cogito*: 'Personally', he states, 'I prefer not having the human subject privileged in its relation to the world'. In the second instance, the structure of the enunciat-ing subject is dissembled, articulating only a partial self: 'A spider', he writes, 'is integrating parts of my body in its cobweb'.[49] Werder not only invokes the formless universe of Bataille's spider and spit, but the collapse of the psychoanalytic subject into the 'body with-out organs' elaborated by Deleuze and Guattari across the breadth of their collective work: their subject, like Werder, recognises no dualism or dialectic between man and nature, plugging 'an organ-machine into an energy-machine, a tree into his body, a breast into his mouth' and here, dismantling limbs, incorporating all into the spider's own field.[50]

If this refusal to entertain a formally delimited metaphysical subject at the centre of its plane of activity (or 'world') is grounded in the provisional play of differential forces that are constitutive of, rather than constituted by, the Deleuzian subject, in the first of his assertions, Werder advances this issue in the form of a critical appraisal of sub-stantialism: 'I propose the field not to be a "material"'.[51] Here, Werder describes 'material' as that isolated object that a tautologous 'phe-nomenological assumption' identifies in order to perceive. Following Deleuze, Werder dismisses not only the empirical or perceptual mode of investigation that privileges the identity of the discrete or differenti-ated object, but also rejects the processes of rendering that favour the substantial over the 'mere operating' of the world. Such an under-standing of 'material', Werder continues, might be identified with a Kantian conception of matter as 'the world's appearance for us'.

According to Iain Hamilton Grant, who provides a second epi-graph, and whose work appears in the text of Werder's accom-panying score, in attempting to circumscribe the 'whole of all appearances' in the form of a 'material nature', Kant proposes to elucidate the furthest recesses of matter, 'the darkest of all things, or darkness itself'.[52] Yet in predetermining 'a whole comprised of the totality of things insofar as they appear', Kant already perpetrates a return to Aristotelian substantialism in the form of a universe 'composed of a plurality of distinct individual entities'. While the objective configuration of Kant's darkness-material necessitates that metaphysics 'ground the doctrine of body', the metaphysical orientation of the natural sciences insists upon a pursuing a 'doctrine of body alone' or 'metaphysics of corporeal nature', rather than a 'complete analysis of the laws governing the possibility of a thing'. As such, Grant suggests, when Kant claims that the analysis of matter has been reduced to 'nothing but moving forces', such forces necessarily remain beyond the remit of both Kant's accommodation and the natural sciences alike: 'we cannot comprehend a priori the possibility of these forces themselves'. While his analysis has reduced matter to 'nothing but moving forces . . .', forces themselves – for Kant, the 'darkest of all things', or 'darkness itself' – 'cannot be part of material nature'. The resultant separation of material nature and matter, Grant explains, induces 'a dualism of body and force' whereby 'transcendental physics mirrors the dualism in the Newtonian natural philosophy': 'the principle of motion' is cleaved from 'the moved'.

This attempt to overturn the dichotomy of the 'thing' and 'non-thing' has many precedents and a powerful counterpart in Werder's own reasoning. In 'The field', Werder proposes that 'silence' offers an alternative 'way of breaking [the] phenomenological assumption' that privileges the isolated object and the metaphysical dominance of the 'moved' over 'motion', 'thing' over 'non-thing'.[53] Hence, Werder's refusal of the language of 'variables, characteristics, properties' takes a specifically non-verbal form: 'I don't talk of predicates . . . of a world'. How, then, does silence function to undermine this opposition for Werder? The composer's encounter with Deleuze and Jullien illuminates the procedure.

7. 'An experience of disinterested observation'[54]

Werder encountered Jullien in 1999, following the publication in German translation of *Eloge de la fadeur*, a short text on the virtues of Daoist and Confucianist affirmations of a non-dialectical metaphysics, and containing a chapter dedicated to the practice of a 'silent' music. This text, widely distributed and highly influential among some of the Wandelweiser collective, situates the bland, the insipid, the flavourless and the silent as avatars of a pre-differentiated fount of being or efficacious blend *prior* to individuation, rather than that which is subsequently compounded or alloyed. These pre-differentiated qualities are provisionally opposed to the categories of the savoury and the flavoursome, which are identified with a Western metaphysical tendency more appropriate to the Cartesian affirmation of the distinct over the indistinct, the particular over the undefined, and the manifest over the formless. Jullien's text levied its most explicit influence on Werder in the latter's widely translated and disseminated summation of compositional strategy and ontology, *Das Klingen der Welt*, which initially appeared in a collection of interdisciplinary reflections on Jullien's philosophy in 2005.[55] If Werder's compositions and texts make scant explicit reference to either silence or Jullien, *Eloge de la fadeur* and its sister tome, *La Grande Image n'a pas de forme, ou, Du non-objet par la peinture*, nonetheless provided the composer with a template for his largely idiosyncratic 'silent music'.

Jullien's configuration of immanence, transformation and becoming, distinct from the restricted distribution of originary being and substantive beings described by the metaphysical dualisms of Occidental philosophy, chimed with Werder's doubts regarding the sustainability of his own work 'within that great European and Judaic culture'.[56] This reluctance also draws upon Werder's familial proximity to the decentred, nomadic and pantheistic Chilean Mapuche culture, which privileges genealogical and spatial proximity over patrilineal ties and, the composer contends, operates without systematic appeal to a unique metaphysical other beyond a loose and dynamic societal organisation. For the Mapuche, social life is conceptualised in relation not to the discrete, individuated unit in the form of personal being or god, but to participation in the plurality and social aggregation of the community.

Werder's rendering of Mapuche culture as a transversal or 'flat' hierarchy is not only reminiscent of Jullien's disavowal of *metaphysical* hierarchy, but also resonates powerfully with Deleuze's philosophy of immanence.[57] Rather than commencing with an ontological model in which existence is regulated by appeal to a transcendental signifier, or indeed the subjection of the methodological other to excavation and spoiling, Deleuze asserts a creative ontology in which the *telos* governing the relationship between Being and beings is overturned and stripped of its oppositional posture. Instead of insisting upon a fissure between the ontic and the ontological, or establishing two separate regimes of Being, Deleuze affirms a 'univocity' in which 'being is said in a single and same sense of everything of which it is said', but with the important caveat that that of which it is said 'differs': being, Deleuze asserts, is said 'of difference itself', but this difference should not be understood as the difference between things, substances or entities.[58] Rather, difference *itself* or *in itself* is that force prior to and motivating dividuation or differentiation, and this crucial privileging acts as the driving force behind a constitutive and perpetual transformation. Such transformation is executed in place of, or instead of, an originary 'ground' defined by presence, identity and stasis inherent to the hierarchical models of Being that Deleuze discerns as disqualifying the possibility of novelty in, for example, Hegel and Heidegger, and that Jullien recognises in the metaphysical dualism of Descartes. Furthermore, in order to render such creative possibility and novelty accessible beyond that which Deleuze calls the 'equal' distribution of unequal, undifferentiated or pre-individuated difference, a *quasi*-opposition is instituted between the Bergsonian categories of the *virtual* and the *actual*. This elaboration, described by Deleuze in the form of 'unequal odd halves', functions merely to provide different perspectives upon the same process of becoming or distinction: the virtual and the actual provide apertures that temporarily capture, on the one hand, the *actual* dominion of empirically identifiable things, subjects, substances and objects, and, on the other, the *virtual*, pre-individuated and impersonal forces and becomings that engender them. Virtual and actual do not oppose each other, then, but merely coexist upon that which Deleuze calls a *plane* or *field of immanence*, describing the 'real' and infinite process and landscape of becoming.

This structure is recapitulated by Jullien in *Eloge de la fadeur*: here, the fundamental philosophical tenor affirms an 'undifferentiated foundation of all things' or 'world beyond' that nonetheless eschews opening on to a proprietary 'metaphysical' world 'cut off from the senses'.[59] Jullien concludes that the Daoist has '[n]o metaphysical preoccupations' but nonetheless posits a 'world' described in its 'elemental capacity' as an 'inexhaustible unfolding' situated at the 'basis of [a] reality [that] serves as the platform upon which all existence rests'.[60] Like Deleuze, Jullien's interrelation of Being and beings establishes its poles upon 'the same plane' rather than founding an unbreachable opposition between them: the plane is a field consisting of two different perspectival elements or stages merely in the sense that the processes of existence, or becoming, consist in an oscillation *constitutive of*, rather than between, these poles. The transformative properties of becoming are thus only apparent in the relief cast

by the emergence and disappearance of forms into the undifferentiated and the silent; Jullien thus asserts that the Daoist merely attends
the 'unfurling and expanding of this world', a world he describes as
'(the only one)', tracking it as it returns 'to its original, virtual state'.[61]

If the Daoist merely attends to these processes, Jullien attempts to
account for the ingress of the virtual and undifferentiated upon music,
a milieu traditionally associated with the actual, and to assess the
implications of such an incursion, since both virtual and actual must
occur, to some degree, in the domain of the sensible. Crucially for our
understanding of Werder's post-2004 work, *Eloge de la fadeur* posits
its most distinctive account of this process in relation to a notion of a
'silent music' which opposes the allegorical and ascetic reticence that
opens Western music on to 'some inaudible, celestial melody superior
to the ones we perceive physically', to a third-century Chinese literature
describing a musical expression that 'extends and deepens' in maintaining, in abeyance, 'definitive realisation' and 'full exploitation'.[62]
Practitioners of such a music remained interested less in 'completely
satisfying' the demands of ear or palette than in reserving execution in
order to 'possess the highest degree of *potential* flavour'.[63] Here, the
musician is unacquainted with the opposition between the audible and
inaudible, but is concerned merely with the maintenance of a maximal
virtuality, a state rendered by Werder in his text on Jullien as 'the totality of all existing sounds' or 'the sounding of the world'. A totality of
potential sounds, Werder continues, 'by far exceeds the small section
audible for human beings'.[64]

What might this ultimately mean for Werder's practice? While
'articulating a sound', Werder admits, 'actualises its potentiality',
it is an awareness of the inherent potential or efficacy in a forgoing
of actualisation, rather than an illustrative acquiescence before or
submission to the process, that ultimately constitutes the power of
a 'silent music'. Just as Jullien asserts that the least seasoned dish
possesses the highest degree of potential flavour, and the unsounded
tone evokes an inexhaustible value, so Werder stresses the process
of 'purging the score [of] contextual compromises'.[65] This is not,
however, a process in which the limits of performance strategy
are determined or defined. Indeed, Werder provisionally posits a
mutual independence between performance practice and compositional imperative: developments in one domain may, the composer
explains, appear 'puzzling' in relation to the other. This opposition
also conceals an important complicity: in suggesting that a perceived
concurrence or correspondence between these divergent strata may
proceed from and result in a 'rather chaotic dynamic', Werder places

a slight but significant distance between his own increasingly non-interventionist performance practices – those that maximise the virtual potential of the score – and those strategies that, in undertaking simple actualisation, do not correspond to the ontological demands of the compositional concept borrowed from Jullien and Deleuze. Indeed, while generously describing and engaging in and with a variety of interpretative strategies, Werder is quick to confide a separate and hermetic regime of realisation: in February 2005 the composer began an ongoing 'private performance' project consisting in realisations of the text score *2005¹* in, among other places, Santiago, London, Paris, Tokyo and Delhi. This, he claims, constitutes 'the most important activity' in which he presently engages, and consists merely in 'roaming the streets . . . looking for a place to be at a certain time' and initially, at least, 'possibly producing [a] few sounds'. [66]

In fact, while the initial 'actualisations' (Werder's favoured term, borrowed 'of course through Deleuze') consisted in occasional and sparse interventions, it soon became 'clear that I would not need to produce any sound' and, furthermore, this being the case, abstention or intervention 'would not make any difference at all' to the *telos* of the work. [67] Indeed, Werder even stresses that a performance 'is not primarily about sound, more about nature', and, later, that a reading of the score is 'discretional', if, indeed, instruction is at all necessary; furthermore, Werder asserts that the very presence of a score remains 'optional'. [68]

At its limits, this procedure, rather than encouraging active participation or abstention, finds its participant simply 'dissolved in this mixture' as one might feel in the midst of 'native woods'. [69] But Werder is not nearly naive enough to entertain the possibility of complete dissolution. 'I'm present, sitting on a bench', he says, 'however easy to miss. I call it actualisation [but] it simply alludes more to a situation that is happening, emerging by itself', and establishing its field beyond the parameters specified by page or stage. [70]

8. 'You have defined the events you have seen primarily (but not necessarily exclusively) by relating them to the event of the field' [71]

Given its extraordinary scope, a brief historical overview of the movement of the concept of field in the social and physical sciences cannot hope to offer a definitive portrait of the field of 'fields', nor even of the field of 'fields' in field theory; nor can it fully penetrate the range of conceptual transpositions that serve to resituate and reconfigure it across the contemporary humanities in general, or music in particular. Furthermore, Werder's compositional and performance practices clearly do not amount to the exposition of a conventional field theory. Yet the concepts it generates are germinated from the same unbroken line of philosophical, artistic, scientific and sociological antecedents that Berger recognises in the resonances between Faraday and Cubism: indeed, if Berger's understanding of the function of contemporary art is predicated upon a diagrammatic redrawing of the 'invisible processes, forces, structures' that constitute and structure contemporary life and account for the 'interplay between nature and ourselves', so Werder articulates a comparable concern for the nature and emergence of material, the interaction between and articulation of those often inaudible elements *as* the interplay between man and nature, reinvigorating the field of musical activity as a fundamentally desubstantialised and dynamic play of the full suite of elements.

Furthermore, the articulation of a field of compositional practice which rejects the privileging of a centralised composing, performing or listening subject and seeks to actualise previously unrecognised, concealed and intermediary forces is strongly reminiscent at once of the mediative continuities of Köhler's field, and of Koffka's concern to undo the false dichotomy of the thing and the non-thing. Hence, in as much as Werder's compositional activity remains concerned with tracing contours of a field in which the opposition of the virtual and the actual, the substantial and the insubstantial are collapsed or dissolved, it intersects uncannily with the historical concerns and impulses of field theory, finding novel ways to traverse and reimagine territory, collapsing enclosures, redrawing spaces, and turning over new and fertile ground.

Notes

1. *New Society*, No. 475 (4 November 1971).
2. John Berger [1971], 'Field', p. 31. All references to Berger's 'Field' are to the essay as reprinted in this book.
3. Ibid., p. 31, p. 32.
4. Ibid., p. 203.
5. John Berger [1969], 'The Moment of Cubism' in John Berger, *Selected Essays*, ed. Geoff Dyer (London: Bloomsbury, 2001), pp. 82–3.
6. Ibid., p. 82.

7. Ibid., p. 92.
8. Ibid., p. 84.
9. Ibid., p. 74.
10. Ibid., pp. 84–5.
11. Ibid., p. 75.
12. Ibid., p. 85.
13. Berger, 'Field', p. 31.
14. Berger, 'The Moment of Cubism', p. 74.
15. On the rich prehistory of the concept of field in the physical sciences before Faraday, see Ernan McMullin, 'The Origins of the Field Concept in Physics', *Physics in Perspective* 4.1 (February 2002): 13–39.
16. J. E. McGuire, M. Tamny and I. Newton, *Certain Philosophical Questions: Newton's Trinity Notebook* (Cambridge: Cambridge University Press, 1983), p. 211.
17. Isaac Newton [1758], *Philosophical Writings* (Cambridge: Cambridge University Press, 2004), p. 102.
18. Michael Faraday, 'Historical Sketch of Electro-magnetism', *Annals of Philosophy* 19 (1822): 108.
19. Quoted in A. K. T. Assis, J. E. A. Ribeiro and A. Vannucci, 'The Field Concepts of Faraday and Maxwell' in M. S. D. Cattani, L. C. B. Crispino, M. O. C. Gomes and A. F. S. Santoro (eds), *Trends in Physics. Festschrift in Homage to Prof. José María Filardo Bassalo* (São Paulo: Editora Livraría da Física, 2009), pp. 31–8.
20. William Thomson [1851], *Reprint of Papers on Electrostatics and Magnetism* (Cambridge: Cambridge University Press, 2011), p. 473.
21. J. Clerk Maxwell, 'A Dynamical Theory of the Electromagnetic Field', *Philosophical Transactions of the Royal Society of London*, Vol. 155, Part 1 (London: Royal Society of London, 1865), p. 459.
22. Ibid., p. 460.
23. Albert Einstein and Leopold Ingold, *The Evolution of Physics* (New York: Simon and Schuster, 1938), pp. 152–3. While it is widely accepted that theories of ether undergo an acute decline with the broad acceptance of Einstein's special theory of relativity, Cantor and Hodge not only state that one of the reasons for the delayed acceptance of the special theory was a continued interest in ether among British physicists, but that theories of ether persist (in quantum theory, for example). Furthermore, Einstein himself, in an address at the University of Leiden in 1920, cautioned that even the special theory of relativity does not compel the renunciation of ether, only the ascription to it of a definite state of motion.
24. Berger, 'Field', p. 35.
25. Berger, 'The Moment of Cubism', pp. 74–5.
26. Kurt Lewin, *Field Theory in Social Science* (New York: Harper, 1951), p. 240.
27. Ibid., pp. 44–5.
28. Ibid., p. 76.

29. Ibid., p. 52.
30. D. Brett King, and Michael Wertheimer, *Max Wertheimer and Gestalt Theory* (New Brunswick and London: Transaction, 2005), pp. 122–3.
31. George Humphrey, 'The Theory of Einstein and the "Gestalt-Psychologie": A Parallel', *American Journal of Psychology* 35.3 (July 1924): 353–9, pp. 357–8.
32. John Levi Martin, 'What is Field Theory?' *American Journal of Sociology* 109.1 (July 2003): 1–49, p. 15.
33. Wolfgang Köhler, *Dynamics in Psychology* (New York: Washington Square Press, 1965), pp. 61–2.
34. Ibid., p. 55.
35. Kurt Koffka [1935], *Principles of Gestalt Psychology* (London: Routledge, 2013), p. 47.
36. Ibid., p. 42.
37. Ibid., pp. 71–3.
38. Ibid., p. 67.
39. Pitirim A. Sorokin, *Sociocultural Causality, Space, Time: A Study of referential Principled of Sociology and Social Science* (New York: Russell & Russell, 1964), p. vii. Sorokin subsequently introduces his own concept of 'fields of meaning' in which 'all meanings, as pure meanings, find a definite location, not in the field of geometrical or sensory space, but in the universe of pure meanings' (p. 124).
40. Ibid., pp. 108–100. In his early work in the philosophy of science, Lewin developed the concept of *genidentity* in an attempt to show that discrete objects with the same properties are not identical, but multiple entities in different temporal phases. Initially, however, Lewin used the concepts of *relatedness* in biology and *affinity* in chemistry in order to construct a genetic antecedency between disciplines seemingly irreducible from the perspective of each. See Flavioa Padovani, 'Genidentity and Topology of Time: Kurt Lewin and Hans Reichenbach', *The Berlin Group and the Philosophy of Logical Empiricism* (New York: Springer, 2012), pp. 97–122.
41. Berger, 'Field', p. 31.
42. Martin, 'What is Field Theory?', p. 17; Koffka, *Principles of Gestalt Psychology*, p. 8. Pierre Bourdieu, who partially extends the dimensional territory of sociology by recourse to a process of critical disinheritance from Marxism-as-science, neatly sidesteps this problematic. Bourdieu's *concept* of field proceeds at once from a resolution 'to truly side with science', and an attempt to transcend classical Marxism by instituting a break with the teleological *propulsion of substances* at the expense of relationships, dismissing the reduction of the social field to relations of economic production, and refusing an objectivism which obscures symbolic struggle. Bourdieu's ultimate rejection of classical Marxism functions with reference to the same conceptual triumvirate of substantialism, reductionism and objectivism rejected by the first generation of Gestalt field theorists. In place, it demands a dynamic

social topology in which the world can be represented as a multidimensional space constructed on the principles of the differentiation or distribution of properties within a given social universe. For Bourdieu, a universe is possessed with the capability to confer power – the underlying principle of all fields – upon its agents. Power thus constitutes a field of fields manifest in the form of different kinds of capital with their own logics and hierarchies distributing and engendering agents according to a relative composition, determination and volume of capital possessed. The productive dynamism of the field is thus traced in the form of the trajectories of its agents as they occupy a succession of positions with respect to their accumulation of various manifestations of capital immanent to the field. Since constitutive properties of a field are always active properties, Bourdieu's field is always a *field of forces*, in which an objective set of power relations are imposed upon all present in the field and are irreducible to the intent of an individual agent or the direct interpenetration of agents. See Pierre Bourdieu, *Outline of a Theory of Practice* (Cambridge: Cambridge University Press, 1977) and Bourdieu, 'The Genesis of the Concepts of Habitus and of Field', in *Sociocriticism* 2.2 (1985): pp. 11–24.

43. Berger, quoted in Hubert Steins, 'Seelenverwandtschaft im Zeichen der Stille: Zur Ästhetik der Edition Wandelweiser', *MusikTexte* 125 (2010): pp. 85–8.
44. Manfred Werder, introductory talk, 'Field Fest', Q-02, Brussels, 15 October 2011.
45. Werder, correspondence with the author, 27 September 2011.
46. Berger, 'Field', p. 35.
47. Werder, correspondence with the author, 29 August 2015.
48. Werder, 'The field' in *Field Fest*, ed. Julia Eckhardt and Ann Goossens (Brussels: Beursschouwburg, 2005), p. 42.
49. Werder, 'The field', p. 42.
50. Gilles Deleuze and Félix Guattari, *Anti-Oedipus: Capitalism & Schizophrenia*, trans. Robert Hurley, Mark Seem and Helen H. Lane (London: Athlone, 1984), p. 4.
51. Werder, 'The field', p. 42.
52. Iain Hamilton Grant, *Philosophies of Nature after Schelling* (London: Continuum, 2006), pp. 67–8.
53. Werder, 'The field', p. 42.
54. Berger, 'Field', p. 35.
55. See Pierre Chartier and Thierry Marchaisse, *Chine/Europe: Percussions dans la pensée. A partir du travail de François Jullien* (Paris: Presses universitaires de France, 2005). Subsequent translations of Werder's text into German and English (the author's own) have followed the composer's later, modified version, which is divested of explicit citation from and reference to Jullien, serving to reconfigure it as a general statement of compositional intent. Crucially, these translations also excise the leading coordinating conjunction of its original title: 'La musique du

silence, ou le "'sonner"' du monde'. A more recent Spanish translation has reinstated the full title.

56. Manfred Werder, personal correspondence with the author, 11 May 2010.
57. Werder, personal correspondence, 11 May 2010.
58. Gilles Deleuze, *Difference and Repetition*, trans. Paul Patton (London: Athlone, 1994), pp. 36–7.
59. François Jullien, *In Praise of Blandness: Proceeding from Chinese Thought and Aesthetics*, trans. Paula M. Varsano (New York: Zone Books, 2004), pp. 24–5.
60. Ibid., p. 45.
61. Ibid., p. 25.
62. Ibid., p. 70.
63. Ibid., p. 67.
64. Werder, *The Sounding of the World*.
65. Werder, *Practice as performer-composer*, unpublished text, 2011.
66. Ibid.
67. Werder, correspondence with the author, 18 June 2010; Werder, *Practice as performer-composer*.
68. Werder, correspondence with the author, 25 August 2008; Werder, Correspondence with the author, 18 June 2010.
69. Manfred Werder, *The Sounding of the World*, trans. Nicholas Melia, http://www.soundsofeurope.eu/wp-content/uploads/2011/11/the-sounding-of-the-world-Werder.pdf (accessed 31 August 2015)
70. Werder, *Practice as performer-composer*.
71. Berger, 'Field', p. 35.

Chapter 2

The Nondescript*

Stephen Benson

'Gonna test a few bonds . . . see how friendly we are.'
Graham Lambkin and Jason Lescalleet, 'Hotdog Harris or
the Road of Remembrance', *Photographs*

The field of the field recording as the latter is conceived in the present volume is often anything but common ground. It is the field of the unusual, the remote or the hard-of-access; of the little known or the not-before-heard; of the 'hidden' or the microscopic.[1] It is the field of the 'Inaudibly Loud, Long-Lasting, Far-Reaching', or of the near silent and the fugitive; a field heard, not infrequently, late in the day or strikingly early.[2] Sounded fields of these kinds are precisely uncommon, in themselves and in respect of their sources, a late reminder of the origins of such transcriptive and archival practices in anthropology and ethnography. And in being variously uncommon they are uncommonly interesting, hence our being drawn to listen and, in response, to make a case for their aesthetic and ideological value, a case based in part on novelty, whether of sound or source.[3] Field recordings thus made and heard propose a sounded ethics of the uncommon.

Elsewhere, however, we find other sounds, resolutely not sublime, the sounds of recorded fields closer in spirit to the field as imagined by John Berger. This field, while not necessarily common ground in legal terms, is 'a common one', figuratively and experientially: a field with 'the same proportions as your own life'.[4] A field, that is, such as we have to hand, un-ironically acknowledged in recordings of domestic spaces and everyday goings-on, of mundane and uneventful happenings, 'immediately recognizable', sometimes, in source if not sound (Berger, 'Field', p. 32). These are the fields, to put it in simple terms,

---

*Accompanying audio recordings are indicated in the following way – d[2.1]b – and available on the publisher's website at: https://edinburghuniversitypress.com/book-writing-the-field-recording-hb.html [click on the 'resources' tab].

of the ordinary not the extraordinary; or rather, these are the fields that implicate and lay claim to something we might call ordinariness. Uncommon they are not. And so, given the often loosely organised, muted and indistinct sounds of these common field recordings, their scrappy fuzziness, what is it that holds the attention, however tenuously, or enables the attention to wander in ways that feel still to be significant and promiseful? Why, given the marked absence of the singular and the novel, should we listen? How are they interesting – 'merely interesting' – these common sounds?[5] And in what register might their interestingness be set to words?[6]

The common field recording is the subject here, together with the matter of the descriptive mode attendant on such soundworks. The object is a serial collaborative work by Graham Lambkin and Jason Lescalleet, a trilogy comprising three named artefacts – *The Bread-winner*, *Air Supply* and *Photographs* – recorded and edited between 2006 and 2012.[7] Both Lambkin and Lescalleet are processual in creative orientation, and prolific, meaning that fine distinctions of quality or value run the risk of appearing at best leaden-footedly precious and at worst tendentiously ignorant of extra-acoustic implications. Their multi-part collaborative project stands nevertheless, for this listener, as one of the most interesting soundworks of recent years. Responding over time to this work, 'gradual[ly] hollowing out an imprint', as Michel Chion says of successive acts of the 'listening-by-listening constitution of an object', inevitably raises questions, both of judgement and quality, and of an appropriate verbal account.[8] 'The field affords me considerable pleasure', that much I can admit by way of beginning. But I hesitate to make value judgements, for two reasons. First, because the received notion of the work, as concept, is potentially anachronistic used here in a field of artistic practice – post-Cagean or experimental music; phonography; *musique concrète*; *audio-vérité*; sound art: whatever we wish to call it[9] – regularly conceived in terms not of an idealised aesthetic object and scenario, but of an ethically inflected form of attentive life, ongoingly inhabited in the inventions of maker and listener.[10] And secondly, because aesthetic judgements can appear tellingly to falter before some at least of the kinds of contemporary artworks discussed in these pages. The faltering would appear to be symptomatic, as if something in the substance of the works themselves resists or frustrates inherited, or at least dominant, ways of sifting and selecting. There is an uncertainty as to the status of the exemplar, the object of close listening, and it is important, because significant, to admit as much.[11] Indeed, uncertainty as to character and quality may well prove to be related closely to the question of appropriate or adequate registers of description.

Hence the 'vague and non-specific' provocation of interestingness and the concomitant call, not for the declaration of judgement, but for the working-through, potentially collaborative, of justification.[12]

The 'tentative approach' to description marked by John Berger in his own account of field thinking is thus appropriate, not least in its echo of the trying-out – the trialling – that is the promise of the essay (p. 32). For now, I can say that Lambkin and Lescalleet's collaboration has produced a work of provoking interest, looser and variously more informal than much contemporaneous practice in this broad area, most obviously that with Wandelweiser affiliations. It is a serial soundwork the cumulative effect of which is suggestive of the pairing of friendship as motivation and ground – as object; a soundwork which in its materials, its field recordings in particular, makes the sounds of friendship, even understands friendship as a matter of sound, albeit not necessarily the 'total sonority' suggested by Roland Barthes as characterising friendship's desirous 'space'.[13] Friendship as sounded here is something altogether more changeful, fleeting and unexpected. To say as much by way of an opening gambit is already to invoke the idiom that is both the property of oneself and a mark of companionship. And idiom unavoidably brings into play the much-disputed category of medium-specificity, an anachronism to pair with the work concept but one which we may also wish not entirely to disavow or to declare as having been overcome.[14]

Inventory

The most noticeable aspect of the work, hence the place to start describing, is its very legibility: the fact of its appearing to invite interpretation, albeit that the invitation comes in the form of words and images, as if thereby to signal by implication the potential difficulty of speaking of the sounds. The framing invitation appears friendly in its miscellaneous openness, a hint perhaps that the two that have made what we hold are happy, or at least willing, to be joined by a third. Such an apparently extrovert orientation to the listener-viewer is markedly at odds with the attitude evident in many field recording-related objects, where a minimalist or abstractionst resistance to the ready legibility of word and iconography tends to preside, of a piece with a reductionist orientation to sound: in winds measure recordings' 'double [field] compilation', *v-p v-f v-n*, for example, with its anonymous white packaging, lowercase typography, affectlessly descriptive titles, and unpeopled and industrial grey photographic image.[15] Lambkin and Lescalleet establish a pointedly different relation to the notion of the field as a commons to that of the artists of this important compilation, one we might call unbracketed; a difference immediately evident but which will take a little time to work through.

A basic inventory of elements is warranted by the proliferation of potentially signifying clues, and by the 'tentative approach' to description under the accommodating sign of which the present account shelters:

Materials: three objects, three titles: *The Breadwinner: Musical Settings for Common Environments and Domestic Situations* (2008), *Air Supply* (2010) and *Photographs* (2013). Four discs in total, numbered one to four, each comprising eight titled pieces.

Scenario and arrangements: 'The material for *The Breadwinner* was recorded at Lambkin's house in upstate NY, over two recording sessions', while 'The material for *Air Supply* was mostly recorded in and around Lescalleet's house in Maine in early 2010'.[16] The first of *Photographs*' two discs was recorded in Folkestone, England, the second in Worcester, Massachusetts, USA – the childhood homes of Lambkin and Lescalleet respectively.[17]

Sources: the cover and design for *The Breadwinner* is an adapted copy of Ariel Peeri's cover for the original LP release of Robert Ashley's opera *Private Parts* (1977).[18] The cover and design for *Air Supply* is an adapted copy of *Air Structures* (1978), an unofficial bootleg recording of Robert Fripp and Brian Eno made in Paris in 1975.

Images: *The Breadwinner*: a single morphed photograph of Lambkin's and Lescalleet's faces, unattributed and uncaptioned. *Air Supply*: an abstract cover image modelled after *Air Structures*; inside, one image of each artist and two of them together, one of the latter of which includes the word 'GENTS', in capitals, matched by 'LADIES' hidden under the enclosed disc. The images in question, striped and slightly sepia in appearance, were made by Lambkin using a 'faulty printer' and hand tinting. The design is again modelled after the images on the cover of *Air Structures*, the photograph on the rear of which has the words 'REST ROOM' in the background. *Photographs*: ten photographs, including one each of Lambkin and Lescalleet as children (with handwritten captions), one of their shadows against a tree and one of them standing in a church doorway, one in which they stand with what look to be close relations (perhaps a brother and a son, or two sons), and one in which they are silhouetted, standing, behind an older man, seated.[19]

Symmetries, pairs and groups: four discs, eight pieces apiece. Individual track lengths, and so total playing time, are identical for discs one and three (the two recorded in and around places associated with Lambkin) and discs two and four (the two recorded in and around places associated with Lescalleet). Track three of discs one and three have two-part titles the first parts of which read as codes: 'E5150' (the title of a song by Black Sabbath) and 'CT20 1PS' (a postcode in Folkestone). Discs one and three include three similarly titled tracks: 'There and Back', 'There and Back Again' and 'Back Again'. Tracks four to six of discs two and four are grouped – '69°F', '68°F', '67°F'; and 'Kingdom 1 (Knobs)', 'Kingdom 2 (Laughing)', 'Kingdom 3 (Submerge)' – while the final two tracks of these discs appear as variations: 'Air Pressure' and 'Air Supply', and 'Street Hassle' and 'Street Cleaner'.[20]

These are some at least of the main visual and verbal marks, signs of the private codes, the minutiae, of friendship, those small things such as only a friend would understand – hence, perhaps, the gesture towards Ashley's *Private Lives* and the various allusions to pop music of the late 1970s and early 1980s. They are in Berger's terms the field ('the *ground*') which '*contains*', and to which our attention is drawn by, the recordings ('Field', p. 35). They invitation is to act the befriending reader, to say what we see in order more securely – and so, perhaps, pleasurably – to establish that we know what we hear. Interpretative breadwinning, however, while unavoidable and part itself of the promise of friendship, risks yet another in a long if largely silent history of the disavowal of sound by writing. Better, thus, to see if we might mark, by descriptively re-marking, how the copying, symmetry and repetition evident in what we can see and read are of a piece with the collaborative twoness of the work as a series in sound. The presiding figure for such essaying is the pair, the partial repeat or copy: two Ls, each an other; each, as marked by duration but not name, the home of two of the trilogy of four; each jointly and separately copied as image across the two twos of the series, with varying degrees of fidelity. All of which counterpointing posits the collaboration of friendship as a form of rhythm; or, to say it again, posits rhythm as itself a form of friendship. 'Gonna test a few bonds . . . see how friendly we are.'

Sounds Formal

Along with the distances travelled in order to make the recordings – 'There and Back Again', 'contingencies overlapping' (Berger, 'Field', p. 32) – the middle ground between these two, hence the channel for the series, is their medium: recorded sound and the air (supply and pressure) of its passage; a medium entirely familiar from a long century and more of exposure, and yet, as encountered here in this name-resisting form, still a little unexpected. The medium via which they communicate holds Lambkin and Lescalleet together in a serial friendship, on which we eavesdrop. Theirs is definitely '*an art of sounds*', albeit one palpably earth-bound rather than ethereal – 'Listen, the Snow is Falling' is the inaugural injunction on the first disc – and the provocation is thus to consider how this particular art might be conceived or made to signify anew.[21] As Berger says, modestly, of his own attempt to 'describe . . . diagrammatically' a common field experience: 'What are the simplest things that can be said about it?' ('Field', p. 32).

The presence of two, both separate and together, is signalled from the start by the twin authorship and then by the many repetitions, full and partial, of the verbal and visual marks. The listener is thereby encouraged to listen out for pairings and for passages between; to think in terms of what is promised by 'Two States' (*The Breadwinner*). Conceived formally, as a unified work in sound – to accept for now the work concept and a degree of structural listening – there is a sense of two different orientations towards acoustic material, two operations, each made audible in relation to the other. The first is a presiding continuity of sound, an all-overness that feels acoustically indivisible and durational; the second, an orientation towards repetition and intermittence, hence towards rhythm. This second characteristic is perhaps the single most striking element of the composition, in part because it is relatively easily articulated, and because it answers acoustically, as one more repetition, the work's framing visual rhythms. 'There and Back', for example, the second piece on *The Breadwinner*, includes near the beginning an arrhythmic tapping or flapping **d[2.1]b**; a soft flapping, slightly hollow-sounding, heard intermittently over the 4 minutes. We shall not be able to say with any certainty what makes the sound, but it serves nevertheless as an anchor point against which we sense the other rhythms and repetitions: some kind of detonation, complete with descending whistle; a sound as if of a ball being bounced; and a short and discretely placed recording, higher-pitched, of the tinkle of metal on glass and in water, sounded repeatedly with an effect pointedly contrapuntal as well as somehow gestural. Sounds, each a rhythmic character, are heard as if from inside a room, within the warmly muffled ambience of which we situate the little motifs one against the other, some as if close, others recessed. The rhythmic field becomes for this listener one of the titular domestic situations, light and modest-sounding, even mildly ironising in tone. The situation of the domestic, as it is happening here or as it is made to happen, sounds as a matter of rhythm.

The series includes a host of other constituent parts that, while various in terms of sound, speed, duration and imagined cause, are heard as a general rhythmic disposition, a marking of intermittency that in the fact of its being repeated, comes to feel significant. These field-recorded rhythms, to speak of them in terms of imagined sources, include, *inter alia*, the common sounds of the creaking of a door ('Listen, the Snow is Falling'), the inhalation and exhalation of snoring ('E5150/Body Transport'), some kind of sawing ('Soap Opera Suite'), shovelling and the engines of passing cars ('Because the Night') and footsteps ('Back Again'). Some of the sounds have clearly been treated after the event of their recording, either looped or extended in duration, but the overall impression is of an abundantly polyrhythmic auditory field.

Against or alongside these passages we hear sounds that are markedly continuous as opposed to intermittent or spaced. These are, most consistently, the ambient sounds registered by microphones, the presiding ground for the acoustic events of many of the constituent pieces. If Lambkin and Lescalleet can be said to have made a field recording of one thing in particular, albeit inadvertently, we might nominate this most common of sounds: the ambient sound of the passage of air and of the immediate acoustic environment. And if we were to nominate a true commons of the field recording as acoustic object, it would be this: same-sounding but endlessly variable in texture and volume, a muffled quasi-presence, animate and yet somehow inert, unrepeatable and yet universal. Description's limit, if we imagine such a framing, is marked by this unmarked sound.

The 'complex', 'continuously sustained' mass of ambient sound, the work's ground, is heard alongside all the other ostensibly non-rhythmic, hence uneventful passages whose dominant sonic character is uninterrupted.[22] This listener registers many of these as field recordings, whether treated or not, distinct from the ground ambience and from the more eventful acoustic happenings that sound as if 'on top' of these two layers. And then very close in character to these assorted field recordings are those sounds more akin to musical drones; sounds, that is, that strike the listener as musical rather than environmental, albeit the work as a whole renders such distinctions moot. These sounds tend to have a gothic, ghostly and ominous character, as if in acknowledgement of the affiliation of drone and threnody.

My language, as it works to disaggregate and give adequate expression to what I hear, is effortful. I can feel its being so. Critical inarticulacy is admissible nevertheless, and worth preserving, as the mark of an aesthetic response such as I am seeking to register here and to work through.[23] More particularly, performatively laboured descriptions such as these are excused on the grounds that they help pragmatically to substantiate with detail a relatively intuitive sense, acknowledged over time, of the twinned formal orientations of Lambkin and Lescalleet's series: the rhythmic and the continuous, or the interrupted and the sustained. We might be inclined to identify these pairs as equivalent to the event and the field, were it not for Berger's caveat regarding the need of each for the other: 'All events exist as definable events by virtue of their *relation* to other events', such that each is the event of the other ('Field', p. 35, emphasis added). The sustained sounds of Lambkin and Lescalleet's fields are arranged rhythmically – interruptively; relationally – against the rhythmic passages, at however slow a tempo; and the sustained sounds, as we know, are ever indigenously and pulsingly rhythmic in texture and in their complex massing. The formal operation in this art of sound, rather than being a twoness in the sense of pairing or binary, is more akin to the marking or spacing of time: the cutting or division of duration and the possibility of such by means of the edit. The rhythmic cut conjoins just as it holds apart. It is the mark here of friendship, but also of the cut made by the recording in the field of the common where friendship is happening.[24]

Sounds Informal

The foregoing description, itself a cutting and editing of its object, is too abstracting to name with sufficient security or suggestiveness a soundwork of such informality, such abundant scrappiness. Nor does it offer any explanation as to why and in what particular manner such sounds might detain us – why, that is, they are interesting. We need now to acknowledge what Michael Chion calls 'the interested nature of audition', our propensity to wonder, as we listen, '"What is that?"', '"Where is it coming from?"'[25] The sounds themselves enjoin us to listen 'causally' and 'figuratively'.[26] Doing so, we sense gradually, almost 'diagrammatically' (to use Berger's word), a small repertoire of field sounds, variously modest, fugitive, funny and obtuse. 'It has a little bit of everything in it', so we are told ('If All Goes Well', *Photographs*). For these are sounds which, heard repeatedly, gather according to what appears to be an overlapping series of anthropo- and eco-logical groupings and scenarios. They are the titular sounds of *Common Environments and Domestic Situations*.

To begin, L and L's common field is elemental.[27] We hear over the time of the collaboration a series of variations on the sounds of each of the four classical elements. The aforementioned airiness is evident throughout, most obviously in the lo-fi field disruptions of the wind, but also in the nondescript ambience of the outside air in which seagulls cry, through which cars pass by and over which bells sound. The end of 'Layman's Lament' (*Air Supply*) is particularly striking, in its apparent move outward and upward from chant-like human sounds into bird-filled open air. Earth, down below all along, is acknowledged in the 'Street Hassle' (*Photographs*) sounds of walking and the shovelling of 'Because the Night' (*Air Supply*) d[2.2]b, and in the repeated drones, each its own texture but all in their rumbling grittiness suggestive of the subterranean – the ancient drone of the ear in the earth rather than the eye in the sky. Fire sounds just once, as a hint of warmth in 'Listen, the Snow is Falling' – an inaugural gesture of comfort and solace – and water too is here, particularly in *The Breadwinner*, with its twin action motifs of bubbling and boiling, and of being stirred.

The sound of the elements is heard as environmental, an ambient signifier of the recordings and the ambience of the recording itself, the artwork, as object. I am reluctant to posit the elemental sounds as primarily locational, so as fixing all the rest, but that is certainly one way in which they imprint themselves and in which we might interpret them. And yet a relation of fixing is perhaps too grasping a response in establishing a default mode of ground-figure arrangement. The elemental-environmental sounds are not separate from or underpinnings for those acoustic signs of the human; rather, the elements are intertwined with the ostensibly human such that each inhabits and is inhabited by the other in a blurring of what might otherwise settle into a too enclosingly defined self–other relation. For L and L most certainly do sound out, in a finely nuanced way but without show or piety, the fact of being human. We hear the common sounds, first, of things being *done* – of liquid being stirred, something or other variously shovelled or cut or drawn; and of walking and assorted unidentifiable fumblings – and of things being *said*, snippets of passing conversation about taxis, banjo playing, food and drink. And against these incidental sounds of the waking hours we hear the sound most unavailable to us in the moment of its making, that of our being asleep, marked here by snoring (what else?), an earth-bound drone-in-waiting, both non-verbal vocal signature and a lamenting reminder of our proximity to unconsciousness (with the hint also of a blokeish practical joke).[28]

The imprint left by the 'listening-by-listening constitution' of the series is characterised once again not by an aloneness or separation, but by a relation between sounds. This relation, in the case of the human-made sounds, is touchingly communal and ritualistic, a marking – again, free of piety or grandeur – of occasions of being together and of being with others. Field recording-oriented artworks can imply a separateness or isolation on the part of the recordist, whether literally, as a being-apart of location, or metaphorically, in a recorded disposition to objects or scenarios variously expressive of a person singularly alone with singular things – alone, that is, with their listening, including the prosthetic listening of the recording technology and the implied future listening of a solo auditor. L & L's field, conversely, is populated, a field of occasion. *Photographs*, the final part of the trilogy, is especially richly communal in acoustic character, as if with the intention of drawing out a particular aspect of the first two parts of the series.

Being together is sounded in two ways in particular, each signifying and acknowledging a form of community. The first is foreheard in the bell of 'The Breadwinner', a motif picked up at the start of *Photographs* ('Loss') and in the chant-like vocal sounds of 'Layman's Lament' d[2.3]b (and echoed in the whistling kettle of 'If All Goes Well'). 'Quested to St Hilda', a field recording of part of a church ceremony, suggests a possible reading of these two apparently isolated compositional elements in terms of a ritualised communality, and of song. We hear a priest's voice and then the beginning of a congregation singing, 'How sweet the name of Mary, . . .'; while a little later, in 'Gold Interior', a fragment of conversation – 'went to listen to the bells last night . . . Baptist church . . .' – further directs attention. Bell- and singing-sounds are treated after the fact, pushed and pulled gravitationally towards what feels over time to be an ever-present possibility of the drone; but then these highly marked field moments imply an origin for the drone not only in lament, as already noted, but also in community and ritual, especially the communal performance of song: song as grounded in the drone or emerging from it, an intermittency inherent as potential in duration.

The second occasion is marked not by song but by food, in particular, by the archetypal ritual of food prepared and shared. This element is pointed up in particular across the twinned discs of *Photographs*, each of which testifies movingly to the occasion of collaboration as happening unshowily within and around the scene of the everyday. The second disc is bookended by rituals of domestic hospitality, beginning with a shared lunch of 'chicken and vegetable soup' – soup with, again, 'a little of everything in it', in case the listener, as silent guest, hadn't already noticed – and ending drily with a review of dessert: 'Jason, were you a fan of the plum pudding?' To which Jason replies, 'No'. (Jason's surname has earlier been figured in relation specifically to cooking, in the brief discussion on the subject of skillets included as part of 'If Truth Be Told' (*Photographs*).) An analogy is sounded between the making and sharing of food, as an act of hospitality, and the making of the soundwork as in this conception a record of collaborative hospitality and domestic invention. Where so much field recording-oriented practice appears to aspire to a condition of auditory uncanniness – the uncommon as uncanny – L and L are at home, making and performing a shared space of invention the achieved ordinariness of which is the feat of the collaboration.[29] The homemade – the made at, in and by the home – is their 'site', their commons, their conjured re-cording: a commonplace act of the heart.[30]

Description's Field

Descriptions such as these, tentative in approach as they are, offer in turn a temporary home in language for what is heard; a home suggested by the sounds themselves, but made, necessarily, by the words through and with which we form, gradually, a relation to those sounds. The relation happens in the temporary home of the description. Ekphrasis – for that is the rhetorical mode – speaks out from a place between the listener and the presently silent soundwork (it is silent now, as I write and as you read), hoping through an act of mediated invention to conjure a presence for the work such that it appears animated anew in language, the same but different. Description, however doggedly faithful or wilfully inventive, testifies to the interestingness of its material; it is, let's say, the re-mark in writing of the interesting, akin to Chion's 'imprint', the 'listening-by-listening constitution of an object'.[31]

The discourse of description, especially as it figures in accounts of the theory and practice of art criticism, both suggests and at times seeks to maintain a considerable distance from interpretation; as if one form of words is able pristinely to indicate, whereas another is burdened with the lesser or greater task, depending on how one conceives the work, of glossing. And yet *descriptio*, a figure of rhetoric, as it finds a place to start and a way of stretching out and going on, is never other than tendentious.[32] Sound's writing, following as it does, and whether it likes it or not, in the wake of the discursive fields of music criticism, can be rather resistant to such tendencies, in particular, to those ostensibly inherent in non-technical descriptive modes:

to the particularities that enable and so characterise scenarios of listening, and to the potential for a graspingly co-optive and normative relationship of listener and listened-to.[33] Hence, for example, Patrick Farmer's recent text-score 'Listening and its not', a direct response to the ostensibly predatory workings of description.[34] Farmer instructs the participant to 'try and write about listening in a way that does not point directly to, or at it', hence to conceive a text in which the originating acoustic matter is constitutively absent for the reader. '[K]eeping distance' is the possibility here, an evasion of dualism and of direct appropriation or projection, and an opening towards the 'overgrown, forgotten, something else': 'A description without sense that may pick up new qualities'.[35]

I mention this provocation as an instance of one strand of thinking within sound studies, and, more immediately, because the present essay, in being avowedly a description with sense (or so one hopes), aspires to precisely that mode against which the not of listening protests. The aspiration thus far to a form of descriptive close listening is, again, strategic, of a piece with a provisional acceptance of medium specificity and the work concept, and in response to the performative contradiction of those paradoxically brief and vague expositions of specific works evident in much writing about sound art. Berger asks of his own field, 'What are the simplest things that can be said about it?', a question that yields a description simple only in the sense that the writing testifies in its movements to an attentive proximity to its object and to a desire to draw its reader into a similar relation.[36] Closeness, as a figure of relation, is just as much a matter of ethics as are distance or resistance. As Lawrence Kramer writes in defence of the 'ordinary language' of common musical discourse, 'The act of description required by the object's inability to speak for itself is an encounter with otherness in the most positive sense of the term'.[37] To seek through instructive intervention to bypass description's grounding register is in one sense tacitly, albeit anxiously, to maintain the dual ideal of a sound object conceived as an other of language, and so of idiom, and, conversely, of an unmediated conveyance between listener, writer and reader.[38] There is no bypassing description's encounter and no need, faced with the scenario, to be anxious or melancholy – or, for that matter, to be idealistically hopeful about the chances of a union of media, hence of an '"overcoming of otherness"'.[39] The question is not, or not only, how we might escape the common predicament, but in what registers of invention it might be inhabited, this avowedly 'artificial thing that exists / In its own seeming'.[40]

And so how further to develop the tendencies in this ekphrasis, towards a *reading* of L and L's soundwork, one that might account for why, given the acknowledged aspects of form and texture, the sounds provoke and are valuable? How to stretch the descriptive tendencies a little further in order to meet by re-marking the marks of a work at once affecting and yet benignly resistant to that language in which affection enters the commons of discourse and so comes to be open to contestation?

The tendency in the description thus far has been towards notating a loose and welcoming openness of elements that have in common a play on the figure of twoness: the copy; the iterated; the pair; the collaboration; the symmetrical; the friends, L and another L. A presiding relationality is heard, again loosely, in the work's performed organising of duration, its play with continuity and interruption, and with the rhythm of the cut or edit by which one becomes the other; and heard also in the repeated sounding of scenarios of sharing and communality, through and within an environment of elements. Serial composition; a looseness of form, accommodating in its gathering of elements ('a little bit of everything in it'); a plethora of anecdotal signs; and, held within these frames, sounded scenes of friendship and domestic sociability, and a presiding attention to the field of the common: would it not be true to say that the constituent parts thus described sound suspiciously akin to those of that most commonplace of verbal art forms, the novel? Yes, the novel, odd as it may seem to suggest such a connection. And if we accept the apparent family resemblance? What conception of L and L's soundwork might be made possible by a description that has tended in this direction, however unexpectedly?

To work out this possibility I turn, as the first step of a brief detour, to Roland Barthes, writing about music and description in Balzac's *Sarrasine*:

> What would happen if one actually performed Marianina's '*addio*' as it is described in the discourse? Something incongruous, no doubt, extravagant, and not musical. More: is it really possible to perform the act described? This leads to two propositions. The first is that the discourse has no responsibility via-à-vis the real: in the most realistic novel, the referent has no 'reality': suffice it to imagine the disorder the most orderly narrative would create were its descriptions taken at face value, converted into operative programs and simply *executed*.[41]

'Something incongruous, no doubt, extravagant, and not musical': this might serve as a thumbnail description of L and L's collaboration, a counterpointing of the disharmony of incongruence and the divergent energies of the extravagant. Barthes considers here a particular aspect of what he had previously identified as 'the reality effect' of descriptive writing in fictional prose, classic realist novels in particular; those passages of writing conventionally understood quietly and faithfully, even a little boringly, to establish and colour a world for the human drama, but which, so Barthes suggests, serve an altogether more tendentious function in corroborating and authenticating the claim made by novelistic prose on the field of the real.

The idea that a realisation of the descriptions of realism would result, not in real-ness but in 'disorder', was neatly borne out shortly after Barthes made his suggestion, and with reference specifically to acoustic markers, by John Cage in his text score, _, _ _ *Circus On* _, described as a 'Means for translating a book into a performance without actors, a performance which is both literary and musical or one or the other'.[42] Cage's proposal, first realised in his own *Roaratorio: An Irish Circus on Finnegans Wake* (1979), is for the making of a new piece from a performance of all the sounds in a chosen literary work, to the accompaniment of a verbal text extracted from the source through a series of processual operations – not a straightforward acoustic conversion of a novel's signified aurality, but certainly an artfully disordered execution of description's signifiers.[43] L and L's work, given its anecdotal and geographical orientations, might be conceived along these lines, as a Cagean realisation without a source text; an acoustic fiction with no originating words.

To do so, however, would require projecting the traces of a prior verbal narrative on to the acoustic material, a narrative for L and L that would account in entirely conventional literary terms for the snatches of conversation that we hear and the various comings and goings that we imagine by means of the recorded sounds. Rather than think of these ingredients as the sounded rustlings of language and so resort yet again to the comforts of one more back translation from sound to word, we might instead hear this work in sound, not as the acoustic version of an imagined novel, but as the sounding out, literally and metaphorically, of an *idea* of the novelistic, taking a cue perhaps from one of L and L's clues: Robert Ashley's *Private Parts*, with its '*meditation*' on the form of opera;[44] the novelistic conceived, that is, as a recording, via description, of the field of common things, a field the commonness of which is acknowledged and affirmed rather than lyricised, atomised or abstracted.[45] This is an idea of the novel inherited most emphatically from the mid- and late-nineteenth century and which has been variously operative and evident in fiction since then; a record of the going-on of the secular prosaic, what in different contexts has been thought of as the everyday or the ordinary or the insignificant (terms far from interchangeable).[46] The novelistic thus conceived is the field of the common, if not in the sense of ownership then in terms at least of a marking of the shared territory of the domestic, in all its parts. Other arts have attended to it, painting most compellingly, but the novel is that form in which the common field of the ordinary, imagined as a form of descriptive attention to quotidian detail, has been most persuasively and lastingly represented, via the same medium as we are all bound to use in the specification of our own prosaic environments. As such, the novel is the form in which, through the common art of description – 'the humblest of intelligent symbolic acts' – a particular conception of the ordinary has been recorded and made known.[47]

The conception in question has been subject to much scepticism: from those reading for the plot, for whom the potentially interminable itemising of space and its stuff is not only tedious but also, and quite precisely, surplus to requirements; and for critics, for whom description is one of the chief constitutive marks of the novel's founding and continued acquisitive individualism. A space or an object described is a space or object made knowable and thereby known. Such is the novel's claim on, and to, the world. Hence, variously but always sceptically, György Lukács on description's detemporalising and dehumanising orientations, Barthes on description's work in the naturalising of culture, and Franco Moretti on description's inherently conservative blocking of history.[48]

Yet there remains the possibility (that at least) of a counter-reading of novelistic description, according to which the novel promises, prosaically but uniquely, a non-acquisitive relation to those environments it details; a marking of the field of the common that does not, in the very act of transcription, make of it something other. The novelised object, descriptively attended, is apparently 'nothing special', of a kind of ordinariness the weak provocation of which declines to offer for the onlooker anything by way of social distinction.[49] It is the thing attended, albeit with mild puzzlement: not only at the object of attention but also at one's noticing and being-with. Attending does not lead towards acquisition or domination, and certainly not to self-confirmingly responsive articulacy. Judgement and knowledge remain elusive; indeed, their remaining so is a mark of the relation, in its relative mildness and indistinctness, and in its being unresolved. Such is the promise, however unrealised or unrealisable.[50]

Sound's Nondescript

I have sought to corroborate the tendency of a descriptive essaying of L and L's trilogy towards the realm of the novel, a realm defined in this instance by an ethics of description and of a common ground. Verbal response and audio object have come thus to be interwoven around description's reach, and its workings. In lieu of an expansive return now to the details of the soundwork, I end with a more generalising summary, beginning with the provocation from Brian Kane that has guided this listening essay:

> If there is such a thing as sound art, 'the message' must be grounded in the sound . . . A theory of sound art must take account of sound art as *an art of sounds*, where sounds are heard in all their sociality. A theory of sound art is ultimately justified by its ability to support the description and production of soundworks at the level where individual sounds matter.[51]

It is the possibility and the possible registers of such a description that I have been working here, with the additional fold of the descriptive itself as that which is performed as well as invited by the sounds in question – the field recording as an act of auditory description. While I agree with Kane that we should seek to 'specify the relation between forms of sociality and the sounds made', such forms may well turn out to be known to us already as existing mediations or representations. The novel is of course one such, perhaps the pre-eminent art, in the West, in which 'forms of sociality' have been imaginatively inhabited and dramatised. Much field recording-based compositional practice appears to aspire to the formal orientation and affective register of lyric poetry, whereas L and L's serial collaboration is a triple-decker: expansive and discursive where the tendency in the art form is otherwise, towards precision, reduction and restriction, however forbiddingly or performatively durational; abundantly signifying rather than veiled and abstracted; and unashamedly parochial and anecdotal where contemporaneous work in sound can appear to resist overt anthropocentrism. The anecdotally discursive frame, novelistically loose in form, gathers and holds organised sounds the field of which is a commons of memory and friendship; a shared sounded ground of two together, structurally and experientially, and of the rhythmed symmetries of difference within sameness. The frame is novelistic and so too the sounded field, the latter in the sense of marking a register of ordinary prosaic matter: an unparticularising sounding of what at this endpoint, and in keeping with the descriptive motif at play throughout this reading, we might nominate as the *nondescript*, a term singularly fitting in the disjunctions of its three meanings: as that which is 'undistinguished or insignificant', or is 'not easily classified . . . neither one thing nor another', or 'has not been previously described'.[52] The nondescript, conceived as an aesthetic category, bespeaks, while maintaining, a perception of the interesting in the trivial, the novel or foreign in the over-known, and the undescribed or undescribable in the not-worth-describing. Or perhaps it is not a relation of one *in* the other, marked here prepositionally, but of one *as* the other; a relation, 'apparently illogical', analogous to that of field and event as articulated by Berger and of sounded continuity and intermittence as performed in the trilogy ('Field', p. 35). More particularly, the nondescript is a word helpfully impervious to the potential normativity of a claim on common ground, a means of resisting privatisation and any tendency towards the proprietorial.[53]

The nondescript, as aesthetic response, is a form of the interesting. It is one field of the interesting, and to that extent it brings us back to the beginning. L and L's collaborative soundwork is nondescript. Therein lies not only its achievement but also the interestingness of its common field and of that field's appeal: its attraction and its call. To describe its nondescript audio-description and acknowledge a sometimes nondescript experience of it, in terms of an inherited, culturally resonant idea of the novel, is to situate the sounds socially and to recognise thereby the wordliness of their resonance. The 'forms of sociality' heard in L and L's work are not in themselves uncommon: how could they be, given what is at stake? They are the relational forms of friendship, male friendship in particular, and of domestic and local communality and collaboration;[54] and the relational forms of the ambient and elemental environments within which sociality comes to happen. The forms are sounded as we listen, causally and figuratively – as we listen for the origin or scenario of the acoustic matter – just as they are when the work is heard structurally and texturally, for the organisation of the material. Sound's novelty, thus sounded, resides not in the forms themselves but in their singular articulation, what we might call their style: the sounded stylings that make and mark a field of the common. Kathleen Stewart, wishing to notate the fleeting happening in everyday life of what she calls 'ordinary affects', looks 'to fashion some form of verbal address that is adequate to their form'.[55] Adapting Stewart, we can say that the field recording thus styled by L and L to describe, thereby effecting, a common ground is one such mode of adequacy, as in its own minor way is the descriptive register of encounter essayed here, the latter being also an attempt to acknowledge 'the interesting's lack of descriptive specificity' while at the same time using that lack as the moving-off point for an account.[56] The trilogy is to 'where the field was' as L is to L: each the other's commons, each resonantly and hopefully nondescript ('If All Goes Well', *Photographs*)

Notes

1. Jennie Gottschalk, looking to summarise the territory, considers a strain of field recording-based practice under the heading 'Finding Hidden Sounds' in *Experimental Music since 1970* (London: Bloomsbury, 2016), pp. 64–71. Artists mentioned include David Dunn, described as attending to 'sounds that are difficult to access', and Jana Winderen, whose own description of her work provides Gottschalk's heading.

2. 'Inaudibly Loud, Long-Lasting, Far-Reaching' is the title of a chapter of Douglas Kahn's *Noise, Water, Meat: A History of Sound in the Arts* (Cambridge, MA: MIT Press, 2001), pp. 201–30. It forms one part of a section devoted to 'The Impossible Inaudible'. See also Joanna Demers's characterisation of some of the work of Toshiya Tsunoda and Francisco López (*Listening Through the Noise: The Aesthetics of Experimental Electronic Music* (Oxford: Oxford University Press, 2010), pp. 113–34). Demers describes the recordings in question as variously 'sparse and long-lasting', 'of long duration and minute detail' (p. 125), with sounds including 'a seven-minute recording of the wind blowing through the rails of a metal footbridge' (p. 126) and 'some sort of electrical signal' heard in a recording 'with a duration of more than seventeen minutes' (p. 128).

3. Will Montgomery writes of Tsunoda as 'direct[ing] the ear towards what is not available to ordinary experience' ('Beyond the Soundscape: Art and Nature in Contemporary Phonography' in *The Ashgate Companion to Experimental Music*, ed. James Saunders (Farnham: Ashgate, 2009), pp. 145–61, p. 155).

4. John Berger, 'Field', p 32, p. 35. References to Berger's 'Field' are to the essay reprinted in the present volume.

5. The 'merely interesting' is Sianne Ngai's term for that peculiarly low-level affective response provoked, for instance, by the 'look' of conceptual art (*Our Aesthetic Categories: Zany, Cute, Interesting* (Cambridge, MA: Harvard University Press, 2012), pp. 110–73, p. 112).

6. According to Ngai, the interesting, as a specific form of aesthetic evaluation, is characterised in part by the call for justification it provokes in others: 'when someone feels compelled to make public his

evaluation of an object as interesting, we seem equally compelled to ask immediately: why?' (*Our Aesthetic Categories*, p. 169). Hence the auto-interrogation ventriloquised here, and tacitly throughout what follows, in reply to the everyday matter of my having been interested by a particular soundwork.

7. *The Breadwinner: Musical Settings for Common Environments and Domestic Situations* (Erstwhile, 2008); *Air Supply* (Erstwhile 059, 2010); *Photographs* (Erstwhile, 2013). *Photographs* comprises two discs. There is also a 7-inch record of additional material from the collaboration ('The Food Chain' / 'Nice Ass' (Glistening Examples, 2011)). The trilogy is the subject of a relatively extensive critical literature online, to a little of which I make reference below. See, in particular, Matthew Horne's review essay, 'Last a Lifetime', published in issue 2 of the online journal *surround* (April 2014): http://surround. noquam.com/last-a-lifetime/. Horne cites a number of other online responses. The richness of this resource is a reminder that art of this kind is made possible and then sustained by the efforts and enthusiasms of small networks and communities involved at all stages in the life and influence of the work, from artist to listener. The co-option of such work in academic and other institutional forums, however benignly intentioned in terms of advocacy and dissemination, is not without its problems, one small way of mitigating which is to acknowledge the already existing critical archive written by those closely engaged, over time, with the life of the art. For a considered but concerned account of what is at stake in the difficult relation between, on the one hand, communities of practitioners and traditions of practice, and on the other, academically or institutionally oriented descriptions of the work in question, see Bradford Bailey's response to Gottschalk's book (https://blogthehum.wordpress.com/2016/09/19/ on-jennie-gottschalks-experimental-music-since-1970/; last accessed 21 September 2016).

8. 'Records replayed often . . . construct an object that goes beyond the psychological and material vagaries of each successive listening. There is as yet no word to denote this gradual hollowing out of an imprint, this listening-by-listening constitution of an object that from then on preexists the new act of listening or rather the new audition that will be made from it' (Michel Chion, *Sound: An Acoulogical Treatise*, trans. James A. Steintrager (Durham, NC: Duke University Press, 2016), p. 214).

9. *Musique concrète* is the term most frequently invoked in online critical responses to the trilogy. There is, however, little consensus regarding nomenclature in these areas of contemporary creative practice, and much said against the reductive and potentially misleading effects of categorisation. For a recent and helpfully pragmatic overview, see the first chapter of Gottschalk, *Experimental Music since 1970*, especially pp. 5–8.

10. Gottschalk, who herself coins the felicitous term 'nonfictional music', uses the concepts of 'change' and 'experience' to mark a shared orientation across a range of audio practices towards work 'more grounded in actual lived experience than in musical tradition' (*Experimental Music since 1970*, p. 4). Compare Michael Pisaro on 'the unexpected ways of sounding and of being' created by what he calls 'experimental music': 'What emerges is an ever-expanding network of possibilities and of friends, a conspiracy against the way things are, a way of saying: there is also *this*' ('Writing, Music' in *The Ashgate Companion to Experimental Music*, ed. Saunders, pp. 27–76, p. 76).

11. In keeping with this uncertainty, it is perhaps worth nominating a contemporaneous and equally 'interesting' work the sounded field of which is not dissimilar to some parts of that of Lambkin and Lescalleet: Anett Németh's *A Pauper's Guide to John Cage* (Another Timbre atb-08, 2010). The idea of a pauper's guide chimes with the non-pejorative weakness and modesty that characterises, for this listener, the soundwork of the common field recording.

12. Ngai, *Our Aesthetic Categories*, p. 117.

13. Roland Barthes [1977], *A Lover's Discourse: Fragments*, trans. Richard Howard (London: Vintage, 2002), p. 167.

14. The 'post-medium condition', exemplified in conceptual and digital art, and in installation practice, has long been a dominant signifier of a generalised contemporaneity in the visual arts. See Rosalind Krauss, 'Sculpture in the Expanded Field' (1979), included in *The Originality of the Avant-Garde and Other Modernist Myths* (Cambridge, MA: MIT, 1985), pp. 276–90; and for a critical and historicising account of the concept, Peter Osborne, *Anywhere or Not at All: Philosophy of Contemporary Art* (London: Verso, 2013), pp. 72–8 and 99–108.

15. *v-p v-f is v-n* (winds measure, 2012). Derek Walmsley notices the 'minimal context . . . minimalist design and . . . long durations' that contribute to the 'hushed reverence' characteristic of much recent soundscape-oriented field recordings ('The Field Recordist as Obsessive', *The Wire* (August 2014), http://www.thewire.co.uk/in-writing/columns/derek-walmsley_the-field-recordist-as-obsessive; last accessed 7 September 2016).

16. http://www.erstwhilerecords.com/catalog/052.html and http://www.erstwhilerecords.com/catalog/059.html (last accessed 1 September 2016).

17. Ngai links the category of the interesting and the serial artwork, according to a shared enactment of 'betweenness' (*Our Aesthetic Categories*, p. 36). On the subject of the series as a distinguishing feature specifically of contemporary art, see Osborne, *Anywhere or Not at All*, pp. 62–7.

18. *Private Parts* is an early version of what became a section of Ashley's television opera, *Private Lives (Private Parts)* (1978–83).

19. The older man pictured drinking from a mug in *Photographs*, so it transpires, is Lambkin's father, while the other men in one of the companion images are not relatives but Tim Goss and Darren Harris, members of Lambkin's old band, The Shadow Ring. They are heard on 'Hotdog Harris or The Road of Remembrance'. I am grateful to Graham Lambkin for help with identifying some of the images, and to Jon Abbey for the original contact.

20. Several of the track titles reference late 1970s and early 1980s music: the aforementioned Ashley opera, Fripp/ Eno bootleg and 'E5150' by Black Sabbath (released in 1981); 'Air Supply' (an Anglo-Australian group prominent at this time); 'Because the Night' (the Bruce Springsteen/Patti Smith song first recorded by Smith late in 1977); and 'Street Hassle' (an album and song by Lou Reed, released in 1978).

21. 'A theory of sound art must take account of sound art as *an art of sounds*, where sounds are heard in all their sociality' (Brian Kane, 'Musicophobia, or Sound Art and the Demands of Art Theory', http://nonsite.org/article/musicophobia-or-sound-art-and-the-demands-of-art-theory; last accessed 2 September 2016). Kane's account of trends in sound studies has informed my thinking.

22. These terms are borrowed, via Chion, from Pierre Schaeffer (Chion, *Sound*, pp. 266–8).

23. Simon Jarvis is one among a number of writers recently to have argued via a rereading of Kant for the 'the equivocal or speculative character of the field of criticism', as a necessary acknowledgement of the constitutively experiential and singular, though common, complexion of aesthetic experience ('An Undeleter for Criticism', *Diacritics* 32.1 (2002): 3–18).

24. I am drawing here on Sarah Wood's essay 'Anew Again', in particular, on her reading, via Derrida on 'the obscure friendship of rhyme', of the senses of sound (in Sarah Wood and Jonty Tiplady, *The Blue Guitar* (London: Artwords Press, 2007), pp. 18–36, p. 24; reprinted in *Creative Criticism: An Anthology and Guide*, ed. Stephen Benson and Clare Connors (Edinburgh: Edinburgh University Press, 2014), pp. 277–92, p. 283).

25. Chion, *Sound*, p. 24.

26. 'Causal listening' is familiar from Schaeffer. 'Figurative listening' is Chion's term for the mode 'that may appear identical to causal listening but that has to do not so much with what causes a sound in reality as with what the sound *represents*' (p. 266). There are of course a number of different versions of these distinctions in the critical literature attendant on sound and phenomenologies of listening.

27. I refer hereafter to Lambkin and Lescalleet by the shared letter of their respective surnames, an alliteration that presides over the collaboration and its sounding of the same-but-different scenarios of friendship. ('[L]ike two capital "I"s, one erect, one fallen, touching while diverging

from another, neither single nor double'. So writes Clare Connors of the shared first letter of Lizzie and Laura, Christina Rossetti's precursory duo of Ls (*Literary Theory* (Oxford: Oneworld, 2010), p. 165.) The relation of the same-but-different, especially as marked in language, is sounded most overtly in the trilogy in a recording of a voice reciting some of the test words used in the Harvard Dialect Survey, an exercise intended to trace variations of dialect across US States ('CT20 1PS / Rinsing Through the Shingles', *Photographs*).

28. The sound of snoring, as well as being one among many drone textures in the work, is a part of the common field of acoustic matter occupied by L and L, and another sounding, albeit congested, of their elemental medium. It is also a pre-emptive acknowledgement of the constitutive proximity of the interesting and the boring.

29. This is not to disavow the previously acknowledged drones of the work, with their variously ghostly and subaquatic character (Horne refers to the 'disquieting atmosphere' of the first two parts of the trilogy, and refers in passing to similar responses from other listeners); and yet even these sounds are frequently framed or interrupted in such a way as to puncture any inclination towards a generic uncanniness of sound.

30. Demers is one among many writers to use site and situation as the organising terms for conceiving recent work in 'sound art', including field recording-based practice ('Site in Ambient, Soundscape, and Field Recordings', *Listening through the Noise*, pp. 113–34). She proposes an understanding of 'site-specific sound art' as 'any art that *in some manner* . . . addresses the topics of site and location' (p. 125). See also, for example, Gottschalk, *Experimental Music since 1970*, pp. 227–81, and Michael Pisaro et al., 'What is Field?', *Wolf Notes 5* (2013): 16–27 (PDF downloaded from: https://wolfnotes.wordpress.com/wolf-notes/).

31. Compare Chion's use of the metaphor of the imprint with that of Sébastien Biset, who applies it specifically to the field recording, which, 'by extending the microphone towards the world seeks to seize the imprint of the immediate surroundings' ('Experimental of Experiential: Exploratory Perspectives and Tactics for Music Conceptualized as Experience', trans. David Vaughn, *Tacet* 2 (2012): 126–53, p. 135).

32. 'The question of description is an exasperating one: not only where to begin to describe, but, at each beginning, why precisely there?' (Louis Marin, 'The Ends of Interpretation, or the Itineraries of a Gaze in the Sublimity of a Storm' [1981] in *On Representation*, trans. Catherine Porter (Stanford: Stanford University Press, 2001), pp. 173–201, p. 178. I have been influenced in thinking about sound's description by Marin's several essays on the far more firmly established matter, albeit still contested, of painting and its verbal description.

33. For a polemical account of the anti-description argument as related specifically to sound, see chapter 5, 'Authoritarian Listening', of François J. Bonnet's *The Order of Sounds: A Sonorous Archipelago*,

trans. Robin Mackay (Falmouth: Urbanomic, 2016), pp. 195–259. The 'verification, decoding, reading' that collectively characterise discursive listening is, for Bonnet, *'a form of deafness'* (p. 204). Marin, faced with a single painted image – Giorgione's *The Tempest* – and considering the chances of description, worries away at a justification: 'Why write to express the pleasure taken in this painting, its particular quality, which varies, however, from one reading to the next? But perhaps it is necessary to write in order to know something about the painting, even though no knowledge is purely knowledge, no factual knowledge is without its own special affect' (p. 174).

34. *Listening and its not* is the title of the score and of an accompanying book comprising a number of texts written in response to the former's instruction (*Listening and its not*, edited by Patrick Farmer (n.p.: SARU & Compost and Height, 2016)).

35. Farmer, ed., *Listening and its not*, pp. 55–8.

36. We might compare Farmer's prompt with the following account by Daniela Cascella: 'When I listen and then I write, the point is in sustaining a double movement of estrangement from, and recognition of, sounds, which does not call for a synaesthesia but for a cohabitation of worlds' (*En abîme: Listening, Reading, Writing: An Archival Fiction* (London: Zero Books, 2012), p. 73). Cascella's double occupancy is performed in various registers over the course of her book (see, especially, chapters 6 and 7).

37. Lawrence Kramer, *Expression and Truth: On the Music of Knowledge* (Berkeley: University of California Press, 2012), p. 19. New or cultural musicology, that wholesale critique of the established traditions of formalist and positivist writing on music, involved in part a turn, or return, to the possibilities as interpretation of the non-technical description of musical works and experiences. Ekphrasis, as one term for such writing, thus has significant potential for a critic of Kramer's orientation (see *Musical Meaning: Toward a Critical History* (Berkeley: University of California Press, 2002) pp. 11–28; and *Expression and Truth*, pp. 13–23). Allied to this potential is a corresponding scepticism regarding what Kramer identifies as an idealising strain in recent philosophically oriented writing about sound and listening, such as is evident in Bonnet's wide-ranging and suggestive *The Order of Sounds*. See, for example, Kramer's reading of Jean-Luc Nancy's *Listening* (*Expression and Truth*, pp. 142–5).

38. Farmer's score might be read as an instance in sound practice of the 'ekphrastic fear' identified by W. J. T. Mitchell as one of three modes characteristic of the historical discourse on the relation between the verbal and the visual. The fear in question is of the 'collapse' of distinctions between the two, with all the 'dangerous promiscuity' that might ensue. 'Hope' – of a benign union of the verbal and the non-verbal – and 'indifference' – as to the ultimate impossibility of relation between media – are the two other discursive tendencies (W. J. T. Mitchell, 'Ekphrasis

and the Other', *Picture Theory: Essays on Verbal and Visual Representations* (Chicago: Chicago University Press, 1995), pp. 151–81). For a reading of Mitchell's essay in relation to descriptions of music, see Kramer, *Musical Meaning*, pp. 16–20.

39. Mitchell, 'Ekphrasis and the Other', p. 156.

40. Wallace Stevens, 'Description without Place', in *Wallace Stevens: Collected Poems* (London: Faber, 2006), pp. 339–46, p. 344. For a brief discussion of the Stevens poem in relation specifically to conceptions of the field recording as itself an act of description, see Pisaro's comments in 'What is Field?' (p. 19). For a fascinating argument in favour of attending acceptingly to our everyday lexicon of sound, see Chion's chapter, 'Between Doing and Listening: Naming' in *Sound* (pp. 212–42).

41. Roland Barthes, *S/Z* [1970], trans. Richard Miller (London: Blackwell, 1990), p. 80.

42. Cage's text score is included in the documentation for the reissue of his 1979 recording of *Roaratorio* (pp. 59–61) (*Roaratorio; Laughtears; Writing for the Second Time Through Finnegans Wake* (Mode, 2002)).

43. The score, potentially performable using any written work, did in fact follow in the wake of *Roaratorio*, a nicely Cagean reversal of the conventional compositional relationship of text and sound.

44. Pisaro describes *Private Parts* as a '*meditation*', 'philosophical in orientation' ('Writing, Music', p. 52). The link specifically with opera, as subject, is my own addition.

45. 'Description as a recording device is one of our most fundamental' (Shirley MacWilliam, 'Pythagoras's Screen', *Parallax* 12.4 (2006): 4–11, p. 7.

46. 'The first event [drawing one's attention to the field] may be almost anything, provided that it is not in itself overdramatic' (Berger, 'Field', p. 34).

47. Angus Fletcher, *A New Theory for America Poetry: Democracy, the Environment, and the Future of the Imagination* (Cambridge, MA: Harvard University Press, 2004), p. 43. Description, in being for Fletcher a singularly humble mode, is 'common'; and 'because it *is* so common, its possible range alludes us'.

48. György Lukács, 'Narrate or Describe?' (1936), *Writer and Critic and Other Essays*, trans. Arthur D. Kahn (New York: Merlin, 1978), pp. 110–48; Roland Barthes, 'The Reality Effect' [1968], trans. Richard Howard, in *The Novel: An Anthology of Criticism*, ed. Dorothy J. Hale (London: Wiley-Blackwell, 2005), pp. 230–4; Franco Moretti, 'Serious Century', in *The Novel: Volume 1: History, Geography, and Culture*, ed. Franco Moretti (Princeton: Princeton University Press, 2006), pp. 364–400.

49. Cascella writes movingly of the apparent ordinariness of the already known in listening: 'Nothing special. What is special about this nothing is how I get there, and what I make of the experience of listening every time I return' (*En abîme*, p. 92).

50. I am drawing freely here, in this over-hasty and -generalising summary, on Hannah Freed-Thall's *Spoiled Distinctions: Aesthetics and the Ordinary in French Modernism* (Oxford: Oxford University Press, 2015), Kathleen Stewart's *Ordinary Affects* (Durham, NC: Duke University Press, 2007) and Ngai's *Our Aesthetic Categories*, the latter specifically for its account of the category of the interesting.

51. Kane, 'Musicophobia', n.p.

52. *Oxford English Dictionary*. It perhaps goes without saying that little of note has been written on the nondescript, Virginia Woolf's 'cotton wool' notwithstanding. One exception is Fletcher's chapter, 'Description', in which 'a major artistic category of the nondescript' is proposed as a means of accounting for an 'uncanny' 'excess' in certain representations of the ordinariness of the natural world, an excess at odds with received registers of the sublime and the picturesque (*A New Theory*, pp. 42–56). Suggestively novel as it is, Fletcher's account, in its reliance on a numinous plenitude, is decidedly at odds with the nondescript as articulated here.

53. Compare the nondescript with a number of similar, although not identical, nominations of recent years, including the interesting (Ngai), the neutral (Roland Barthes, *The Neutral*, trans. Rosalind E. Krauss and Denis Hollier (New York: Columbia University Press, 2005)), and the *quelconque* (the history and several formulations of which are summarised by Freed-Thall, *Spoiled Distinctions* (pp. 6–12)). Joanna Demers makes a not unrelated case for the 'meaningless' in music and soundwork ('On Meaninglessness', *Journal of Popular Music Studies* 23 (2011): 195–9).

54. Novels on the subject of male friendship are surprisingly rare. If L and L's serial work is in one sense a sounding of certain ideas related to novelness, it is more specifically a piece in the form and substance of which male friendship is variously acknowledged, dramatised and performed. One element of the experience of friendship over time is, of course, loss, in its different forms, together with what endures through memory – including the resonant music of childhood – and what can stand as memorial. While I have not concentrated on these aspects here, they are repeatedly sounded in the trilogy, movingly so, as testified to in much of the online commentary (see Horne, 'Last a Lifetime').

55. Stewart, *Ordinary Affects*, p. 4.

56. Ngai, *Our Aesthetic Categories*, p. 241.

Chapter 3

Text-Score-Text

Will Montgomery

This essay is about words and sounds. It addresses the concept of 'field' and considers how it informs the relationship between literary texts and text scores, particularly in the context of recent work by the composers Michael Pisaro and Manfred Werder. Field is invoked in the sense of field recording (that is, a non-studio recording); as the delimited scene of intensified experience (as suggested in John Berger's 'Field'); and as the acoustic and conceptual terrain in which sounds and words make themselves felt. A particular focus of this essay will be poetic texts, as it is my contention that poems and text scores sometimes operate in similar ways, generating effects that cannot be described in textual or conceptual terms. How does one move between words and sounds? For Pisaro, text scores both elicit and prescribe performance: '[The text score] is asking for translation. It is also an incitement to action.'[1] Can such action be captured in a field recording? Werder has written of the difficulties of translating experience into recorded sound: 'how to render or to evidence mental constructions or processes that are rather non-transferable (as a content) but are nevertheless present'.[2]

What is described, then, is an aesthetic presentation of an experience in which meaning and non-meaning coincide.[3] The relationship between the two is at the heart of that between poetry and music, text score and performance. In what follows, I seek to open the discussion of sound and meaning on to the literary, arguing that text scores that engage with poetry, or that have para-poetic qualities of indeterminacy and condensation, explore the relationship between sound and meaning in distinctive ways. For my purposes, poetry is meaningful-sensible with an accent on the former, and music as meaningful-sensible with an accent on the latter. The text score exploits qualities of contingency that are specific to both of the domains it encompasses. The score's very status as an artwork is equivocal because of the temporality it embodies: is it the work or merely the prefiguring of the work? The temporal trajectory of the score is to point towards a future realisation that is other to itself. In reading a text score, as opposed to a mere text, the performative rendering of the text is always at least implied, even if one's interest in the piece is primarily theoretical or historical. The poem, on the other hand, whether sounded or voiced inwardly, is encountered in a present. Yet its associative resonances extend laterally across contemporary culture and downwards vertically into literary history. The qualities of opacity and ellipsis that characterise the poem of the modernist tradition give the text scores I am discussing a quality of potentiality. My suggestion, then, is that there is a particular generative energy to the text score when the score has poetic or para-poetic qualities. This arises from its insufficiency: it points towards its own realisation in another medium; it is not viable as a vehicle for the clear communication of concepts; it does not make clear the terms on which its translation into the acoustic sphere might take place. And, travelling in the opposite direction, the performance of the score, even if only imagined, always gestures back towards the words that give rise to it and which condition the sounds in ways that apply in no other compositional or improvisational domain.[4] The parapoetic score acknowledges the errancy of language, opening new possibilities for composer, reader, performer and audience.

* * *

The Wandelweiser group's fascination with silence as a philosophical and compositional question is often discussed, but there has been less attention to the literary entanglements of this body of work, or to its remarkably various use of field recording. Their use of these compositional elements allows them to explore a kind of directed indeterminacy. Field recording's openness to the density of incident in ambient recordings is, in my view, a potential complement to the linguistic uncertainty staged by the poetic utterance. Cage's *4'33"*, with its implicit injunction to hear the world, prefigures the use of field recordings in contemporary composition and performance. Yet it is also a crisp and open text, an orientation towards the sounds of the world that is instigated by words.[5] Several of the Wandelweiser composers have expanded the referential and associative range of a score by working with text that offers no instructions to the performer. Antoine Beuger has often worked with literary and philosophical texts. Jürg Frey's *24 Wörter* is a series of settings of single words, and his *Landschaft mit Wörtern* is a series of ultra-minimal pastoral text scores.[6] Eva-Maria Houben's *druids and questions*, discussed elsewhere in this volume, engages with an Emily Dickinson poem and a text by Charles Ives.[7] However, the two composers I want to discuss in detail are Michael Pisaro and Manfred Werder. Each uses a range of literary and philosophical texts. Pisaro incorporates field recordings into many of his scores and recordings. Actualisations of Werder's work, including those made by the composer, have often used field recording as a means of responding to the composer's insistence that we encounter the fullness of the world in its sounding.

In his essay 'Eleven Theses on the State of New Music' (written in response to a text on aesthetics by the philosopher Alain Badiou), Pisaro considers Cage's *4'33"* as an 'event' in Badiou's sense of the word.[8] This is a fundamental and revolutionary break, or, in Pisaro's words, a 'rupture (event) from which a truth procedure (the long term evaluation of what an idea is capable of) follows (or might follow)'.[9] Pisaro explains how *4'33"*, far from being a museum piece, opened a range of possibilities that are still being explored:

> If one were to posit *4'33"* as being in the neighbourhood of an event (if not an event unto itself) – the question would be how to pursue the consequences of this occurrence along the infinite path of its trajectory. Of course, there are many answers to the question of how this can be, has been, and currently is being pursued. One can remain faithful in a vast diversity of ways, as is demonstrated by the music of Christian Wolff, David Tudor, Morton Feldman, Alvin Lucier, Robert Ashley, James Tenney, George Brecht, La Monte Young, Max Neuhaus, and many others, right on up to the present day. In retrospect it is the body or corpus of this work that confers the status of 'event' on what began with Cage. 'Cage' is the name under which this work has continued (and continues).[10]

Pisaro is careful to state that, although this practice follows from Cage's ideas on indeterminacy and non-intention, it remains one of careful and systematic experimentation, not 'the nihilistic "anything goes" proposition that it is sometimes held to be'.[11] Both poetry and field recording are resources for indeterminacy in Pisaro's work. The aesthetic potential that is opened by *4'33"* might be compared to Berger's field – a delimited space in which a particular enquiry can unfold. While many of Pisaro's scores use loosely spatial terms to steer instrumental sounds – 'low', 'long' and so on – field recording brings a many-layered unpredictable acoustic event into the compositional frame.

There is no aspiration in Pisaro's use of field recording to create the kind of nuanced, quasi-musical representation of place to which soundscape recordists often aspire. Pisaro's *Transparent City* works, for example, are built around unremarkable 10-minute mono urban field recordings. In these pieces, Pisaro combines the ambient recordings with sine tones that subtly steer the experience of listening. The sounds of traffic are reconfigured around the sole quasi-musical element and the ear hears them differently, drawn by a harmonic magnet. Does the combination of basic tones with generic urban recordings release an incipient musicality that neither element possesses alone? Does the project tell us more about the breadth of musical sound or the potential in the everyday? Field recordings also feature on such recorded works as *Fields Have Ears (6)*, *Asleep, Street, Pipes, Tones*, *The Middle of Life (Die ganze Zeit)* and the 3-CD set *Continuum Unbound*. The latter's point of departure is a 72-minute recording made at sunset in Congaree National Park in South Carolina. This is presented unedited on the first CD. The second CD combines 24 field recordings made at different locations in the park with loosely scored sounds realised by Pisaro's collaborator Greg Stuart. The third contains contributions (mostly field recordings) made by five collaborators arranged in 72 sections. The sequence thus moves from a particular place and time to an increasingly fragmentary and polyphonic structure, in which Pisaro considers how ideas of contingency and discontinuity might be expressed in an ordered musical composition. Field recording is used in different ways: as the record of a sunset; as the record, in 3-minute sections, of movement through the national park; and as the record of quite other places, rendered through recordings of sand and wind made by collaborators working independently of one another. Pisaro's notes on the project make it clear that his enquiry is not simply into the auditory potential of the park. The work has its conceptual origins in a text by Badiou that makes frequent reference to two poems entitled 'Anabasis', one by Saint-John Perse and the other by Celan. Motifs of movement are woven, via Xenophon, Perse, Celan and Badiou into a tripartite composition. Poetry and philosophy, in this case, provide a framework for the overall endeavour.

Pisaro has noted that

> experimental music . . . raises, again and again, fundamental questions about the conditions (that is the mechanics, the system of reference, the function and process) of writing: as an exploration of what the hand can do, as a way of giving performers directions, as a frame of reference for sounds, as a model for certain kinds of musical behaviour.[12]

While this elegantly indicates the gestural potential of the mark-making of the composer, it perhaps does not take account of the expanded referential potential in such acts of writing.[13] The poem is the utterance that most tests the meaning-making capacity of language. In the parallel practice of the poem, the text score finds its most potent analogue, in which the lucid instruction for performers dissolves under the pressure of entirely different conventions of reading and writing. Pisaro puts poetry to many different uses. The notion of a thick cloud of sound in which single points are indistinguishable is important to *A Wave and Waves,* which takes John Ashbery's long poem *A Wave* as inspiration and which features 100 instruments.[14] The composition becomes a means of thinking about the relationship between the one and the many, conceived as that between a punctual event and densely layered sound. A motif abstracted from a set of verbal triggers is realised in acoustic terms: in Ashbery's poem, the successive mutually qualifying renderings of a meditative but wandering mind achieve a cumulative effect that is not dependent on the viability of any single utterance. In Pisaro's view, the poem can be read as 'the breaking-down of an event into its molecules, without mitigating its collective force'.[15] The relationship between granular detail and collective force is readily apparent in the composition.

Another recent release, *The Middle of Life (Die ganze Zeit)* (2013), contains material by the German-language poet Oswald Egger.[16] There are readings, in several languages (English, French, Japanese, Korean and Icelandic), of the first line from Eggers's *Die ganze Zeit*, which, in turn, is a version of the first sentence of Dante's *Inferno*. In this case, unusually for Pisaro, the poetry is actually voiced in the recording. Egger was recorded in fields near his home. Rural field recordings and fragments of a recording made by the musician Graham Lambkin thicken the texture of the piece. These recordings, with their distinct spatial contexts, serve to amplify and complicate the referential axes opened up by the polyglot rendering of the poetry. In *July Mountain* a short late poem of the same title by Wallace Stevens functions as a verbal backdrop that guides some of the compositional choices. Field recordings made in the mountains of southern California accumulate into a layered edifice of sound that it is impossible to apprehend with any clarity. Stevens's 'constellation / Of patches and of pitches' is rendered with twenty field recordings, ten instrumental parts and piano. The poem uses a vocabulary of multiplicity and becoming – 'Not in a single world, . . . Thinkers without final thoughts / In an always incipient cosmos' – that is continuous with some of Pisaro's theoretical preoccupations. The poem is included in the score but is not presented as part of the instructions to the performers. Although it is integral to the score, the poem does not give any clear purpose beyond offering an orientation to the performers. Pisaro is interested in translating not only the referential axis of the poem (piano, the 'constellation' of 'patches and pitches'), but the ways in which it escapes interpretation. This elusive late poem points to untranslatability, an excess of meaning that finds its analogue in the sheer proliferation of acoustic events in the matted threads of sound that are presented to the listener. There is an analogy to be drawn between the excess of acoustic incident created by the layering of ambient recordings and the poem's invocation of a state of becoming. However, the translation between domains is, of course, not achievable and their relationship remains one of productive friction and mutual interference.

Pisaro's most systematic recorded engagement with poetry is in his *harmony series*. This comprises 34 text scores based on poems, nos 11–16 of which have been issued on a Wandelweiser CD.[17] The poems are mostly by American authors, and most of these belong to a minimal or reductionist current within modernism: Gertrude Stein, Wallace Stevens and Robert Creeley among them. Some of the ideas are explored in more than one way, so, for example, the instruction 'for from six to thirteen musicians playing sustained tones' applies to compositions 7a, 7b and 7c (settings, respectively, of works by David Markson, William Carlos Williams and Wallace Stevens). The compositions of *harmony series* usually break down into sections that correspond to the number of lines in the source poem. The various versions of *harmony series* 7, for example, contain 13 sections. David Markson's 'Half-cracked' and Williams's 'The Locust Tree in Flower' each runs to 13 lines, while the Wallace Stevens poem is '13 Ways of Looking at a Blackbird'.

Almost all of the *harmony series* pieces use tones of unspecified pitch. These are often sustained and are often described as 'soft' and 'pure' (the word 'pure' occurs 24 times in the score). Silence and pauses play a large part in the work. Although the exact duration of sounds is not always specified, tones overlap in unpredictable clusters. Each realisation of a piece will give rise to new harmonies, often microtonal ones. Pisaro co-opts structural features of the poems in order lightly to orient a series of works composed of unpitched tones and silences. These pieces can sound very different from one another, as the Wandelweiser disc attests. There are some recurring preoccupations: sound, silence, temporality, being-in-the-world. Yet, although the meanings of the words are rarely directly significant, the choice of text betrays Pisaro's interest in the referential instability of poetry – an expressive potential that is analogous in this strand of music-making to the acoustic indeterminacy of the field recording.

Even though the text of the poems is never rendered directly by the performers, the presence of the poems in the scores brings a distinct sensibility to the works, which would be quite different without the poetry.

Pisaro's closest collaborator Greg Stuart goes some way to explaining the pressure exerted by the unvoiced poems of *harmony series*. There are, he says, three stages to the translation process adopted in *harmony series*. First of all, the shape of a poem is 'traced' in a stencil-like way to provide numerical markers – five lines might translate to five performers or five minutes, for example. Secondly, the 'internal forces of the text' are mined for compositional pointers. This translation to the field of the acoustic is done in as direct a way as possible, avoiding expressive or 'evocative' interpretation. In the final stage, realisation, a 'mist is sprayed' as the musicians make choices in performance: 'one starts to know (or sense) what sounds are correct to play, even when there are no explicit rules for how they are to be chosen'. Stuart remarks that a distinct and complex 'weather system' is set up in each realisation of these poetry-inflected scores: 'On the other side of the stencil we are in unknown world – sun-distant, alive – immersed in a gently spinning mixture of tone, noise and silence'.[18]

In this work, poetry is not heard as song, and there is no attachment to lyric. Neither is poetry treated as a resource for expressive realisation. Rather, structural and conceptual features of the poem are transmuted into musical terms. There is ample scope for a response to the poetic text to inform discussions between musicians prior to performance. The requirement for tones of indeterminate pitch or tuning instructions means that melody is absent, and that each realisation will result in new, unforeseeable harmonies. It is here, I think, that this series re-encounters poetry. There is a parallel between the intrinsic plasticity of language and the unending harmonic potential of these works. I would argue that this drawing together of aesthetic commitments, between clusters of words and clusters of tones, referential sounding within a language system and harmonic sounding within a musical system, is a subtle and non-reductive means of thinking and experiencing the relationship between words and sounds. The meaning-bearing potential of the poems is not reduced through specific interpretations; rather, the poems' potential for generating meaning is enhanced through these new, acoustic articulations.

In the *harmony series* scores, no one could mistake the poems for musical instructions, or the instructions for poems. However, placed together, they function as a composite. It is unlikely that a blindfold listening could identify the text behind any given realisation. None-theless, the poems determine parameters of the score, and exert a lin-guistic pressure on the performative realisation of the poem. Rather than ceding priority to either text or music, the score places these incompatible phenomena in parallel. While the end result, in record-ing or performative terms, is musical, the poems pre-exist and circum-scribe the musical realisations, inserting the realisations into a field of reference that they cannot fully escape. Pisaro levers these strange textual fragments into an adjacent disciplinary space in which they become sounding boards of acoustic possibility.

The most open-ended of the *harmony series* pieces is no. 17, which is based on an 18-line text by Kenneth Rexroth. This is one of the more direct realisations, arising from the lines 'I sit quiet / Anywhere Anything / Happens'. The score asks the following of the performer:

In a large, open space (possibly outdoors).
For a long time.
Sitting quietly.
Listening.
A few times, playing an extremely long, very quiet tone.[19]

The piece is dedicated to Manfred Werder. It has none of the struc-tural qualities of the other pieces. The text has a more direct rela-tionship to the instructions in the score than in other *harmony series* works. It is simply a textual clearing that provides for a person sit-ting playing a long, quiet tone a few times. The text is presented in para-poetic fashion, one sentence per line. No musical parameters are fixed and the choice of tone, and the interpretation of 'long' and 'very quiet', are left entirely to the performer. In a note to the various reali-sations of the piece collected by Compost & Height, Pisaro acknowl-edges that this piece is unusual in the series, as it does not propose the generation of multiple tones. Instead, questions are asked by the performer: 'What, in the sum of things occurring now, do I hear, and how do these things harmonize themselves? How can I express my relation to this harmony as a tone? What effect does this have on my continued listening? How will I spend my time? Do I experience the void or just imagine it?'[20] Most of the realisations of *harmony series* 17 are achieved through field recordings – the only way of capturing the active and alert immersion in environmental sound that the score recommends. The location of the work (the score? the performance? the recording? – none seems adequate on its own) is complicated by compositions such as this and the field recording may best be under-stood as both work and documentation.

Crucially, in this piece the performer is at the same time a listener – quite possibly the only witness to the performance. I want to turn now to the piece's dedicatee. Although Werder's work can be positioned within the event score / text score tradition as developed by Cage, Ono, Wolff, Brecht, Tenney and others, it might be better to see him not as a composer at all but as an artist working across the fields of sound, text and performance. The piece *2005[1]* inaugurated the series of minimal text scores that Werder turned to after moving on from his monumental *Stück 1998 Seiten 1–4000* and his performer series project (a series of nine 4,000-page scores that are gradually being performed in successive discrete performances).[21] The short text scores continued with elliptical evocations of particularity (e.g. *2007[1]*, 'a day a sound'). Werder then began publishing short, list-like pastoral para-poems such as *2008[3]* ('a hill / a valley / a mountain range / a lowland / a plateau / a river delta / a fjord') and *2008[6]* ('spider / air / eucalyptus / wasp/ petals / rain'). All of these scores were published online as PDFs with a simple, standardised layout and font.[22] In 2009 he began his experiments with found text drawn from poetic and philosophical works.

What Pisaro describes in the score for *Only* is a version of Werder's performance practice, which, in Werder's words, seeks to 'break the dyad of performer and listener'.[23] To this end, many of his scores contain no instructions at all for the performance. To take an example from a series of scores he calls 'found sentences', Werder's *2010[1]* reads, in its entirety: 'the rarity of the *énoncés* // that immediate transparency that constitutes the element of their possibility' (note: English texts are given in this essay but many of Werder's scores use German or French and some are bilingual). The two phrases that make up the score are quotations from Michel Foucault's *Archaeology of Knowledge* on the *énoncé* (or 'statement'). In choosing these decontextualised fragments on the contextual nature of meaningful utterance, Werder isolates an idea of potential within everyday experience. G. Douglas Barrett has discussed Werder's suppression of the first clause in Foucault's sentence: 'We shall try to render visible, and analyzable, that immediate transparency that constitutes the element of their possibility'. This phrase is rendered almost entirely opaque, even to the reader with a passing awareness of the source text, by Werder's elision. Instead, argues Barrett, Werder's score 'contemplates its discursive potential as a musical work; it enunciates a kind of self-cancellation of its own ability to speak'.[24] Beside this possible meta-statement, though, is a desire to think about the relation between meaning and sound. The phrase 'the rarity of statements [*enoncés*]' derives from a passage on 'the incomplete, fragmented form of the enunciative field, the fact that few things, in all, can be said, explain that statements are not, like the air we breathe, an infinite transparency'.[25] Werder skews Foucault's text, offering it as an inexplicable fragment, a textual opening that provides an ambiguous frame for listening. If we look at the source, we see that 'transparency' is to be understood as 'the air we breathe'. In addition to the negative movement of self-cancellation discerned by Barrett, with its risk of Beckettian impasse, there is a positive attachment to meaning-making. The fragment 'that immediate transparency that constitutes the element of their possibility' indicates the uncontainable multiplicity of the sounding world as experienced in every actualisation. *2010[1]* shares with other of Werder's scores a desire to explore the manifold ways in which an enigmatic textual fragment can orient the performer/listener towards the world. Werder's score is comparable in its means of operation as the poetic text. The qualities of obliquity, condensation and opacity that animate much poetry of the modernist line are what gives this score its suggestive power. Like an unmoored citation occurring in the work of Ezra Pound or Charles Olson or Susan Howe (or countless others who have explored citation), the words radiate new meanings in their new context. The phrase 'the element of their possibility' no longer refers to the discursive range enabled by the *enoncé*, it indicates the possible conditions of acoustic experience. This may only be discernible to the performer, who may, in any case, be the only witness to the piece.

One immediate priority in Werder's work is to lead performer and auditor into an awareness of the incommensurable scale of the everyday – an awareness comparable to the attention to incident recommended in Berger's 'Field' essay. A typical performance by Werder of this and other pieces in the series closely resembles what is outlined in Pisaro's *harmony series* 17: Werder sits quietly in a public space for several hours.[26] Sometimes he may use a small pipe to make a tone, and sometimes he does not even do this. Werder's quiet attentiveness directs attention to the light conditions, the temperature, the vegetation, the built environment, the crossflows of human activity both seen and heard. Yet it should be emphasised that Werder nowhere publishes recommendations for others to adopt this performance practice. Works such as Pisaro's *harmony series* or *July Mountain* combine poetry and instructions for musical performance. In Werder's *Found Sentences* and *Found Words* series, however, the cited material is the only available instruction in the piece. The work of the composer ends with selecting a text written by another.

In such works, references to philosophers such as Foucault, Badiou, Iain Hamilton Grant and Quentin Meillassoux, or poets such as Francis Ponge and Fernando Pessoa, provide contextual pointers to the interpreter. Much as the massed citations of a modernist poetic text encourage the reader to make archival forays, so Werder's scores offer his interpreters the option of investigating the conceptual hinterland to his work. It is usually possible to find currents of thinking that intersect with Werder's: the interplay between text and phenomenal experience in Ponge, for example, or Grant's interest in directing philosophical attention towards the object-world. Yet, these are fragments, not a synthesised portmanteau of aesthetics, and they are oriented towards Werder's encounter with sound. His shards of contemporary philosophy and poetry provide thus a bridge from the meaningful to the sensible, gesturing at conditions for a listening experience that cannot be fully articulated.

For Werder, such scores act as a point at which various unstable vectors meet: word, world, performance, interpretation. 'The plane of the score,' he writes, is 'a field of incidence – unassignable unpredictability.'[27] These scores make a small textual clearing that can open on to an artistic action of any kind or any duration. They can be read as standalone texts, as found poems, as the catalyst for a creative act. Through his use of citation, Werder complicates the authorial role assigned to the composers of text scores, placing himself at a further remove from the text offered to performers. The performer might want to take the decontextualised fragment at face value, or to research other texts by the writer cited by Werder. The relation between words and sounds is entirely up to the performer. Yet the resulting performance, whatever it is, will not be the same as a piece generated independently of the score. These texts are simultaneously scores that function like literary fragments, and literary fragments that serve as scores. Werder thus blurs the lines between score and poem, performance and listening, composition and appropriation.

On his artist's webpage for the Sounds of Europe field-recording project, Werder briefly outlines a distinct interpretation of 'the field'.[28] A quote from Ponge opens the text: 'The field, as well, is a way of being. Let's decide to drift there, today.'[29] The world, for Werder, is unyielding and indifferent; it cannot be captured and it is not to be understood in relation to the mind of the artist. He writes, 'I propose the field not to be a "material". "Material" would be . . . what a phenomenological assumption once more identifies as isolated objects to be perceived . . . There is no outside the field. It also includes the digital silence in the editing of a "recording" as a possible frame, as far as it unconditions this specific reality, as one conceptual form of the field.'[30] If there is a residual Romanticism, discernible perhaps in his use of Grant's reading of Schelling, it is revisionary and self-aware, comparable perhaps to Gerhard Richter's seascapes and cloudscapes – paintings of photographs that insistently pose the question of their own mediatedness. The world is not to be understood as an object of contemplation – objectivity itself as a means of isolating the field for human attention is ruled out.

This is where Werder's work extends and contemplates the notion of field advanced by Berger. While Berger is interested in the phenomenal attributes of aesthetic attention, Werder wants to remove the frames imposed by the perceptual process in order to arrive at an 'unconditioned reality' independent of the human perceptual frame, where 'all is permanently drifting in its own right'. It is clear from Werder's work that, while field recording offers mediated access to the sounding world, his practice goes further, unsettling the subject/ object relationship embedded in the recordist/listener dyad. 'There is no outside the performative,' writes Werder.[31] He asks us to imagine a world that is utterly – almost unthinkably – independent of the human perceptual and conceptual apparatus. Attending to the 'transcendental' 'surface' in *2011*[4] ('depths are not the transcendental, but rather the transcendental is the surface of the world, while both are physical', a quotation from Grant) means cultivating an openness to the overwhelming excess of the world, or what Werder, in his 'Text Scores – Statement (1)', calls 'sensing and experiencing the vertiginous infinity of mere occurrence'.[32] The world, for Werder, is not an object, nor is it an arrangement of discrete objects somehow arrested in time for our apprehension. What Werder asks us to do is to put the spectator–performer relationship in suspension and try to imagine – against all possibility of actually experiencing – the reality that unfolds all around us and independently of us. The field is not viewed, Berger-style, from the car at the level crossing, the field encompasses and engulfs the perceiver. Werder begins his short statement 'The Sounding of the World' with a remark that places the human within this larger frame: 'It is possible to conceive of music as the totality of all sound – a totality far exceeding the thin sliver audible to man. This totality of all sound – of which we are part – is the sounding of the world.'[33]

Field recording has played a key role in the realisation of Werder's works, even though the field recording, heard in another setting, is not equivalent to the experience it documents. A recording of an open-air performance of a Werder piece might involve only minimal sounds from the performers, as in the version of 2006^1 on the Skiti label, or no sounds at all from the performers (as in the realisation of 2007^1 on another Japanese label, Futow).[34] Each of these scores requires attention to the singularity of a particular time and place. 2006^1 reads 'a place, natural light, where the performer, the performers like to be / a time / (sounds)'; 2007^1 reads simply 'a day a time'. While sounds are invited, albeit parenthetically, in 2006^1, 2006^2 offers interpreters as open as possible a clearing in which to operate. Werder remarks in a sleeve-note to 2006^1 that the piece is 'not about exploring new sounds, but exploring a new relation to what the world sounds'.

Jason Kahn's version of 2005^1 ('place / time // (sounds)') for the winds measure label, is ambitious, with eight CDRs of urban field recordings.[35] No musical sound is made by the recordist, who observes a determinate procedure of his own invention. Kahn made a recording at the same time every morning in Zurich railway station for a month. These are presented as thirty-one recordings, each exactly 18 minutes long. There is nothing distinctive or remarkable about the recordings themselves. What is of interest is a 'new relation' to such sounds that the project proposes by re-presenting the everyday in a long series of identical temporal frames. In between score and realisation, is interposed the interpretative choices made by Kahn. Such works make collaborators out of interpreters. The CD Werder made with the Japanese field recordist and sound artist Toshiya Tsunoda, *detour*, is unusual in that no score is used. The work layers a number of different field recordings as it seeks to represent the respective physical and mental processes of the two recordists in a particular environment. Tsunoda remarks in a liner note that the work proceeds 'by recording various layers such as our directions of eyes, our thoughts, our orientations towards the place'.[36] The clearly untestable proposition of the work is that the corporeal and cognitive experience of the two recordists, flickering states of being at best, colours the recordings in distinct ways.

Another CD release, *Im Sefinental*, recorded by Werder with Stefan Thut and released by Wandelweiser in 2009, is simply a pair of near-identical pastoral field recordings. Each features running water and each is nondescript.[37] The first is a rendering of Thut's *aussen raum* ('an area outside: several times / between sound and noise'). The second is Werder's 2008^3 ('a hill / a valley / a mountain range / a lowland / a plateau / a river delta / a fjord'). Thut's score recommends a reflection on the distinction between sound and noise, without indicating what that might be. The pastoral orientation of Werder's text, enmeshed as it is in the overdetermined vocabulary of Romanticism, serves as much to underscore the distance between words and world as it does to bring them together. The recordings of these very different scores, made in Sefinental, a mountainous area in rural Switzerland, on the same day in October 2008, are almost impossible to distinguish from one another. At one point in the Werder actualisation, a stone is dropped to the ground – a tiny incident which nonetheless inserts a performative act into the recording. This pair of field recordings seem, in this case, to ask a polemical question of the text score: what happens if two distinct texts yield a near-identical result? The sound of the stone dropping 23 minutes into the Werder piece may or may not carry weight for performer or listener. The twinned realisations are a provocation that through a polemical reduction procure a bare level of sufficiency for the scores. The recordings cannot be heard on their own terms, divorced from the words that engender them. The point of the release seems to be to insist on the interdependence of the word and world, performance and interpretation, artwork and document.

None of these CDs could be thought of as musical in any conventional sense. Yet neither are they comparable to soundscape recordings. Some, such as *Im Sefinental* and the futow disc, even contain rumble from wind hitting the microphones, a form of undesirable sound that most soundscape recordists would eliminate at the editing stage. The compositional context in which the recordings exercise their polemical potential is integral to how they work. The recording is just one facet of the contingent relation between words, space and performers that is examined.

Performers of Werder's work are typically respectful of the performance tradition and the preoccupation with silence that the Wandelweiser composers share, even though these points are never indicated in the text-score series that I have been discussing. Words cannot bring the world into being: they can only present a trace of that world. So, a score such as Werder's *2008*[6] – 'spider / air / eucalyptus / wasp / petals / rain' – is more a testament to the world's unavailability than a conjuring in pastoral language of Nature. Music, like language, becomes a provisional means of rendering the flux of the world.

Werder's minimal text scores offer a suggestive frame for the world. As Werder suggests in a reflection on text scores, words function more as contextual markers than as the vehicles of thoughts:

> Language is not a function of frontal and explicit communication and has far more to do with locating oneself in an environment than with communicating whatever contents to others. Thus, as I reject a frontal or explicit communication, the entire complex of a score's potentiality

arises differently . . . I would say that the score keeps being the referential instance, even if I personally realise the score now and then, or propose a certain reading. This reading is my way of dealing with the score; however, there are certainly others.[38]

In a gesture that brings the score within the suggestive ambit of a poetic text, Werder presents the score as a complex of 'potentiality'. Werder's suggestion is that a mode of non-explicit communication might be a particular means of activating a given field for a performer/listener. The score can be read in many different ways, but this does not mean a free-for-all – it remains a decisive and determinate anchoring point for a mode of performance that typically frames an intensified mode of attention to the multiplicity of the everyday.

*   *   *

To conclude, I wish to say a little more about the relationship of both poetry and text scores to concepts of field, including field recording. Field recordings are deployed in different ways by the artists I have discussed. They become part of a musical or quasi-musical arrangement in Pisaro's CDs; they typically function as the document of a realisation in Werder's. In both these cases, field recording provides a quality of indeterminacy: the excess of incident that both invites and resists objectification within the artwork. For Werder, an immersion in indeterminacy – world as de-aestheticised world – is the central issue:

> Each place is intrinsic multiplicity and doesn't need any intervention of ours. So, I try to approach a place regarding a performance almost unnoticeably, unimposingly. I think when performing I'm looking for a situation where for a certain time something like 'the world' would appear. Not one to look at or listen to. Not one to project concepts on to. One to be part of.[39]

While for Pisaro, field recordings are undeniably put to musical ends, such audio derives its unsettling force from the quality of 'intrinsic multiplicity' that it brings to an unfolding sonic environment. Location recordings function not as an index of place, but as an undoing of place. Similarly, the aesthetic potential of the text score resides as much in polyvalence and indeterminacy as in the determinate instructions to musicians. Pisaro's insertion of poetic texts into scores is one way of drawing attention to this instability; Werder's use of decontextualised 'found' materials is another.

Poems in *harmony series* exist in an oblique relation to the musical instructions, throwing a particular filter or texture over the interpretative process. In Werder's case, the absence of musical instructions opens up an entirely new way of reading – the poetic fragment *is* the score. Each is a way of loosening the control that the composer has over the performance, allowing the words in the score to function in ways that could not be anticipated. Pisaro uses structural features of the texts – the number of lines, for example – considering the visual appearance of the poetic text on the page. Non-semantic details colour the score as much as the meaning. Each text has a contextual history – a particular use for the radical energies of modernist experimentation – that steers interpretations of the *harmony series* scores. In Werder's case, the directive function of the score melts away entirely – he looks for a 'structural matter of fact' rather than a 'prescription for action'.[40]

Place played a major role in modernist poetics. We might think of epic examples such as long poems by Olson or Williams, or the reductionism of Robert Creeley, Larry Eigner, Robert Grenier or Thomas A. Clark. In a recent study, Lytle Shaw reads across fine art and poetics to elaborate a vocabulary of place and site. He argues that neither 'place' with its promise of empirical tangibility, nor the more contingent and open term 'site' is sufficient. The apparently naive ambition of place-oriented writing in the work of an Olson or a Williams – naive, that is, to those who were affected by the 'linguistic turn' in the 1970s and 1980s – nonetheless contains an ability to destabilise discursive boundaries:

> As poets became experimental historiographers and ethnographers of place, as they took poetry into an expanded field of buried historical and immediate social relations, they also necessarily engaged the authority of those disciplinary fields traditionally used to frame, contextualise and historicise these literal spaces. One of the most fascinating results of these excursions into new fields . . . is [a] series of generative recodings of disciplinary terms and practices.[41]

For the radical writers discussed by Shaw, an investigation of place necessarily becomes a critical investigation of the various discourses that frame and organise our understanding of our environment. For a poetics that is attentive to these discourses, the 'occasion of framing, measuring, charting is also the occasion of unbinding measure'.[42] I would suggest that, in the encounter between text and world, score and realisation, what Shaw calls 'unbinding measure' is proper both to the para-poetic workings of the text score and to the use of field recordings in such compositions. The strange linguistic energies of a score such as Werder's *2009[1]* – 'dost // rue // araucaria // ore // lewfü' – are brought into contact with the unpredictability of the world. As Werder argues, the language of the score mobilises the 'precise though chaotically indeterminable economy of each letter and its impact on the world'.[43] In Pisaro's case, the temporal structure and detailed recommendations to musicians in *July Mountain* are exceeded and undone by the stacked field recordings that they engender and the elusive words of Wallace Stevens.

When text scores propose to organise sound, they do so in a way that provides a peculiar presentation of the relationship between words and sounds, which, as François J. Bonnet argues, can never be thought independently:

> To seek 'to listen to sound for itself, as sound object' is precisely to introduce formal determinations, 'powers of language', into the enterprise of reduction. In listening to the sound 'as object', one precisely does not listen to the sound for itself . . . Sound always speaks to us. There is no reduced, pure consummate listening. Such a listening targets the voice of sound, and not sound itself.[44]

If sound always speaks, if it cannot be disentangled from the network that embraces it without objectifying it in a way that robs it of its very specificity as sound, then we might view the text score as offering a particular way of appraising the entanglement of the sensuous and the meaningful. Sound both resists and elicits verbal responses. Typically, when sound and text meet, the sound precedes the interpretation. The text score reverses this order: acoustic events are prescribed in advance by words. The inherent instability of the word – its very inability to describe sounds – causes such scores, however detailed, to be more open than conventional music notation. As soon as we describe a sound that we have heard, it is in the past. The score offers a route to the future, a prescriptive rather than a descriptive language, however open-ended that prescription might be. Words taken on a primary, generative status, rather than a secondary, after-the-fact one.

John Berger's description of the delimited space of the event is marked with his address to the field: 'the wire around you is the horizon'.[45] The para-poetic text score opens a new kind of acoustic potential that develops Berger's vision. The uncertainty of the word liberated from its status as instruction multiplies the possible fields of operation. At one level, the score itself is an object of readerly interest: the words on the page look towards a form of actualisation that can only be imagined by the reader. In the actualisation itself, particularly in the case of Werder, listening becomes a performative act. Berger's phrase 'contingencies overlapping' may helpfully apply to the works I have been discussing, which are not sealed and self-sufficient as score, actualisation, performance or document.[46] Field recordings memorialise a particular time and place, but they may also expand the range of acoustic possibility open to composer, performer and listener, introducing everyday indeterminacy to the musical realm as an analogue of the interpretative flexibility of the para-poetic text. Berger's field is, notably, on a hill, tilted towards him 'like music on a music stand'.[47] The most effective of the works I have been discussing greatly complicate that tilted manuscript, leading to multi-layered assemblages of word and sound, meaning and sensation, present and potential.

Notes

1. Michael Pisaro, 'A Lot of Silence', audio recording of a talk given at the Writing Sound symposium, Oxford Brookes University, 2012, available at https://wolfnotes.wordpress.com/2013/02/02/writing-sound/ (last accessed 25 October 2016).
2. Liner note to the CD *detour*, a collaboration between Werder and the Japanese sound artist Toshiya Tsunoda. Toshiya Tsunoda and Manfred Werder, *detour*, CD (Erstwhile 071, 2014). The CD is discussed by Pisaro in his chapter in this volume.
3. John Cage's 'sound in itself' and Pierre Schaeffer's *objet sonore* each sought, in different ways, to bracket off the sensuous features of acoustic from cultural meanings. More recently, and arguing against Cage and Schaeffer, Seth Kim-Cohen mounts a polemical attack on the concept of 'sound in itself' (*In the Blink of an Ear* (London, New York: Continuum, 2009)). For Christoph Cox, sound is a continuous anonymous 'flux' that both precedes and exceeds human expression (Cristoph Cox, 'Sound Art and the Sonic Unconscious', *Organised Sound* 14.1 (2009): 19–26). Brian Kane, on the other hand, rejects the 'onto-aesthetics' of Cox and others, arguing for the continuing validity of a conception of auditory culture ('Sound Studies without Auditory Culture: A Critique of the Ontological Turn', *Sound Studies* 1.1 (2015): pp. 2–21). And, for the composer François J. Bonnet, reduced listening of the kind advocated by Schaeffer fails because the conferral of objecthood on the *objet sonore* inevitably orients it towards a system of representation (*The Order of Sounds: A Sonorous Archipelago* (Falmouth: Urbanomic, 2016).

4. Unlike musical manuscript, text scores are often made available in performance situations, sometimes even projected above the performers. They are also often reproduced online and in CD booklets.

5. Liz Kotz, *Words to be Looked At: Language in 1960s Art* (Cambridge, MA: MIT, 2010), especially chapter 1, pp. 13–58.

6. Jürg Frey, *24 Wörter*, CD (Edition Wandelweiser, 2015) and Landschaft mit Wörtern (B-Boim, 2009).

7. Eva Maria Houben, *druids and questions*, CD (Edition Wandelweiser, 2011)

8. Michael Pisaro (2006), 'Eleven Theses on the State of New Music', available at http://www.timescraper.de/_michael-pisaro/11theses-12-06.pdf (last accessed 14 September 2016).

9. Ibid., p. 5.

10. Ibid., p. 4.

11. Ibid., p. 4.

12. Michael Pisaro, 'Writing, Music' in *The Ashgate Research Companion to Experimental Music*, ed. James Saunders (Farnham: Ashgate, 2009), p. 28.

13. Pisaro notes that his first encounter with experimental music was with John Cage's *Winter Music*, which turns the imperfections on a piece of paper into the points from which musical notation is created. Pisaro, 'Writing Music', p. 27.

14. The juxtaposition of figures of uncountable multiplicity and grids or graphs is common in Pisaro's work. See, especially, *A Mist is a Collection of Points* (New World Records, 2015) and *Ricefall (2)* (Gravity Wave, 2010).

15. Michael Pisaro, sleevenote to *A Wave and Waves* (Cathnor 009, 2010).

16. Pisaro translated Egger's work for the respected West Coast small press Green Integer. Oswald Egger, *Room of Rumor: Tunings*, trans. Michael Pisaro (Los Angeles: Green Integer, 2004).

17. Michael Pisaro, *harmony series 11–17* (Edition Wandelweiser 0710, 2007). Twenty-two versions of no. 17, which is based on a text by Kenneth Rexroth, were recorded by various recordists and musicians in late August 2009, and are available at the Compost & Height website: https://wolfnotes.wordpress.com/2013/01/02/michael-pisaro-only-harmony-series-17/ (last accessed 23 September 2016).

18. Stuart's note is available on the Wandelweiser website: http://www.wandelweiser.de/_e-w-records/_ewr-catalogue/ewr0710.html (last accessed 24 September 2016).

19. The score and Pisaro's note are available at the project page for *Only (harmony series 17)*, cited above.

20. Ibid.

21. Multiple versions of *2005¹* were commissioned by the UK record label Another Timbre and published online in 2013. These are available at http://www.anothertimbre.com/werder2005(1).html (last accessed 5

October 2016). The present author submitted a recording as part of this project and has released two other realisations of compositions by Werder on CD.

22. Werder has recently begun issuing printed scores that depart from the generic Times New Roman hitherto used, such as the six he contributed to issue four of Ryoko Akama's *Reductive* journal (November 2015). These are presented with the Courier font, text ranged right and faded – they appear to have been made with a physical typewriter with little ink left in the ribbon.

23. Manfred Werder and Simon Reynell (2013), 'Interview with Manfred Werder' available at http://www.anothertimbre.com/werderinterview.html (last accessed 2 September 2016).

24. G. Douglas Barrett, 'The Silent Network – The Music of Wandelweiser', *Contemporary Music Review* 30.6 (2011): 449–70, p. 465.

25. Michel Foucault, *The Archaeology of Knowledge* (New York: Pantheon, 1972), pp. 119–20.

26. The present author witnessed such a performance of *2010¹* by Werder in an east London churchyard in 2010. For a description of a more conventional performance of this piece, see Douglas Barrett, 'The Silent Network', pp. 449–50.

27. Manfred Werder, 'Text Scores – Statement (1)' in *Word Events: Perspectives on Verbal Notation*, ed. John Lely and James Saunders (London and New York: Continuum, 2012), p. 379.

28. Manfred Werder, 'Description of work with field recording', available at http://www.soundsofeurope.eu/artist/manfred-werder/ (last accessed 13 December 2016).

29. Ibid. The phrase comes from Francis Ponge's *La Fabrique du Pré* (discussed in our introduction). This is a book-length collection of drafts and fragments that provide the material for Ponge's relatively brief poem 'Le Pré' ('The Field').

30. Ibid.

31. Ibid. See Cage's 1955 article 'Experimental Music: Doctrine': 'If, at this point, one says, "Yes, I do not discriminate between intention and non-intention: the splits, subject-object, art-life, etc., disappear, an identification has been made with the material, and actions are then those relevant to its nature."' In John Cage (1978) *Silence: Lectures and Writing* (London: Marion Boyars, 1978), pp. 13–17, p. 14.

32. Werder, 'Text Scores – Statement (1)', p. 379.

33. Manfred Werder, 'The Sounding of the World' (2011), trans. Nicholas Melia, available at http://manfred-werder-archives.blogspot.co.uk/2012/03/sounding-of-world.html

34. Manfred Werder, *2006¹*, CD (Skiti, 2006); *2007¹*, Manfred Werder, CD (futow, 2010).

35. Most of the versions of *2005¹* in the project initiated by record label Another Timbre in 2013 also incorporate field recordings. However,

with Werder's agreement, these realisations were limited to a maximum of 15 minutes. A second stipulation – that actualisations 'should result in an audio recording that is suitable for repeated listening' – seems to go against the open spirit of Werder's work.

36. Note to Toshiya Tsunoda and Manfred Werder, *detour*, CD (Erstwhile, 2014).
37. Stefan Thut and Manfred Werder, *Im Sefinental*, CD (Edition Wandel-weiser, 2009).
38. Manfred Werder and Simon Reynell, 'Interview with Manfred Werder', n.p.
39. Sleevenote to Manfred Werder. *2005¹*, CD (winds measure, 2012). Also available at http://manfred-werder-archives.blogspot.co.uk
40. Ibid.
41. Lytle Shaw, *Fieldworks: From Place to Site in Postwar Poetics* (Tuscaloosa: University of Alabama Press, 2013), p. 7.
42. Ibid., p. 259.
43. Werder, 'Text Score – Statement (1)', p. 379.
44. Bonnet, *The Order of Sounds*, p. 116.
45. John Berger, 'Field', p. 31. All references to Berger's 'Field' are to the essay as reprinted in this book.
46. Ibid., p. 32.
47. Ibid., p. 33.

Part Two

The Poetics of the Field

Chapter 4

Rubies Reddened by Rubies Reddening*

Michael Pisaro

Geosound

Field recording, composition and poetic text are three forms of writing.[1] Each form of writing already involves a kind of translation. In the broadest sense, a field recording is sound written by the Earth, or a part of it anyway, on to – or into – the apparatus of the recorder. The device translates vibration into electrical impulses that are at some point translated back into vibration, having undergone a significant change appropriate to the medium of performance or playback. The composer writes symbols on paper meant to represent sounds and silences – or at least the potential for these. This has to be translated by a performer into actual sound, which will inevitably be different to some degree from what a composer might have imagined. The written text also represents sounds that will have to be translated by the mind of the reader into actual or virtual sound. An image described in a text is sketched with a degree of abstraction that asks the reader to fill in the spaces.

I am interested in the linkages that can be formed between pairs of these forms of writing, and want to discuss these in two compositions I have been involved in creating: *crosshatches*, a recording project with Toshiya Tsunoda, and *July Mountain* for field recordings and percussion.

I want to talk not just about the how the music was written and how it was conceived, but especially about its connection with something I am going to term *Geosound*. Geosound is sound in relation to the Earth.[2] Geography tells us about the terrain of the Earth and how human cultures inhabit it. Geosound as I conceive of it, must tell us about the sonic terrain and the musical cultures that arise on the Earth. It must make explicit the usually implicit connection between the place where we are situated and how this place conditions the sounds we make.

---

*Accompanying audio recordings are indicated in the following way – d[4.1]b – and are available on the publisher's website at: https://edinburghuniversitypress.com/ book writing the field recording hb html [click on the 'resources' tab].

This way of theorising sound is new (or it seems that way to me) and thus must be, for the moment, somewhat provisional. Although I have long been interested in the concepts and ways of producing music discussed here, until recently it was difficult for me to find a theoretical container that would allow me to think through the locational issues the work had raised. The springboard for this new way of thinking was the 2010 publication of a number of the journal *Collapse*[3] devoted to the Earth and to 'geophilosophy', a term invented by Deleuze and Guattari in their book *What is Philosophy?*[4] The work in this volume was inspiring enough that I began to consider a set of concepts that might belong to the idea of Geosound. Over the course of the 2012/2013 academic year I led a seminar on the topic at the California Institute of the Arts, where some of the concepts discussed below crystalised.

In the introduction to the 'Geophilosophy' issue, Robin Mackay writes: 'we turn our gaze back towards our home planet to ask how, as products of the Earth, philosophers, scientists and artists have attempted to encompass it in thought; and how the philosophical enterprise of thinking "the whole" has been, and continues to be, determined by our belonging to the Earth.'

Location

I use the word 'location' to refer to a specific point in the world. It can be mapped with a system of longitudinal and latitudinal coordinates. It can be described precisely not just by where it is, but how it looks and how it sounds from the vantage point of the viewer and auditor. The sounds on the ground are *local*.

If the ground-centred point on Earth is the physical location, what is a sonic location, and how do we know we are there? Our two ears, especially the pinna or folds on the edges, are excellent locators in space, based on very subtle high-frequency information.[5]

The sonic model for location could be the *microphone*. The microphone might be conceived of as an instrument designed to detect vibration from something that approximates a point: the diaphragm of the microphone. When the microphone puts our ears in the location of that point we hear more or less what it hears: the sonic traces of the location.[6] When I stand at a certain point in the city or in the field, set my microphone on the stand pointing in a certain direction, and turn on the recording, the uncountable number of sounds available at that point leave their trace. The sounds from everywhere in range enter through that point.

Location prioritises perception over conception. Our ears are focused on the myriad features of that time and location as we attempt for once *not* to filter out sounds we would otherwise ignore. While this kind of work, especially Tsunoda's *Extracts from the Field Recording Archive*, might be beautiful it is not poetic – in the sense that the work does not need to pass through many language filters on its way to our ears. Field recording in this vein asks to be taken at face value: we place the sound within the limited context given. The set-up or background of location recording is often fairly easy to describe with barebones text. In addition to the information gathered, I believe we ultimately hear such location recordings as *music* of an ephemeral sort, not unrelated to the way we hear improvised music. (With field recording post-perception is the entry point of the poetic.)

Incidentally, what I have been calling a *field* is a map of locations. In my music I have often pictured 'the field' as a kind of grid with locations adjacent to each other. Perhaps the original model for something like this comes from Leibniz's concept of monads as adjacent beings. That is, as Leibniz in the *Monadology* conceives it, individual beings are contiguous – there is no space between one being and another. (In this case, being is considered in the abstract – it is not the same thing as human, person, animal and so on.) The implication is that being is always in contact with or touching other beings. Similarly, the field is a place where we experience sets of things continuously affecting one other. We experience sums and confluences. The relative isolation of a single sound in a field is an illusion created by proximity.

Space

The starting point for my idea of sonic *space* is Gaston Bachelard's *The Poetics of Space*.[7] The space, according to Bachelard, is indoors. Our original encounter with it is our childhood home, if we are lucky enough to have grown up in a house. Its deep ancestor is the hut, there to offer protection from the elements, to offer a simple shelter. The 'house' as Bachelard describes it also has to do with comfort and familiarity. A house might contain multiple spaces. The space of a basement is a very different space from an attic. But this shelter allows for something else. 'We comfort ourselves by reliving memories of protection. Something closed must retain our memories, while leaving them their value as images . . . The house shelters daydreaming.'[8] Although it would have to form the basis of a different topic than what I am discussing here, I would say that the musical remnant of this concept of space resides in the idea of chamber music, and then eventually the home stereo system. The practice of field recording, with some exceptions, seems to be largely about transporting the outdoor field into the indoor space. The implications of this are far-reaching. I believe that it is this fact that serves to set the stage for the use of field recording as *composition*, about which I will have more to say towards the end of this essay.

In sonic terms, we can say that the space has *resonance*. A resonance is the report of a sound given by the surfaces, the walls, the floor and ceiling and everything else, soft or hard, that happens to be there. A work like Alvin Lucier's *Vespers* can tell us a great deal about the sound of a space. In the piece, a group of blindfolded musicians use Sondols (handheld pulse oscillators) or some other instrument that emits a strong *click* to determine their location through echolocation. The musicians then begin to develop flocking patterns of movement as a result of Lucier's instructions. These patterns can be seen as patterns of the discovery of a sonic space and as fields that are activated *within* the space.

The resonance of a space can darken or brighten or otherwise filter a sound. A sound projected into a space carries a code of that space. (That is how electronically added reverb works, after all. It imposes the resonance coding on to the input.)

A small concert hall can have a feeling of space. Its design might be viewed as a way of protecting sound (and people), and in some cases of successful design or good fortune, fostering daydreaming in that form of sound we call music.

One field recording/*musique concrète* artist who has made extensive use of the concept of space in Bachelard's sense is Graham Lambkin. His *Salmon Run*,[9] for example, is fascinating in this regard, as it combines a feel for the privacy of interior spaces with the idea of home listening – especially to classical chamber music.

crosshatches: Location + Space

The collaborative composition *crosshatches*[10] was made over a period of about fourteen months – from the beginning of 2011 to April of 2012. Tsunoda and I were quite familiar with each other's work and wanted to work together, but we had to learn *how* to work together. Toshiya offered to make a graph representing sound shapes in time as a starting point. I then took this graph and divided the sounds into categories for noise and for pitch-based material. Toshiya recorded noise in a variety of ways and I created a series of chords, mostly using recorded and multi-tracked guitar. We then combined the audio into an hour-long alternation of sound and silence, maintaining this internal subdivision of pitch and noise. We liked the result, but it was not 'a piece'. So we agreed to make a *second* set of recordings using the material on this hour-long track. Having a hunch that Toshiya would make outdoor field recordings, I decided to record all the sounds I wanted to use in a single space: the Wild Beast Concert Hall on the CalArts campus, Valencia, California.

The final, eight-part composition is something one could visualise as a wire running across a complex landscape upon which are hung individual moments derived from our sets of recordings. It is in effect a continuous crosscutting (or crosshatching) between and among the indoor space and outdoor locations, many of which contained or recorded our original sets of sounds. In some instances, Toshiya embedded chamber sounds I had made into recordings made in the field – by allowing speakers to play back those sounds into the field. In some cases, I took recordings he sent and played them back into the space where I made most of my own recordings.

Although the listener can judge for herself, I think that the *clarity* of the contrast between the two types or categories creates movement between Location and Space. That is, we listen with a sense of 'openness from a point' (location) at some times and of 'protection within a room' (space) at other times. One could say the tendency of the field recording as document is inflected by the dream space of the shelter. There is also the possibility that by opening these two categories in such a clear way, the composition establishes gradations between these points. One clear instance would be where (in part 2.4) Tsunoda placed small speakers playing back recordings I had sent him inside ceramic containers, which were then half-buried in sand near the beach and recorded. This must somehow fall between the two categories I have defined. There are several other instances on this recording and in subsequent works by both Tsunoda and myself that seem to play with this continuum.

Two of the works indebted to this way of thinking are Toshiya Tsunoda and Manfred Werder's *detour* and my *Continuum Unbound*.[11] In *detour*, Tsunoda and Werder present what on first listen seems like a transparent set of field recordings. In fact, however, the piece is a layering of recordings. There is one in a field by a pond that runs for the whole duration of the disc and then a series of shorter recordings layered on top of it. The location for each of these shorter recordings represents a specific point of attention by the person recording. To render this *location* as a *space*, Tsunoda and Werder reasoned that they could not just record from a central position, but had to also take into account the accidents of attention: how we are directed by circumstances to look and listen to collections of points in our surroundings. Close listening reveals that these layers added come and go. There is something prismatic about the way they alter the perception of the fundamental layer – by directing our ears to some new region of sound while we remain conscious of the whole assembly.

This leads to a moment at around 40'25" where the scene appears to change rather dramatically: a strange, seemingly electronic sound takes over and runs until the end of the piece. In fact, it is a very close recording, using a stethoscope placed on the ground, of an insect. We continue to hear the long recording by the pond dimly in the background. This unexpected confrontation with the micro-world beneath the world we think we inhabit leads to a decisive alteration in our sense of the location. We realise that when the microphone moves our sense of *proximity* changes. And there are infinite degrees of proximity. The point of the microphone is revealed to be part of a continuum and our sense of naturalness disintegrates in the face of the real.

This disintegration of the sounding world is what *Continuum Unbound* attempts to hear. The work consists of three 72-minute parts. The first part, *Kingsnake Grey*, presents a single recording of the Congaree swamp in South Carolina at sundown. As I listened to the result, I became fascinated by how the apparently continuous processes that one might anticipate as the sun goes down were continually interrupted, restarted and disturbed in such a way that made the trajectory seem almost chaotic. In the second part of the work, *Congaree Nomads*, twenty-four locations from the same area were sequenced in 3-minute segments. A developing and increasingly continuous layer of bowed percussion runs concurrently with the field recordings. My hope was to achieve something like what Oswald Egger calls 'discrete continuity' – a situation where disjunction and conjunction of sound are heard to be in a shifting and unstable balance. This final piece, *anabasis (1)*, was an attempt to hear how five musicians could *create* a kind of discontinuous continuity. It required each of the musicians to make the sounds for their part of the score without knowing what the others would do. Then as the parts were assembled I listened for and created strategies for *unbinding* what had been bound together by the mixing process. This produced a result that had many sections and breaks in a piece whose overall trajectory was clear: a sequence of sounds defined as moving from sand to wind to tone to waves. In the terms of this essay, *Continuum Unbound* moves from a 'pure' location recording through the superimposition of multiple locations within the space of a harmonic music, and ends with what I will now define as something called 'place'.

Place

Marcel Proust, at the beginning of Part Three of *Swann's Way*, describes how the heart of the narrator begins to palpitate as he sees the hour of departure of the train to the seaside resort town of Balbec. The list of names of the towns the train passes through fills him with joy. Proust meditates on the power of a place name to encapsulate and enhance his images of the places mentioned.

A place, as I am using it here, has a *name*. It is thus tied in an important way to words, to language. A place is a collection of locations and spaces, often in a kaleidoscopic mixture of the large and the small, the indoor and the outdoor, the public and the private, and even the real and the virtual. (Perhaps my awareness of this last is heightened by the fact that I live near Hollywood.) Paris is a place; so is Los Angeles. Sometimes a place has a language or code and a set of referents of its own – for example the semi-real, semi-fictional place worked out in gangsta rap in Compton and South Central in the late 1980s and early 1990s.

In 'July Mountain', Wallace Stevens says that our world (that is, a place) is made up of 'pitches and patches'. It is a hybrid which we assemble collectively, so that when we use words like New York or Istanbul we have a shared idea of what is referenced. As must be clear, a place is already partially a poetic entity. Recordings can be made *in* a place, but there is no recording *of* a place.

July Mountain

> We live in a constellation
> Of patches and of pitches.
> Not in a single world,
> In things said well in music,
> On the piano and in speech,
> As in a page of poetry –
> Thinkers without final thoughts
> In an always incipient cosmos.
> The way, when we climb a mountain,
> Vermont throws itself together.[12]

d[4.1]b; d[4.2]b

One example of a composition in which *place* is central would have to be John Cage's *Roaratorio*.[13] The composition upon which the piece is based, '____, ____ ____ *circus on* ____', is a set of instructions for turning a book into sound. Since Joyce's *Finnegans Wake* is centred on Dublin, a great deal of the assemblage that Cage constructs involves that city.[14] But as a glance at Louis O. Mink's *A Finnegans Wake Gazetteer*, which Cage used to determine the location of the field recordings, confirms, there are a huge number of other places referenced in the book. Thus, in concentric circles, Ireland, Europe and the World appear as places, with many intermediate gradations between.

Place is a poetic concept, a composition and an assemblage. Place sprawls, leaches, grows in all directions and cannot be limited to one medium. As Deleuze and Guattari argue, geophilosophy (that is, the territory of the concept) requires both deterritorialisation and reterritorialisation. I think the same can be said for place. Place is not static; it is continually undergoing change and transformation. It may be that sound is therefore a natural partner to an aesthetics of place, since it too cannot be recouped – only summarised. The mental image we retain of a collection of sounds continues to transform itself in our minds, in many cases, long after we have heard the composition in which the sounds are placed.

Description without Place

But what, exactly, is Vermont doing is *July Mountain*? And how does *it* throw *itself* together? Is it a place or something else? I think that another of Stevens's ontologically oriented poems, 'Description without Place', has something to say on this topic. It might also serve as an introduction to the work I will introduce at the end of this section: my own composition called *July Mountain*.

In 'July Mountain' Stevens says that place is always in formation out of an 'incipient cosmos'. To my mind this carries an association of a kind of chaos that, from an infinite abyss of possible images, throws up opportunities for recognition. Stevens likes to use places and place names as stand-ins for something else, in order to dislocate – or deterritorialise – them. In the 'Anecdote of the Jar' something happens to 'Tennessee' that has never happened to it before. Is Tennessee really a 'slovenly wilderness' or is it a stand-in for the *idea* of wilderness?

'Description without Place' concerns itself with the relation between 'seeming' and 'being'. Stevens begins: 'It is possible that to seem – it is to be/ As the sun is something seeming and it is.' The poem slyly investigates the being of mental constructs, the ontology of concepts. The 'sun' referenced here is not only the astronomical object, but also the words for this object as used in the poem. At the seam of this seeming is another kind of zone, where verbal constructs, perhaps stemming from experiences in the actual world take on a luminescent virtuality.

In seeming, something dislocates itself from the precisely local (in my terms, a 'location') and becomes something else, beyond even the collection of related images I am calling 'place': a description without place.

> If seeming is description without place,
> The spirit's universe, then a summer's day,
>
> Even the seeming of a summer's day,
> Is description without place.[15]

Stevens says that this description is '[a] little different from reality: The difference we make in what we see.'

This is the work of a poet: using language to make a difference, creating an artificial thing not from scratch, but as a vector hinged to the seam of the real. A poem or a piece is a collection of sensations that are not on the same plane as the actual world. It is the plane of composition, which behaves differently from the cause and effect of our day-to-day lives.

What I find striking about the poem is the speed Stevens discovers in what he calls description. Because it is artificial, taking place in the world of 'its own seeming', it is more intense that 'any actual life could be', 'more explicit than the sun'. This would be the world of the concept, a place where, as Deleuze says, thought occurs at infinite speed – because the component parts of the concept are adjacent, energy can be exchanged between them instantaneously.

In Stevens's conjuring of this world, words and images flicker before our eyes. The nearly matched doubles in the poem are placed upon one another in such a way that they do not resolve – one term intensifies the next, the way the seeming-sun fires the one we experience.

That is why '[d]escription is revelation'.

In *July Mountain* I wanted to capture the movement from the apparent reality of a situation (a collection of location recordings, forming a 'mountain place') to a synthetically assembled world of its own seeming. In Stevens's 'July Mountain' this is where we arrive as Vermont throws itself together: no longer the place Vermont, no longer a false facsimile but somewhere else entirely. One word for this – borrowing it from Julian Barbour's *The End of Time* – might be 'configuration'. Another word that comes to mind is 'orchestra'. To close this section, I will quote the end of *Description without Place*, which addresses itself to the potential of art as manifold intensification:

> . . . a cast
>
> Of the imagination, made in sound;
> And because what we say of the future must portend,
>
> Be alive with its own seemings, seeming to be
> Like rubies reddened by rubies reddening.[16]

Postscript: The Poetic Assembly, a Constellation

'Description without Place' might be a way of describing a whole category of compositional work I (and certain others) have done with the aid of poetry. It is a zone where the 'seeming' that poetry can bring to a situation is used to condition the performance and the structure of music. It may be worthwhile to give some background to the foregoing discussion of Stevens and *July Mountain*.

Without digressing into the entire history of the poetic influence on music in the West and elsewhere, it will suffice for now to say that certain figures in Western music: Machaut, Gesualdo, Monteverdi, Schütz, Beethoven, Schumann, Debussy and Schoenberg, among others, are unimaginable without the impact of poetry on their work. But starting with John Cage another perspective on the use of poetic impulse in music takes place. From, at the latest, *4'33"* and then onward, those writing words on the page to make scores have an increasing awareness of the power of poetic imagery as instruction; as a way to influence the making of sound and as a way to generate music. This is something other than quotations at the top of the score and the setting of text in song. It is as if the passage *through* text is the only way to get at certain sounds or certain ways of making works. *0'00"* (John Cage, 1962) is a literary work that exists in tandem with the world of sound it brings into being. It is both a set of instructions and the very object that generates sound – in that the task Cage chose, as the first performer of the piece, was the amplified writing of the score text itself. The text scores of Christian Wolff, Yoko Ono, George Brecht, Pauline Oliveros and Alvin Lucier, along with many others, seemed to open up a multitude of ways of using poetry (or text) in music.

In my *harmony series* (2004–6), a collection of thirty-four text scores for open instrumentation, I began to use poetic texts *within* the descriptions of musical events and performance instructions. The temporal layout of the pieces takes the *structure* more than the meaning of the poetic text as a task in translation. For instance, in the piece called *The rain of alphabets*, I try to reproduce in sound something like that additive complexity achieved by Inger Christensen in her monumental work from 1981, *Alfabet*. The work is constructed by using the Fibonacci sequence to determine the number of lines in each poem. The poems are aligned with the individual letters of the alphabet, and each poem uses its assigned letter to head lists of things that exist. Christensen stops at the letter N, the fourteenth in the alphabet, because the number of lines thereafter would become unwieldy. (Since Christensen omits the 0 and the first 1, the sequence is: 1, 2, 3, 5, 8, 13, 21, 34, 55, 89, 144, 233, 377, 610 – the next numbers would be 987, 1597, 2584, 4181 and so on.) In my piece there are fourteen sections that grow progressively in length and in which each section adds one performer – thus moving from a solo to fourteen musicians. Perhaps the extended quotation from Christensen's poem embedded in the score has some impact on decisions that the performers will make.

This way of thinking has can be found in the large set of my pieces that deal explicitly with the formal properties and conceptual framework of specific poems: for example in the Ponge cycle,[17] a series of six works based on Lucretius[18] and several works written in tandem with Oswald Egger.[19] My close colleagues Antoine Beuger and Manfred Werder have pursued their own ongoing investigations as well.[20]

All of this work, it seems to me, occupies a zone where sound and text continue to operate upon each other, generating concatenations of consequences that play out in both realms, no longer so geocentric; not quite Vermont or Tennessee. Perhaps this sort of thinking about place begins with Mallarmé, who in *Un coup de dés*, writes: 'Nothing / will have taken place / but place / except / perhaps / a constellation.' Although we are still in middle of our various projects, it is fair to say in verbal music *beyond* place, we are in the realm of the constellation.

Notes

1. This essay is derived from a talk I gave at the Centre for Creative Collaboration on 12 November 2012, under the auspices of the Contemporary Poetics Research Centre, Royal Holloway University of London, and was subsequently published in issue 5 of the online journal *Wolf Notes*, edited by Patrick Farmer and Sarah Hughes. As part of the talk, I was asked to present examples from the works discussed, which must surely aid the reader in understanding the relationships presented here.

2. Perhaps sound is more of the air than the earth, since that is the medium of vibration our ears understand. In any case, until I can segment the air into aerographical regions, the Earth will have to do as a locator. I did once have a fantasy that we would be able to feel sound with our feet: I wanted to design a very peculiar room that had corrugated rubber floor through which vibration could be produced. This has so far gone unrealised.

3. *Collapse VI*, ed. Robin Mackay (Falmouth: Urbanomic, 2010).

4. Gilles Deleuze and Felix Guattari, *What is Philosophy?* (New York: Columbia University Press, 1994).

5. Recent work by Toshiya Tsunoda experiments with 'separating' the ears, by recording with one left-ear microphone from one person, and from a right-ear microphone in another person some metres away. In the terminology I am using here it is a bit like stretching a location until it becomes something like a space. An extended consideration of this and other aspects of Tsunoda's work by the author can be found here: http://surround.noquam.com/membrane-window-mirror/ (last accessed, 17 May 2015).

6. There is also a point (or, more properly, duration) of time. It is equally crucial to the character of the writing/recording. The question of *temporal* orientation in the sounding world is too large for this essay and will be addressed at another time. This topic's guiding lights will be the poet Oswald Egger, the philosopher Vladimir Jankélévitch and the scientist Julian Barbour.

7. Gaston Bachelard, *The Poetics of Space* (Boston: Beacon Press, 1969).

8. Ibid., p. 6.

9. Graham Lambkin, *Salmon Run*, CD (Kye, 2007).

10. Michael Pisaro and Toshiya Tsunoda, *crosshatches*, CD (Erstwhile, 2012).

11. *detour* (Erstwhile, 2014) and *Continuum Unbound* (Gravity Wave, 2014).

12. Wallace Stevens, *Collected Poetry and Prose* (New York: Library of America, 197), p. 476.

13. John Cage, *Roaratorio (Ein irischer Circus über 'Finnegans Wake')*, CD (Wergo, 1994).

14. A discussion of how the work was constructed can be found in the notes to the release of *Roaratorio* on Wergo.
15. Stevens, p. 300.
16. Stevens, p. 302.
17. *Pieces on texts by Francis Ponge* (Edition Wandelweiser, 2004), derived from 'Le pain', 'La mousse', 'Pluie', 'Le cageot' and 'L'huître', from *Le Parti pri des choses*.
18. So far, the series, which will eventually include one piece for each of the six books of *De rerum natura*, includes: I. *Lucretius Monody* (for solo voice, 2008/9), II. *Lucretius Alap* (2012, for 18 strings), IV. *Lucretius Melody* (for mezzo-soprano, viola and two electric guitars, 2015/16) and VI. *Lucretius Counterpoint* (2007, for four voices, flute, violoncello and percussion), all with Edition Wandelwesier.
19. These include: *A Sea of Ptyx* (2001, reader, marimba, guitar), *Twelve Gardens* (2003, reader and twelve musicians), *Tag und Nacht sind zwei Jahre* (2003, reader, percussion, guitar), *20 songs / le clavecin des prés* (2008, soprano and orchestra), all with Edition Wandelweiser, and the disc *The Middle of Life (Die ganze Zeit)* (Gravity Wave, 2013).
20. Extensive documentation and discussion of a very wide stream of this work can be found in the excellent *Word Events: Perspectives on Verbal Notation*, ed. John Lely and James Saunders (London: Continuum, 2012).

Chapter 5

Pitch 🔂 of Inhabiting: Thoughts on the Practice of Sound, Poetry and Virno's 'Accustomed Place'*

Carol Watts

In Montaigne's essay 'An Apology for Raymond Sebond' he recounts an anecdote from Plutarch about a magpie's facility for mimicry. A captive magpie is sitting in a Roman barber's shop, and in the street outside a group of musicians pass by, 'blasting away on their trumpets'. The effect on the bird at first seems traumatic. The magpie appears 'pensive, mute and melancholic', and onlookers assume that it has become frightened and confused, 'making it lose both hearing and song at the same time'. But then, after a day goes by, the magpie begins to reproduce the sounds of the trumpets perfectly, replete with their pitches and timing, and 'quit with disdain all that it was able to do before', including its stock of imitated speech. In the bird's silence, it turns out, is no simple mimicry, but a form of meditation and 'apprenticeship', an 'inward' preparation of voice.[1] There is something virtuosic invested in the magpie's reproduction of passing sound. Later in the same essay, Montaigne returns to consider the trumpet itself as an instrument. Just as a tree routes moisture through its roots to manifest variously in trunk, leaves and fruit, he suggests, the singular nature of air is analogously 'diversified into a thousand kinds of sound' by the trumpet. Is this a property of the 'fashioning' of the senses, or of the object itself? Montaigne asks.[2] There is a parallel here between the captive magpie and the philosopher, in that black-box gap for thought notated in the fermata of my title,[3] in the process of hearing and recording a sonic complexity through the senses.

I begin with this anecdote not as an entry into Montaigne's understanding of the human and the animal within Renaissance natural theology, but as a way into thinking the relation between writing and

---

*The accompanying audio recording is indicated in the following way – **d[5.1]b** – and is available on the publisher's website at: https://edinburghuniversitypress.com/book writing-the-field-recording-hb.html [click on the 'resources' tab].

field. By 'field', I mean not simply field recording, with assumptions about its mimetic practice and faithfulness to the capture of sound in particular locations, nor solely in a delimited conceptual sense, field as relating to 'event' as it is explored in John Berger's 1971 essay,[4] but field as the space of a *milieu*, where nature interferes with nature, in Foucault's terms. 'Field' becomes in this light a space of uncertain variability to which we are biologically and materially bound, and a zone of articulation among forces of physical nature and the 'artifice' which functions as the nature ('second nature') of the human species.[5] Increasingly, this distinction is under pressure, not least in the current thinking of world ecology, and the bio-imbrication of the virtual or synthetic and the real, in which the boundary between 'nature' and 'artifice' is itself an expanding and living morphological margin. How does this expanding milieu, then, as an acoustic environment, become an active part of a translated and compositional act, whether that of a field recording or poetic text? How might that composition itself collaborate in – 'hear' – the constitutive making of field, or become part of its thought?

In the sketch of the magpie there is, I initially want to suggest, a recognition of an imagined shared poiesis or making, one that loops between encounter, an attention of thought as a listening, and multiplicities of sound and their performance. It suggests a switching point or transposition, between a live hearing or recording instrument (one that is ascribed depth and interiority and the ability to think) and sound emanating from an environment that is on the move, a transposition that may have its own durational lag of time, and always already be shaped by the chance of other intricating and noisy circuits. Rather than a pure mimicry of human sound, as if abstracted from environment, the magpie is involved in a complex exchange with the inhabited street and air, like its current avian counterparts who have adapted the frequencies of their birdsong to the sound of aircraft and car alarms, caught like all other species in an ecosystem shaped by the resonant insistence of noise.[6] But what is at stake in this instance is not just adaptation to habitat. The magpie 'becomes' trumpet for the onlooker, though what is trumpet for the magpie is uncertain. Its mimicry is captured in a universe of sound in which, in Montaigne's words, 'We ourselves, our faculty of judgement and all mortal things are flowing and rolling ceaselessly.'[7]

This looping movement may hint at that sense of 'incipient cosmos' which Wallace Stevens addresses in his poem 'July Mountain', discussed elsewhere in this collection, one that poetry reaches through 'a constellation / Of patches and pitches' rather than any representational description of the world or metaphorics of approximation. We live in such a constellation, Stevens suggests, and 'Not in a single world', and thus place comes to constitute itself: 'The way, when we climb a mountain, / Vermont throws itself together'.[8] The question I will pursue is what kind of constellatory world is set in motion by the anecdote of the magpie, and further, how the implications of its inhabiting might be explored. In what follows I will track a curious and in some sense performative route, in which the *practice* of poetry, sound and place is held to be actively central to that exploration. Beginning with the virtuosity of the magpie and a further versioning of 'July Mountain', through Paolo Virno's work on the praxis of an 'accustomed place', I will move to a consideration of Mei-mei Berssenbrugge's poem 'Hearing' in her collection *Nest*, and the inhabiting of language and environment imagined there. In a final section, the magpie returns in the practice of my collaborative text and sound work with Will Montgomery, *Pitch*, which draws on field recording and fragments of Luigi Nono's *Fragmente – Stille, an Diotima*, to address the inhabiting of an accustomed place once more.

Magpie as Virtuoso

Recent bioacoustic research into the mimicry of birds like the magpie suggests that Montaigne's anecdote is more verisimilar than it might appear. Rather than a low-level reproducing of chatter or sound, like a simple imprinting, somehow of a piece with usual (and erroneous) accounts of a magpie's streetwise thievery of shiny things, its mimicry suggests a complex repertoire. Not only do magpies reproduce the frequencies and the precise duration of imitated sounds, but they are also selective in drawing sounds from their acoustic territory, and, as the philosopher noted, able to learn. 'This species has a very highly developed auditory perception and great musical discriminatory abilities', writes Gisela Kaplan. She explains that recent avian neuroscience has revealed the magpie's internal capacity for the registry of sound as memory, such that it can then check its 'encoded version against the song it then sings'. The gap noted in Montaigne's story, between the bird's encounter with the trumpet music and its later complex rendition, is a recognised phenomenon: 'There is a known delay in reproducing any learned vocalization of up to 48h but thereafter it is copied in its entirety'. 'The thousand kinds of sound' associated with the trumpet may well have been in the compass of the magpie, and its mute 'apprenticeship' dependent on the auditory feedback mechanism that is now known to be one cognitive key to its virtuosic performance. If this is mimicry, it is far from 'mindless', Kaplan points out.[9]

The ancient anecdote may contain scientific truth, yet it nonetheless also carries a fantasy of virtuosity that also has a number of real directions of travel. One is suggested by its acknowledgement of that sensuous internal space within the shock or confusion of a sonic encounter, which provides the opportunity in its seeming silence for an inward adaptation, moving, let's say, from hearing to a processing, and ultimately to a fully mimetic performance. As if, to pursue the analogy with field recording, it might be possible to arrive at a precise rendition of an acoustic environment, whatever the gap between the ear, with its 'physical latency of hearing', as Berssenbrugge will describe it in her poetry,[10] and the 'non-cognitive listening'[11] of microphone recording. This is a bird that is doubly captured, both captive – subjected and tied to place – and captured by passing sound. Yet its internalised routing turns out to be an active sampling of what is passing in the street and in common. Something of the world in its exteriority is looped and returned with its performance, at once recognisable and uncanny.

The magpie story also sets in motion an equivalence between the meditative bird and human thinker, since Montaigne is throughout his 'essay' concerned to point out the mimetic and relational exchange between species of all kinds.[12] What makes the magpie virtuosic in this light is not so much the quality of its performance, which mimics the musical sounds that supplant the everyday human chatter of the barber's (which it reportedly leaves behind with 'disdain'). This distinction between the imitation of vernacular speech and the accomplishment of musical form is clearly part of the freight of this story, and one that should be questioned.[13] Rather, the magpie operates like a marvellous hinge between the human and avian environments, as if it offers a secret key to a common boundary. How to approach that boundary – less a line than a 'thickness' perhaps – is a question here.[14] Montaigne's vision of the multiple differences and correspondences of the perceptual and behavioural worlds of birds and other species, from elephants to shellfish, has what now might seem an ecological or ecosophical charge, not least in its reduction of the privileged viewpoint of the human observer whose unreliable senses cannot penetrate them. This is not a 'single world', as Stevens's poem declared, but rather hints at a complex of *umwelten* that the biologist Jacob von Uexküll understood in musical terms. As Giorgio Agamben describes:

> Where classical science saw a single world that comprised within in all living species hierarchically ordered from the most elementary forms up to the higher organisms, Uexküll instead supposes an infinite variety of perceptual worlds that, though they are uncommunicating and reciprocally exclusive, are all equally perfect and linked together as if in a gigantic musical score.

The magpie's receiving of and precise response to 'carriers of significance' in its own environment would be a playing of that 'keyboard on which nature performs the supratemporal and extraspatial symphony of signification', in Uexküll's description.[15] What makes this virtuosic, perhaps, is the way magpie mimicry brings that performance through selection into view: a translation of trumpet, from air and its diversifying into 'thousand kinds of sound' into an interior sensuous object for the bird – one that takes time to 'prepare' and which remains opaque except to itself – into a reproduction of a 'real' trumpet-object. It is a performance marking the virtuosic convolution of bird and human, entering into the thought of a field or milieu. This might be seen as a form of poiesis, and it arrives eventually as an uncanny auditory misrecognition, a perfect repetition of trumpets sounding where there are none. Misrecognition, here lived as a constitutive imaginary, part of the everyday inhabiting of a milieu.

Moving to an 'Accustomed Place': Sound and Inhabiting

In *July Mountain*, their sound composition responding to the Wallace Stevens poem of the same name, Michael Pisaro and Greg Stuart create a dense immersive experience for the listener.[16] The acoustic texture of the piece appears to be created from multiple layered field recordings, so that 'place' constitutes itself through the accretive assembling of 'patches and pitches', just as the poem might suggest. It is *as if* the ear could come to distinguish numerous composite elements within the overwhelming atmosphere of frequencies here, moving from hearing to the localisation effects of a more accustomed listening. So, to follow this logic, the listener might build a potential relation to the total complexity of signals and noise emanating from what seems to be a specific environment.[17] The result is a transpositional inhabiting of 'place' – a place we might call July Mountain – an *as if* that carries certain anthropological assumptions, geographical and spatial expectations, perceptual freight. However, all is not as it seems. As the score makes evident, a morphing has taken place long before the ear realises. The field recordings have been gradually replaced by percussive human-made sounds, so that by the end there is no vestige of recorded 'field' remaining. If a sense of 'place' persists (and for this listener it appeared to), something nonetheless has rendered it radically indeterminate, 'thrown together' not by walking or climbing, but by another kind of passage. When does that transposition within the notion of field take place definitively? Pisaro notes that even in performances of the piece by musicians it is difficult to tell:

> the whole interest of the piece really lies in this transitional state, in the fact that no matter how many times you come back to it you find that your idea of the mixture between, let's call it the 'given', that is field-recording, and 'produced' doesn't resolve itself. You could never find that point in which you're convinced that now we're entering the world of produced, it's always coming too late, you're always already there. By the time that you think there are still field-recordings there aren't and you think that the percussion must have started up by now but it hasn't.

In addition, Pisaro notes in the same interview, the digital algorithms in the black box mixing the composition are unable to resolve this uncertainty. 'When you have this incredibly high density of an event, on a perceptual level it will never compose itself. No matter how much control is exerted by the person there is simply too much information to really control.'[18]

What then is the nature of the sonic passage through 'July Mountain', in which the switching point between field recordings and human percussive sounds is continuously uncertain? It is perhaps reminiscent of a Möbius strip, in which seemingly dual or exclusive distinctions – interior/external, natural/artificial, human/extrahuman, real/virtual – are walked along a live single surface. This is perhaps a form of 'place-*binding*', as Tim Ingold defines it, but one that simultaneously renders that inhabiting virtual.[19] For the listener, this experience may come as a kind of delayed revelation, perhaps even latent shock, that the saturated 'environment' emerging through the ear and other senses might have had no indexical bearing nor points of anchorage in the 'given', except in that duration of experiencing a performance. What might it mean to think this unsettling in terms of a milieu, in which there is continual interference between nature and nature? If a sense of place persists, it may draw (in my magpie reading) on an everyday virtuosity of auditory selection within that thickness of information, one that makes an inhabiting of such a sensory overload possible, and also on an essential misrecognition, which makes the world of this switchable imaginary livable. Yet what kind of 'place' might this be? What kind of livable?

In his analysis of the 'emotional situation' of the contemporary lifeworld, 'The Ambivalence of Disenchantment', the philosopher Paolo Virno discusses a form of overload that has sonic dimensions, a 'hearing without listening'. He sets out the condition in the form of a 'parable':

> A person stands at the edge of the sea, intent upon nothing. He hears the sound of the waves, noisy and continuous, even after a certain time he is no longer listening. That person perceives, but without being aware of it. The perception of the uniform action of the waves is no longer accompanied by the perception of self as perceiving subject. This perception does not at all coincide with what in philosophical jargon is called apperception, or the consciousness of being in the act of perceiving. At the graying edge of the waves, the person standing there absorbed is one with the surrounding environment, connected by a thousand subtle and tenacious threads. The situation, however, does not pass through the filter of a self-reflexive 'subject'. Rather this integration with the context is that much stronger the more the 'I' forgets itself. . . . The experience of the person on the beach suggests . . . that we belong to a world in a material and sensible manner, far more preliminary and unshakeable than what seeps out from the little we know of knowledge.[20]

Far from being a marginal condition, Virno argues, this situation is one of general surplus, a 'superabundance' of information and signals 'received without ever being distinctly and consciously perceived' (p. 29). He describes an environment shaped by the chatter of information and media technologies, the bombardment of 'miniscule perceptions' and 'impressions and images that never give rise to an "I"', which are nonetheless systemic, and continuously mutable (p. 30). A condition of 'hearing without listening' overwhelms everyday experience. 'The individual hears more than he or she listens to, and perceives more than she or he apperceives'. In this imbalance, the relation to the world is also transformed: 'Consciousness of the self is always comprehended and delimited within a horizon delineated by this perceptual excess, an excess that locates us within an environment that is never "our own"' (p. 31).

Virno prompts the question of how generalisable this 'modality of experience' is and for whom, with its identification of the end of a society of work and an adaptation to 'an essentially abstract environment' in which chatter has built its 'offices' (pp. 29; 16). It is his understanding of this 'perceptual excess' and its relation to place that I want to sketch. A pervasive condition of 'hearing without listening' is a sign of a fundamental *uprooting*, in his view. With uprooting, comes exilic thought:

> Exiles and emigrants, our sense of identity is bitterly tried, precisely because the flow of perceptions that never take root in the self-reflexive conscience is growing disproportionately. This perceptive *surplus* constitutes, moreover, the operative way of taking one's place in an unknown environment. But uprooting no longer evokes actual exile or emigration. It constitutes, rather, an ordinary condition that everyone feels because of the continual mutation of modes of production, techniques of communication, and styles of life. (p. 30)

Such an intensive and endless uprooting transforms the relation to an environment, and with it the 'harmonic' balance traditionally drawn between perception and apperception, that counterpoint between a particularity of finite existence and the transcendence that allows thought to 'open onto the universal' (p. 30). Instead, Virno argues, '[t]oday's modes of being and feeling lie in an *abandonment without reserve to our own finitude*', that leaves us unable to move 'outside' to reflect on that condition. Yet the more abstracted that state of uprooting, the more sensuous and material the attachment to location, and paradoxically, to belonging as such:

> The abandonment to finitude is inhabited by a vigorous *feeling of belonging*. This combination may seem incongruous or paradoxical. What kind of belonging could I mean, after having unrelentingly insisted on the unexpected absence of particular and credible 'roots'? . . . And yet alienation, far from eliminating the feeling of belonging, empowers it. The impossibility of securing ourselves within any durable context disproportionately increases our adherence to the most fragile instances of the 'here and now.' What is dazzlingly clear is finally belonging as such, no longer qualified by a determinate belonging 'to something'. Rather, the feeling of belonging has become directly proportional to the lack of a privileged and protective 'to which' to belong. (p. 31)

In this paradoxical dynamic of uprooting (with its perceptual overload of 'hearing without listening') and intense attachment to the 'here and now' is one potential key to the passage through the soundscape of *July Mountain*. The sense of 'place' that persists – beyond the constellatory patches and pitches that might suggest, briefly, a rooting in the sense of a specific environment 'thrown together' by field recordings and the ear – moves us towards a virtual and contingent experience closer to a form of action than the constitutive recognition of a 'given'. This is then less a form of poiesis, than a praxis, as Virno might see it.[21] His definition of an 'accustomed place' captures the paradoxes at work here:

> Exodus moves towards an 'accustomed place' continually reconstituted by one's own activity, an 'accustomed place' that never preexists the experience that determines its location, nor that, therefore, can reflect any former habit. Today, in fact, habit has become something unusual and inhabitual, only a possible result, and never a point of departure. (p. 32)

Virno's account, extended in a wider ecological sense attentive to the damaging inroads of sonic and informational excess, has repercussions for all the inhabitants of a lifeworld, not only the human ones. That moment in which Montaigne's magpie 'loses' both hearing and song in the shock of encounter returns now as a potential for a more persistent fragility, rather than adaptation; a shared contemporary crisis in what Linda Russo has called 'listening-being'.[22] In this notion of an 'accustomed place' is an activity that might thus illuminate the locational praxes (and stakes) of field recording in their most expanded sense, which also suggests why the anecdote of the magpie retains something of a virtuosic pull on thought. Rather than a perceptive surplus, or deafened shock, in that gap following the moment of environmental encounter, there is an active routing through other modes of extra-human, and non-human experience which turns finitude into a more imbricated attention to relational limits and boundaries, an ecological thinking. So magpie mimicry becomes more than an instance of poiesis as I first saw it. Rather, it suggests a relay of sameness and alterity in the here and now, the sometimes infra-thin, sometimes chasmal borders sounding in the exchange of kinds of sentience and performance. A 'margin', in the words of Mei-mei Berssenbrugge's *Nest*, 'where dwelling and travel are not distinct'.[23]

Inhabiting *Nest*

It is at this point that I want to turn to poetry, as a compositional practice that participates in such an expanded field. I think of poetry at times as a highly attuned recording surface, even as a skin (not just a surface for sensation and inscription, but an expansive organ that has the capacity to hear and metabolise). As such it picks up on interior and external frequencies, and the 'thousand subtle and tenacious threads' experienced on Virno's shore. Poetry's relation to field recording is not for me fundamentally concerned with an equivalence of representation or description, or even primarily to be grasped via a metaphorics of analogy, but is rather about an active poiesis both sometimes share, closer to the praxis of an 'accustomed place', as Virno describes it, in which an environment is repeatedly reconstituted and returned. Poetry in this light is less a 'work', than a continuous practice of embodied thought, inscription and performance. It has in common with field recording an improvisatory passage through the world-as-field and the stakes of its sounding and inhabiting.

Mei-mei Berssenbrugge's sequence of poems *Nest* is centrally concerned with what it means to dwell – in language, in a house, with others, in a landscape, in thought. As a poet of Chinese and American-Dutch descent, she gives the question of inhabiting a 'mother tongue' and its relation to perception sustained conceptual attention, in writing that responds to the phenomenological environment of New Mexico in which she lives. '[H]ome reproduces itself at risk in unfamiliar conditions', she writes, observing that 'It's a complicity of smell and space, wet surfaces, tears, local as margin, other projected as remodeling, nonspecific, recreational lines, tent poles' (p. 52).[24] This piling up of sense material, feelings, abstract vectors and constructions is characteristic of the measure of this poetry, which works through irrational cuts or curious parataxes, and bolts and durations of affective states, as if picking up material with multiple antennae. *Nest* explores inhabiting through intensities of uprooting and belonging, I would argue, in which the making of an 'accustomed place' is continually played out.

The first poem in *Nest*, 'Permanent Home', opens with the words 'I seek a permanent home', and later declares 'Give a house the form of an event' (p. 15). What kind of 'event' is a house? At times, as in 'The Retired Architect', it suggests a 'building' that life might ideally conceive 'to loose in space':

> I tried to complete a life circumstance, like a building I aspired to loose in space on used land.
>
> I made a shape against the sky on flat land, like a cut in the weeds, but I got bored and didn't finish. (p. 31)

The building of a house 'on used land', like a life, is continuously provisional, subject to the affective sway of energies, or misrecognition, 'what we'll accept as being there' (p. 29). Habits don't appear to anchor it: 'I make something, which as it changes and falls apart, offers no clues to itself before' (p. 31). 'Real is a span of visibility, inasmuch as your flesh is not chaotic, *of* a contingency' (p. 26). In this contingent environment, fragments of perception surface, as if they carry tenuous or forensic instances of the 'to which' in belonging that Virno describes as so precarious and lacking, now abstracted: 'He delicately rotates his hands to an emotion that's like a place' (p. 25).

John Berger's essay 'Field' ends with a sense of the commensurability of life and the 'event' of field: 'The field that you are standing before appears to have the same proportions as your own life'.[25] But in Berssenbrugge's poetry these proportions are nowhere secure nor their ground always discernible, even as they are rendered sensitively in the here and now. What might it mean to live in a world overwhelmed by perceptual information? 'Information is not memory' (p. 30), a poem declares, and continues, in these long planar statements, with their steady tonality, like small strips of duration:

> I see reflected light, while behind me in the dark is a proliferation that's biological or life-based, in the sense of a vested interest.
>
> I have to focus in front, then back; it's not transformation.

This is not a world that is to be transformed by a synthetic poetic vision, owned by a receptive lyric subject seemingly settled in its potential. Rather the 'I' is immersed in registering of a finitude that is the space of life. With its 'opaque provenances' (p. 52) and the occasional freedoms afforded by time's 'ethos', this subject inhabits the gap between 'matter and representation' (p. 55). Sometimes that representational pull generates dramas, film stories, the creating of domestic pets, or singing along. It can't get a distance from the chatter of 'hearsay' (p. 64). Or succumbs to plangent sentimentality, like kitsch.[26] The more present the I, the more intense might appear the seeking out of a phenomenal field that offers in its dwelling more than 'poor immunity' (p. 51).

The last three poems, all entitled 'Safety', underline one protective gesture behind the seeking:

> So, I continue to calculate my house, its significance as a holding place for something to look at (image, word), building would illustrate. (p. 67)

'Holding place' carries the sense of a repository for gathered and assembled objects, however provisional. Also, more significantly, it suggests a maternal embracing, which surfaces throughout the sequence:

> Let mothers catch them, raccoon, Labrador bitch, girl, interspecies conservative mothers, arms out like foliage, no locomotion of their own. (p. 54)

A nest, then, is also a holding place, an active form of making which gathers the fragments to create habitable spaces. If it signifies a maternal protection, a construction woven from kinds of building matter, it is composed of shards and found elements that for all their sheltering are also exposed to – indeed part of – the outside and its 'proliferation'. Belonging takes place there; there's pharmacological health to be found perhaps in a nested capacity for immune response, what is taken in from the outside. At times *Nest* seems to discover resources here, like the vision of a family:

> The surface of the visibility of a family doubles over its whole extension with invisible reserve. (p. 23)

Elsewhere the familial 'reserve' might seem in short supply, with 'no ethos of being together, like cards from a disoriented gambler' (p. 33). 'The fragment, "my lost home" belongs to this grounding mistake of a family', she writes. If the leaving of home is something 'difficult to admit', its occupation is also uncertain, as is revealed in 'Nest', with alterity at the heart of the sequence:

> The foreign woman occupies a home that's impersonal, like the nest of a parasite. (p. 47)

The constellatory 'nest' of fragments I have been drawing together from Berssenbrugge's sequence of poems hints at the continual building and decomposition of an 'accustomed place'. Sometimes these fragments gather, like a gift: 'the potlatch settles around me in a house' (p. 55). At other points that house doesn't coalesce, remains unsettled. The subject who inhabits this condition also accretes or changes as if by a physics. Sometimes she is 'a luminescent skin of being herself, subject, wife, envelope of human limits of things' (p. 55). Or part of a web community of emotions and screens, in a 'screen simulation' (p. 55), where 'words leave no trace, like a bird in the sky' (p. 63). Or she might be rendered viscous, like light, like honey:

> Domestic space oozes light through a loophole, mother to mother, so close I can't catch it through myself. (p. 48)

'Don't let her ooze through loopholes we inhabit like migrants', she writes. If this writing tries out nomad affinities, 'states of dwelling undetermined', it also tracks a palpable and sticky maternal inheritance and future care. In a poetry so conceptually attuned to the visible and invisible, to the abstractions of images and planes, it is *hearing* that becomes one dynamic in the grasping of the stakes of this habitation.

Hearing the bird, time

The first lines of 'Hearing' begin with silence or, rather, a voice where there is no speaking:

> A voice with no one speaking, like the sea, merges with my listening, as if imagining her thinking about me makes me real. (p. 53)

In Virno's parable of the shore, the sea is a sign of the condition of an overwhelming 'hearing without listening', such that the 'I' forgets itself. In *Nest*, the maritime nature of hearing is in its tender and maternal holding-in-mind, 'response, not perspective' (p. 55), as if love is a condition for the 'I' to become 'real'. 'What's called *hearer is hearing*', she writes in an earlier poem, imagining an 'exemplary listener' (p. 43). In 'Hearing' she focuses on this condition, and the desire for protection that might imagine it. 'Hearing: transparency arms arc over, glass nest for her young'. In this nesting embrace might be access to a trust in environmental holding, or an ecological wish for it, which hearing makes present as a 'physical latency', like memory, or in some kind of reserve, a sense of 'deep matter'. In the case of the voice which does not speak, 'Its matter is attributed to its passing away, a transcendence whose origin has come apart'. This fundamental maternal reserve without origin may be the 'mother tongue' itself, which is linked here with 'the plane of the sea'. It also has a Buddhist dimension, in the maternal form of Kuan Yin, part of Berssenbrugge's Chinese 'immemorial history' perhaps. Kuan Yin is the Bodhisattva of compassion, and 'hearer of all cries'.[27] After being named briefly in 'Nest', she appears to surface here, and translate into the effort of more local belonging:

> I found I could take words from one discipline and intersect them with another, such as generous feeling with listening to supplicants.

> Empty space intersects with the dignity of stars, of homelessness, health ruined by addiction, to help supplicants.

> Trying to be part of the neighbourhood, school activism, etc., with a serene demeanour not caught in form of fairy or butterfly wing calmly breathing, alternating with the physical situation, someone ill, someone tortured.

Hearing is the fractality of fragments occurring (as they disintegrate). (p. 56)

A movement is discernible here, from a cosmic 'transparency', a world of immanence, to the decomposition of hearing as a 'fractality of fragments occurring'.[28] Tracked in the fragment of a bird falling 'out of the air, through the anti-weave, into the anti-net, delineating anti-immanence', whose calling seems at first incorporated into a sonic net of communication:

> The plane tips up and completes our world with transparency, synapse between birdcall and hearing it, pink and shade facets of waves, butterfly on tongue.

only for the text to move from 'matter to representation, for more agency, point of presence', as the birdcall is sutured into the disintegration of 'my hearing':

> . . . bird falling along a stitched in-and-out of my hearing it call and its ceasing to exist. (p. 55)

That synapse between sound and its hearing, like the gap for internal adaptation in the magpie story, becomes an existential question. The bird exists or does not according to the auditory perception of the 'I'. Perhaps the reverse is also true for the bird. There's a falling perhaps, from the 'glass nest' of (maternal) hearing into a state of finite being that needs to document itself along with 'the bird, time' (p. 63). The poem seeks agency here for a 'non-transparent self', that of an 'I' caught in the affective labour of belonging with others, in a world that includes violence and precarious life, 'someone ill, someone tortured'.

In such an abandonment to finitude, as Virno might put it, Berssenbrugge's fractality of hearing becomes less about a 'glass nest' for protection, than a boundary relation to others, as the poem declares:

> My hearing touches my limit on all sides, a community exposed. (p. 53)

The question of who inhabits that accustomed place, and what might constitute a community of those who belong there, emerges here as an ethical challenge.[29] It runs through the sequence as one of its ambivalent emotional vectors. An earlier poem registers a sense of being overwhelmed: 'A ringing, overflowing sense of others collapses us, with no representable condition of belonging' (p. 40). But hearing is then offered, later, as a form of adjustment, like a finding of frequency in that ringing:

> Hearing attunes to an open place, window, absence, a stranger's arrhythmic walk in open time, then my walk. (p. 44)

Sustaining a being with others is hinged in this contingent occurrence of a walk 'in open time', and what is sounded there. 'Now I know better; community's not meant to protect me; it's exposure to others, a window' (p. 44), she writes. If hearing is attuned to that exposure, and the arrhythmic movements of others, it also walks its own singular foreignness. What then does it mean to be 'with' others in such a walking? Who are the others? In the final poem, 'Safety', 'being with' suggests both a potential for confessional trial and an enigmatic hospitality:

> Being with each other, we want to reveal and reveal, conceal nothing, but there's the sense something does not get across, a secret.

> In this sense, hospitality between us is a secret interior, instead of reality being the plaintiff. (p. 71)

This is a writing that itself moves towards disclosure – in that it continually finds the quietly attuned and singular means to *declare*, as if a being-listened-to. Yet the 'secret interior' discovered here as untranslatable – what can't be carried across – nonetheless remains like a reserve. If what Berssenbrugge calls 'forgiveness' is part of a 'chain of oxidation' here within the experience of dwelling, it may lie in that hospitality for the other who can't be known, a 'being with' which also includes non-recognition, the absolute alterity of a 'being-without'.[30] How that otherness and exposure to community are central to the acoustic contingencies of a milieu leads me back to the magpie, and to the question of writing and field with which I began.

On the Shore: *Pitch*

In the last part of this essay I want to return to the acoustic praxis of composition in this expanded sense, and its constitutive making of 'field'. I have suggested that Virno's auditory conception of an 'accustomed place', like the 'hearing' of Berssenbrugge's poetry, extends to the wider ecological stakes of an inhabiting of 'one's being in this wild present', in the poet Leslie Scalapino's phrase. In her reflection on what an 'eco-logic' of writing might be, Scalapino posits a relation between 'writing and the outside':

> I'm not proposing that one's language, sounds, conceptual shapes alter events outside. Rather, writing can note that one's/their sounds and conceptual shapes are events – that are also along with events in the outside. A poem may place these together. As such one's conceptions alter oneself and being, and alter their and one being outside.[31]

The placing action of poetry Scalapino describes might also hold true for compositional process of field recording. My sense of this is derived from an ongoing partnership, as a poet working with sound, with the sound artist Will Montgomery. Our audiowork *Pitch* **d[5.1]b** is for me an earlier working through of materials and 'conceptual shapes' that have gained further articulation in this essay. This collaborative practice also returns me to Virno's shore, and the magpie, for a final time.

We made *Pitch* in 2010 as a response to a call for work relating to Luigi Nono, celebrated during the Huddersfield Contemporary Music Festival that year.[32] *Pitch* combines field recordings, voice and processed audio samples, including material taken from Nono's *Fragmente – Stille, an Diotima* (1980). We both gravitated towards this late string quartet, in which the composer uses numerous unsung text-fragments from Hölderlin, which are present in the score but not available to the listener. The poetic fragments are not instructional, but there to be silently internalised by the performers, as 'inward' song.[33] At the time of making *Pitch* the meanings of these selected fragments, which Nono describes as 'BOLTS of sensations'[34] were less important than the act of their withholding. For Juliana Hodkinson, 'this retention of something expressive from the listener' is along with the work of fermata the 'constitutive silent aspect' of the work.[35] It is this retentive interior space, and its occupation, that hold my attention now.

Nono's work is focused on the act of listening:

> Very difficult to listen to others in the silence. Other thoughts, other noises, other sounds, other ideas. When one comes to listen, one often tries to rediscover oneself in others. To rediscover one's own mechanisms, system, rationalism in the others.

And this is a violence of the most conservative nature.

. . .

Perhaps one can change the rituals; perhaps it is possible to wake up the ear. To wake up the ear, the eyes, human thinking, intelligence, the most exposed inwardness.

This is now what is crucial.[36]

Bringing Virno's 'hearing without listening' into the compass of this work seemed to me to set off a dialogue. I was aware of a possible parallel between the Italian composer and philosopher, in that *Fragmente – Stille* was seen by some as a move 'inwards' away from the explicit political content of Nono's earlier practice,[37] while Virno's post-autonomia work on immaterial labour has been regarded as an 'angelic' turn.[38] Both seemed to be responding to, and also resisting, an earlier romantic utopianism, at a time of defeat. In Nono's case, this takes place through the fragment form, and in the location of his quartet as an engagement with Beethoven, whose instruction 'mit innigster Empfindung' (with deepest feeling) is repeated throughout the piece.[39] In Virno, the prospect of awakening, either through a form of metaphysical transcendence or political hope, has been subsumed within cynical forms of instrumentally adaptive behaviour. Moreover:

> Because what is in question is not a long, dark parenthesis, but a profound mutation of the ethos, of culture, and its modes of production, it is misguided to ask how far we have lasted through the long night, as if expecting an imminent dawn. Every light we will ever find is already here in the so-called darkness. We need only accustom our eyes. (p. 26)

In Nono, a rigorous attention to the 'exposed inwardness' of listening has a political charge, one that is concerned with 'redistributions of the sensible' as Paulo de Assis describes it.[40] If those redistributions might seem to address the condition of our 'material and sensible' belonging, imagined by Virno at his allegorical shore, they are nevertheless deeply implicated there in the ambivalent disenchantment of contemporary experience. How to recover resources of resistance to this violence while acknowledging the force of this ambivalence, and the cynical capture of adaptation within it, is the question of Virno's exilic politics.

In the making of *Pitch* as an audiowork, this context was present but suspended. Practice thinks through collaborative instincts, finds its own improvisatory lags and attentions. The 'hearing' of non-knowledge through another's process is part of the exchange. I know now that Will took *Fragmente – Stille* and compressed it to a fraction of its original length. At a later point he used granular synthesis to smash and splinter the material, to work with the ideas of extreme fragmentedness that had emerged from engagement with Nono, including the composer's work with tape and electronic sound. At the same time the shaping concept of the 'accustomed place' that I had initially introduced began to play out more explicitly between us in the gathering of sound recordings from locations associated with 'home': the wheezy orchestral strains of his air vent in a block of flats; the lowing bass notes of buses on London's Kennington Road; torrential rain from the vicinity of the same; a magpie call I captured on my laptop from an open front door. That call is to me synonymous with the sound of my neighbourhood, and yet it is, as Deleuze might put it, an acoustic sign of an 'any-space-whatever'. In this way, place comes to work through the attachments of belonging and non-belonging, sonic fragments of a virtual space that is yet to be actualised, and where 'that which happened in it' is subject to 'an extinction or a disappearing'.[41]

While this sonic environment took compositional shape, we began to integrate my vocal occupation and the embedding of text. The high-pitched grains of the Nono-derived soundscape seemed fleeting and speedy, as if they passed the ear like small splinters of jangling birdcall; percussive material suggested rustling pulses of breath, like life signs on a palm: vf vf. Words and sounds were whittled back to a score. The text built itself for me around an interiority of hearing, and the vibratory bones of an open ear. Sometimes the ear is a lung; sometimes it thinks without intention, as if with the hand. Will introduces the voiced texts with digital sound fragments cannibalised from my voice, playing with Nono's name and negativity – no no – which are then clipped short and repeated as if barely making it to echo beyond the consonant. The text then begins with vocalised indrawn breath, which transmutes into the opening vowel sound of 'accustomed place', and flatter tonal modulations and repetitions, until 'eyes adjust':

> no no
> ne ne
>
> a [indrawn breath]
> a [indrawn breath]
> accustomed place
> pitched up

        no daybreak
        or exchequer

        in
        in
        inner
        an
        anv
        anv
        vf [short breath out]
        anvil

        eyes adjust

The text resists transforming itself at each step into a narrative line, as if there is a stuttering effort to maintain place as attention, in refusing the recursive 'afterwards(ness)' that might also produce a subject. Stasis is active here, like a waiting. It has dimensions of weakness, and force, as Nono describes of the fragment.[42] Later, for Will, this recalled his interest in Morton Feldman's sound world, the simulation of stasis and a heightened sense of 'what comes next' as a miniature crisis. Recent work by Wesley Phillips on Adorno and Nono has made me return here to spatiality in *Fragmente – Stille*, and the way it pressures narrative time: the stakes of Adorno's 'passage of time which is holding its breath'.[43] Nono's work in *Pitch* becomes compressed and splintered. Time breaks in, but the waiting is unstable and breath hesitant and shallow, as if the voice does not know how to occupy that holding.

        st
        st
        stays here

        numerous

        a [indrawn breath]
        a [indrawn breath]
        afterward

What or who 'stays here' is also 'numerous'. The reference to George Oppen was intentional, not only to his sense of collective being, but also what might be imagined and unacknowledged on the shore, as *Of Being Numerous* reveals: 'To dream of that beach / For the sake of an instant in the eyes / The absolute singular / The unearthly bonds / Of the singular / Which is the bright light of shipwreck'.[44] Yet the word 'numerous' also carries a feeling of langorousness, as sound sensually discloses in the mouth, like a physical intimation of duration where there is none to be had without knowing nevertheless. As if this is all the word can manage. There is something toxic, highly illumined and monetised about that beach in *Pitch*, in which the fascination for that bright light of shipwreck *is* the shiny matter wrongly attributed to the desire of magpies, *is* the stuff of poetry or media images. 'Relentless gleam' is borrowed from my collection *Sundog*, with its 'wilder sunned/ spots'.[45] It moves towards what is withheld:

> vf [short breath out]
> vf [short breath out]
> relentless gleam
>
> bodies on the shore
>
> un
> un

At the centre of *Pitch* are 'bodies on the shore'. On a hot day in July 2008 two Roma children, Cristina and Violetta Djeordsevic, drowned in the sea off a beach near Naples, where they had been with their cousins selling 'trinkets' carved by Nigerian immigrants. Their recovered bodies were laid out on the sand, and left for some hours under towels while picnicking and sunbathing continued around them. Shock at this indifference was reported by the international press, who might also be said to have participated in its spectacle.[46] Photographs and video of the beach, with its hubbub and sea sounds, remain online. Their death happened during an intense period in a long history of repression of Roma people in Italy, when Berlusconi's government had been involved in a campaign to fingerprint the whole community. Roma camps had been burned out. The mother of the two girls later told an interviewer that the girls had been fingerprinted not long before their death: 'Cristina was angry and scrubbed the ink from her thumb. She understood everything. She knew we were being treated like animals. She died knowing she had no real hope of a better life'.[47]

It is this drowning on the shore, withheld in the matter of *Pitch*, which motivates its hearing. Even the opening negativity of the piece, the play on Nono's name, is undone by it: un un. Caroline Bergvall asks what kind of testimony is attempted here. '*Pitch* nestles in the contours of protest work. Its language is the persistent unpinnable shiver left by shock and loss of articulate response and agency. Its crippled reduced movements stretched between articulate and diffuse sounds inflect the hidden rage of the piece.'[48] This environment isn't a holding place. Protection is torqued into racist exclusion, hearing's 'exposure to community' is face-to-face in ever wider distributions of the 'non-human' and stateless. Returning to this event eight years on, it remains part of a larger and catastrophic homelessness wrecking on global shores. 'Nothing goes on behind the backs of the new cynicism (except we need to remind Paolo Virno of what always went on beyond cynicism, what was always without home and shelter, was always outnumbered and outgunned)', write Stefano Harney and Fred Moten in *The Undercommons*.[49] Virno's vision of the auditory experience of the person on the beach meets a more populated shore, breached by the waves in other ways.

'An auditory and political landscape attempts to escape from *Pitch*'s veiled sonic gestures', writes Bergvall, whose powerful work *Drift* is a deep echoic engagement with the wreckage.[50] How then to continue to occupy that environment with its opening onto the unsettling of accustomed places, the contingencies of holding and abandonment and the violence of the imaginaries we live by? Or in the magpie practice of writing and field, sound and poetry, what in the sonorous time of this 'wild present' is looped and returned beyond adaptation, 'to alter their and one being outside'?[51]

Notes

1. Michel de Montaigne, *The Complete Essays*, trans. M. A. Screech (Harmondsworth: Penguin Books, 1991), pp. 519–20.
2. Ibid., p. 677.
3. This fermata is taken from Luigi Nono's *Fragmente Stille – an Diotima*, which is discussed in the final section of this essay.
4. John Berger, 'Field' [1971], pp. 31–5. References to 'Field' are to the text as reprinted in the current book.
5. Michel Foucault, *Security. Territory. Population: Lectures at the Collège de France, 1977–78*, trans. Graham Burchell (London: Palgrave Macmillan, 2009), p. 23.
6. See H. Slabbekoom and M. Peet, 'Birds sing at a higher pitch in urban noise', *Nature* 424 (2003): 267.
7. Montaigne, *The Complete Essays*, p. 680.
8. Wallace Stevens, 'July Mountain' in *Opus Posthumous: Poems, Plays, Prose*, ed. Milton J. Bates (New York: Vintage Books, 1990), p. 140.

9. Gisela Kaplan, *Bird Minds: Cognition and Behaviour of Australian Native Birds* (Clayton: Csiro Publishing, 2015), pp. 98–9, p. 100 Fig. 7.3, p. 101.

10. Mei-mei Berssenbrugge, *Nest* (Berkeley: Kelsey Street Press, 2003), p. 56. Many thanks to Mei-mei Berssenbrugge for permission to quote from *Nest*, in the format afforded by the page layout here. The Kelsey Street Press edition sustains a longer line.

11. Lawrence English, 'Relational Listening: The Politics of Perception', *Ear/Wave/Event* 2 (2015), http://earwaveevent.org/article/relational-listening-the-politics-of-perception/ (last accessed 14 March 2016).

12. Montaigne's account of animals and thought is part of a longstanding philosophical debate often hinging on human speech, in which magpies among other corvids play an exemplary part. Dante saw the speech of magpies as embodying 'a reproduction or imitation of sound' without 'the power of speech', while Descartes's Cartesian account refutes Montaigne, seeing the magpie as capable of a mechanical behavioural learning, but incapable of thought. See Bernard Siegert, *Cultural Techniques: Grids, Filters, Doors and Other Articulations of the Real* (New York: Fordham University Press, 2015), pp. 56–8, and René Descartes, letter to the Marquess of Newcastle, 23 November 1646, in *Philosophical Writings: Volume 3, The Correspondence*, ed. John Cottingham, Robert Stoothoff and Dugald Murdoch (Cambridge: Cambridge University Press, 1991), pp. 303–4.

13. See, for example, the magpie's relation to the 'blasting' street sounds in the light of Ian Biddle's account of the isolation of creative labour from the hubbub of 'the outside or the street', in his 'Visitors, or The Political Ontology of Noise', *Radical Musicology* 4 (2009), http://www.radical-musicology.org.uk/2009/Biddle.htm, para 6 (last accessed 11 March 2016).

14. 'Consider boundaries as a thickness rather than a line': Gilles Clément's statement is an epigraph within Jonathan Skinner's 'Thoughts on Things: Poetics of the Third Landscape' in *The Eco Language Reader*, ed. Brenda Iijima (New York: Nightboat Books, 2010), p. 34.

15. Giorgio Agamben, *The Open: Man and Animal*, trans. Kevin Attell (Stanford: Stanford University Press, 2003), pp. 40, 41.

16. Michael Pisaro and Greg Stuart, *July Mountain (Three Versions)*, CD (Gravity Wave, 2010). My own listening is responding to the 'California version'. Audio excerpts are available on the publisher's website: https://edinburghuniversitypress.com/book-writing-the-field-recording-hb.html [click on the 'resources' tab].

17. Indeed, the instrumental version of *July Mountain* provides the percussive part without the twenty field recordings, and invites listeners to make their own version of the piece.

18. Michael Pisaro, 'What is Field?', followed by a discussion chaired by Will Montgomery, with contributions from Carol Watts, Drew Milne and Paul Bavister, *Wolf Notes* 5 (2013), p. 25, p. 22.

19. Tim Ingold (2013), 'Against Space: Place, Movement, Knowledge' in *Boundless Worlds: An Anthropological Approach to Movement*, ed. Peter Wynn Kirby (Oxford and New York: Berghahn Books), p. 33.

20. Paolo Virno, 'The Ambivalence of Disenchantment' in *Radical Thought in Italy: A Potential Politics*, ed. Paolo Virno and Michael Hardt (Minneapolis and London: University of Minnesota Press, 1996), p. 29. All further references by page number in the text.

21. Virno's Aristotelian distinction between poiesis as production (realisation in an independent object) and praxis as ethical-political action finding realisation in itself (like the practice of a musician or dancer) is set out in his *When the Word Becomes Flesh: Language and Human Nature*, trans. Giuseppina Mecchia (South Pasadena: Semiotext(e), 2015), pp. 22–3.

22. Linda Russo, 'Listening-Being: Some Unnamed Species of Porous Poems', *Jacket 2* (14 June 2015), http://jacket2.org/commentary/listening-being (last accessed 4 February 2016).

23. Berssenbrugge, *Nest*, p. 46. All further references are included as page numbers in the text.

24. This recalls Jacques Derrida's discussion of hospitality (perhaps in play here), which associates 'mother tongue' with 'the home that never leaves us': 'The proper or property, at least the fantasy of property that, as close as could be to our bodies, and we always come back there, would give place to the most inalienable place, to a sort of mobile habitat, a garment or a tent'. *Of Hospitality: Anne Dufourmantelle Invites Jacques Derrida to Respond*, trans. Rachel Bowlby (Stanford: Stanford University Press, 2000), pp. 73, 89.

25. Berger, 'Field', p. 35.

26. See Natalia Cecire, 'Sentimental Spaces: On Mei-mei Berssenbrugge's *Nest*', *Jacket 2* (May 2011), http://jacket2.org/article/sentimental-spaces (last accessed 14 March 2016).

27. Berssenbrugge reflects on Kuan Yin in 'Mei-mei Berssenbrugge and Charles Bernstein: A Dialogue', originally published in *Conjunctions 35* (Fall 2000), available at http://epc.buffalo.edu/authors/berssenbrugge/bernstein.html/ (last accessed 14 March 2016).

28. Berssenbrugge draws on Deleuzian accounts of immanence, which contribute to the shaping abstraction of her writing. Her poetry recalls here the section in *A Thousand Plateaus* on 'becoming imperceptible', which relates the 'cosmic' practice of Chinese poets and the making of a 'communicating world' via Woolf to the worlding of the moment: 'the moment is not the instantaneous, it is the haecceity into which one slips and that slips into haecceities by transparency' (Gilles Deleuze and Félix Guattari, *A Thousand Plateaus*, trans. Brian Massumi (London: Continuum, 2004), p. 309). 'Eliminate the too-perceived, the too-much-to-be-perceived', the text suggests, and through the abstract lines and pieces that remain 'one makes a world that can overlay the first one, like a transparency' (ibid., p. 308).

29. For Virno, this may be 'a community of all those who have no community' in Bataille's terms. Virno, 'The Ambivalence of Disenchantment', p. 33. For Bataille's position on community, see, for example, Jean-Luc Nancy, *The Inoperative Community*, trans. Peter Connor et al. (Minneapolis and Oxford: University of Minnesota Press, 1991).

30. I have in mind here Simon Critchley's discussion of 'being-without' the other in his critique of Jean-Luc Nancy's *Etre singulier pluriel*: 'With Being-With? Notes on Jean Luc Nancy's Rewriting of *Being and Time*', in *Ethics, Politics, Subjectivity: Essays on Derrida, Levinas and Contemporary French Thought* (London: Verso, 1999), p. 252.

31. Leslie Scalapino, 'Eco-logic in Writing', in Iijima (ed.), *The Eco Language Reader*, pp. 61, 60.

32. *Pitch* is an audiowork which runs to 8.26 minutes. It was exhibited in the worksetting gallery in Huddersfield, December–January 2010–11, and was streamed on French webSYN radio, curated by Caroline Bergvall, 25 November–2 December 2010. It is included on CD in *Out of Everywhere 2: Linguistically Innovative Poetry by Women in North American and the UK*, ed. Emily Critchley (Hastings: Reality Street, 2015). It was first published online here: http://delirioushem.blogspot.co.uk/2011/12/pitch.html.

33. Nono indicates that 'the players should "sing" them inwardly, in their autonomy, in the autonomy of sounds striving for a "delicate harmony of the inner life"'. Quoted by Juliana Hodkinson, 'Presenting Absence: Constitutive Silences in Music and Sound Art since the 1950s', PhD Thesis, University of Copenhagen, 2007, p. 111. http://www.julianahodkinson.net/sites/default/files/writings/Hodkinson%20phd_indmad.pdf (last accessed 5 March 2016).

34. Nono in a letter to the LaSalle Quartet, quoted in Carola Nielinger-Vakil, *Luigi Nono: A Composer in Context* (Cambridge: Cambridge University Press, 2016), p. 171. The range of fragments and their location in the piece are usefully set out in this book.

35. Hodkinson, 'Presenting Absence', p. 111.

36. Luigi Nono, *Scritti e colloqui* (Milan: Ricordi; Lucca, LIM, 2001), ed. Angela Ida De Benedictis and Veniero Rizzardi, I, 522. Quoted in Paulo de Assis, 'Con Luigi Nono: Unfolding Waves', *Journal for Artistic Research* 6 (2014), https://www.researchcatalogue.net/view/51263/65676 (last accessed 5 March 2016).

37. On Nono's 'late turn', see Wesley Phillips, *Metaphysics and Music in Adorno and Heidegger* (New York: Springer, 2015), p. 109. The shift in Nono's work towards the generalised 'other' is also addressed in Robert Adlington, 'Whose Voices? The Fate of Luigi Nono's "Voci destroying muros"', *Journal of the American Musicological Society* 69.1 (2016), p. 66–7.

38. Antonio Negri and Michael Hardt argue that Virno, like other post-autonomia thinkers, addresses the new forces of production in 'angelic'

terms, positing affective and immaterial labour 'almost exclusively on the horizon of language and communication'. See Michael Hardt and Antonio Negri, *Empire* (Cambridge, MA and London: Harvard University Press, 2000), pp. 29–30.

39. The Beethoven instruction, from his Quartet in A minor, Op. 132, 'Sacred Song of Thanksgiving to the Deity in Lydian Mode', had been considered as the title for *Fragmente – Stille, an Diotima*. The piece was commissioned by the city of Bonn for its 30th Beethovenfest. Nielinger-Vakil, *Luigi Nono*, p. 153.

40. De Assis, 'Con Luigi Nono: Unfolding Waves'. The concept of the sensible related to Nono's practice here is developed from Rancière's discussion of sense perception and what is held in common. See Jacques Rancière, *The Politics of Aesthetics: The Distribution of the Sensible*, trans. Gabriel Rockhill (London: Continuum, 2004).

41. Gilles Deleuze, *Cinema 1: The Movement-Image*, trans. Hugh Tomlinson and Barabara Habberjam (London: Athlone Press, 1986), p. 120.

42. See Nono's reflection on the fragment form in Nielinger-Vakil, *Luigi Nono*, p. 186.

43. Phillips, *Metaphysics and Music*, pp.109–10.

44. George Oppen, *New Collected Poems*, ed. Michael Davidson (New York: New Directions Books, 2008), p. 163.

45. Carol Watts, *Sundog* (London: Veer Books, 2013), p. 22.

46. On the 'erasure of the humanity' of the two girls in the popular media, see Anca M. Pusca, *Post-Communist Aesthetics: Revolutions, Capitalism, Violence* (London: Routledge, 2015), p. 134.

47. Dan McDougall, 'Why do the Italians hate us?', *The Observer*, 17 August 2008: http://www.theguardian.com/lifeandstyle/2008/aug/17/familyandrelationships.roma (last accessed 11 March 2016).

48. Caroline Bergvall, 'Indiscreet G/Hosts', in *(.)*, ed. Imogen Stidworthy (London: Matt's Gallery; Maastricht: Jan van Eyck Academie, 2012), p. 24.

49. Stefano Harney and Fred Moten, *The Undercommons: Fugitive Planning & Black Study* (New York: Minor Compositions, 2013), p. 52.

50. Bergvall, 'Indiscreet G/Hosts', p. 24. See her *Drift* (New York: Nightboat Books, 2014).

51. Scalapino, 'Eco-logic in Writing', pp. 61, 60.

Chapter 6

Druids Fielding Questions: Eva-Maria Houben, Emily Dickinson and Charles Ives*

Dominic Lash

In 2011, the German composer Eva-Maria Houben (a longstanding member of the Wandelweiser composers collective) released an album entitled *druids and questions* on the Edition Wandelweiser label.[1] The CD contains a single hour-long track consisting of recorded organ sounds (played by the composer) together with other sounds, arranged and superimposed – it is described on the sleeve as 'electro-acoustic music with recorded organ sounds'.[2] Also on the sleeve are references to two other works of art. When one opens the cover panel one sees on the left the text 'Listening to Charles Ives, The Unanswered Question', while on the right are the concluding lines of a poem by Emily Dickinson: 'Yet a Druidic Difference / Enhances Nature now'.[3] We are invited to consider three different approaches to material, its deployment and differentiation, each of which raises interesting questions about scale and about boundaries. The multivalence of the word 'field' might indicate a way of approaching the issues raised by following Houben's suggestion and considering these three works in relation to one another.

* * *

In a remarkable aesthetic manifesto cum analytical essay cum prose poem, written to accompany his 1966 recording *Unit Structures*, pianist Cecil Taylor begins with 'an opening field of question, how large it ought or ought not to be'.[4] Size is closely related to boundedness, and boundedness appears to be central to many of the various ways the word 'field' has been construed. Often seen as something unbounded and hence all-pervasive, a field was defined in physics by Richard Feynman as 'any physical quantity which takes on different

---

*The accompanying audio recording is indicated in the following way – d[6.1]b – and is available on the publisher's website at: https://edinburghuniversitypress.com/book-writing-the-field-recording-hb.html [click on the 'resources' tab].

values at different points in space'.[5] Charles Olson's claim that 'composition by field' – a poetics limited only by the breath and the edge of the page – is cognate with an 'open' way of working looms large in much contemporary poetics as well as writing on post-Cagean sonic practices.[6] This openness is combined with an absence of hierarchy, or at least with a 'flat' sort of hierarchy, and both openness and flatness are generally taken to be opposed to manipulation and didacticism, to leave room for the listener or reader to explore as they see fit.

And yet these understandings of what field might mean, or what a field might be, are not universal. John Berger very explicitly insists that his idea of a field is characterised, precisely, by its boundedness: 'It must be an area with boundaries which are visible – though not necessarily regular; it cannot be an unbounded segment of nature the limits to which are only set by the natural focus of your eyes.'[7] The infinite need not be unbounded: there are intensive as well as extensive infinities. There are, in fact, so many different applications of the word that I am sceptical about the possibility of extracting a coherent account that would cover them all without remainder. Still worse would be any attempt to give 'Field', with a suitably solemn initial capital, something of the status of a metaphysical concept.[8] It would be mistaken, at best, to consider equivocation and ambiguity as evidence of metaphysical richness. In what follows I will in fact barely mention the word 'field', but will instead attempt close readings of these three pieces of music and poetry and the ways they activate the very same questions about boundary, hierarchy, size and scale which make the notion of the field, for all its nebulousness, such a stimulating object for thought.

Initial connections

Eva-Maria Houben herself is a minimalist, not in the quasi-historical sense this has come to have in music (referring primarily to the work of Terry Riley, Steve Reich and Philip Glass), but in the sense that she minimises the amount of material she introduces into her compositions, severely circumscribing it so that its texture can be explored with an intense closeness, every tiny difference being magnified in importance. Charles Ives was most definitely a maximalist: anything and everything can and often does enter his music, frequently all at the same time.[9] Emily Dickinson, on the other hand, was a miniaturist, which is something rather different. Her themes are as wide of that of any poetry, but are expressed through a focus on small objects and apparently innocuous situations, deployed in short, intense and highly crafted poems where, as with Houben, no detail is without potential significance.

The most immediately obvious connection between Ives's composition (originally written in 1906 and revised in the 1930s) and Dickinson's poem (the earliest known holograph of which dates from 1866) is a shared reference to druids. In Ives's foreword to the score of *The Unanswered Question*, he specifies the symbolism of each of the instrumental groupings deployed in the piece (strings, flutes [or treble woodwind choir] and trumpet). The strings represent 'The Silences of the Druids – Who Know, See and Hear Nothing'.[10] In neither Ives' or Dickinson's case is it apparent exactly what the druids are intended to represent: associations with some kind of profound and probably ancient mystery are clear enough, but neither case is straightforwardly a reference to pagan religious practice (whether historical or mythic). It is not even clear whether the druids that Ives refers to are human – they are contrasted with 'the flutes and other human beings' – and the same may be true for Dickinson.

Other themes link Ives' composition and Dickinson's poem, and provide hints as to the significance they have for Houben. In both works the relationship of the individual to the group is in question – or, rather, of the individual to a wider collection of individuals so large as to be considered a mass rather than a group (is an indistinctness between individual members characteristic of a field?). In the chamber orchestra version of *The Unanswered Question*, a solitary trumpet calls across quartets of strings and flutes; in the full orchestral version, the string quartet is replaced by full orchestral strings (including basses) and the flutes by a full treble woodwind choir – but the trumpet remains a solitary voice. In Dickinson's poem, there is a confrontation between a 'Nation' – albeit 'minor' – and the 'loneliness' of an individual. The individual, however, is a human, while the Nation is a population of insects – crickets, to be precise.[11] Hence drastic divergences of scale are also a theme of the poem, as they are of Ives' composition, where the trumpet represents 'The Perennial Question of Existence', which continues to sound even when the flutes have given up their search for 'The Invisible Answer'. But neither the poem nor the music merely examine cosmic themes, nor even cosmic themes as revealed in the workings of nature. They are also both concerned with human activity – behaviour and invention. Dickinson's poem alludes to human actions (thinking, resting) and religious practices, both Catholic and Protestant, while Ives has his 'flutes and other humans' engage in characteristically human pursuits: hunting for an answer, fighting, mocking and eventually giving up. He also uses different harmonic practices (which are, of course, historically contingent human inventions) to represent each of the three actors in his piece: triadic harmony in the strings, expressively melodic atonality in the trumpet and dissonant chromaticism (culminating in a chord of four semitones stacked on top of each other) in the flutes.

Dickinson's crickets

This is the full text of the Dickinson poem in question, numbered 1068 by Thomas H. Johnson and 895 by R.W. Franklin:

> Further in Summer than the Birds –
> Pathetic from the Grass –
> A minor Nation celebrates
> It's unobtrusive Mass.
>
> No Ordinance be seen –
> So gradual the Grace
> A pensive Custom it becomes –
> Enlarging Loneliness –
>
> Antiquest felt at Noon –
> When August burning low
> Arise this spectral Canticle
> Repose to typify –
>
> Remit as yet no Grace –
> No furrow on the Glow,
> But a Druidic Difference
> Enhances Nature now –[12]

This poem is one of a whole group of late summer poems, and the emotions connected with the passing of summer had long held a prominent place in Dickinson's imagination. When she was sixteen she wrote to her friend Abiah Root:

> How swiftly summer has fled & what report has it borne to heaven of misspent time & wasted hours? Eternity only will answer. The ceaseless flight of the seasons is to me a very solemn thought, & yet Why do we not strive to make a better improvement of them?[13]

Even for a poet known for such practices, the poem makes a very full use of ambiguity and contradiction. 'Pathetic' means able to bring about a relationship of feeling (as in sympathy or empathy), but may also suggest the pejorative tone the word has come to possess (though this is not generally attested until the twentieth century).[14] 'Mass' is certainly ambiguous, referring as it does both to a Catholic eucharist and to the group of crickets, which is so large as to seem more like a unified body than a collection of specific individuals.[15] 'Ordinance' is very definitely a Protestant term designating rituals such as baptism and communion and specifically designed to serve as an alternative to the more Catholic 'sacrament', though its provenance is hard to pin down more precisely amongst the rich variety of forms of Protestantism that thrived in nineteenth century New England. An ordinance is a behaviour expressive of faith, as opposed to a sacrament, which is in Catholic teaching an efficacious sign of divine grace.[16]

'Grace' is therefore an intensely charged word in the poem, with an enormous weight of theological significance and indeed tension behind it, complicated still further by its musical connotations – a grace being a type of musical ornament.[17] Both 'Ordinance' and 'Grace' are, however, present in the poem via a kind of negation.[18] The 'Ordinance' is 'not seen' – it is uncertain whether this is because it is hidden or because it does not exist. Similarly the 'Grace' is 'So gradual' as to be barely perceptible. But what is the consequence of this? 'A pensive custom it becomes' – does this mean that the crickets' song turns into a thoughtful ritual, or – perhaps more likely – that it suits the speaker's habit of thoughtfulness? Also unclear are the consequences of such a custom – does 'Enlarging Loneliness' mean increasing and hence exacerbating it, or encompassing more, and hence alleviating it? Is the speaker made more aware of their separation from, or their unity with, nature?

To find that August is 'burning low' at 'noon' is strange because the sun at midday in August is still high in the sky. The sun is implictly compared to a candle ('canticle' even sounds like 'candle'), which once again makes vastly disparate scales confront each other, and which we can't help but read as to some extent bathetic – is the sun no more than an overgrown candle? Presumably the high summer makes the speaker only too conscious of its transformation, and hence the fact that summer is coming to an end. This might be seen as a dialectical change, in a broadly Hegelian sense. That is, by becoming most fully itself – most summery – summer is in fact passing into autumn. This change is all but imperceptible – there is 'No furrow on the Glow'. The normal object of furrowing, when metaphorically extended, is 'brow', which would have fitted the rhyme-scheme here (more fully than 'Glow', in fact) and is thus a kind of shadowy presence emphasising the speaker's 'pensive' state.

The very passage of time itself also maintains a shadowy presence in the text: the poem marks temporal change by describing an unchanging moment. The crickets' song exists in a continuous present ('celebrates'), and the 'Druidic Difference', though only mentioned at the poem's end, is in fact operative throughout. It is perceptible 'now', but there is nothing to distinguish the 'now' at the poem's end from the moment described at its beginning. The 'Difference' lies in the dramatic irony of the change the speaker knows is impending, which is read back into the scene even though there is nothing materially present to signal it ('No ordinance', 'No furrow on the Glow'). Unlike an earlier draft where sunrise and sunset were explicitly mentioned, here they hover as a suggestion: 'burning low' cannot but suggest evening, even though the explicit reference is to a point in the year (late summer) rather than in the day, and 'furrow' may evoke the 'shadow' conventionally associated with evening.

But perhaps the beginning of autumn within the summer need not be merely an opportunity for melancholy. On the contrary, it 'Enhances Nature now' – the perception of change adds to the present moment, precisely because the sensation of transitoriness enhances the momentariness of the moment: a sensation of eternity would detract from our inhabiting of the moment (*as* a moment). This is emphasised by the alliterating 'D' consonants in 'Druidic Difference', unusual in the poem as a whole. Their percussive edge gives the impression of marking an ungraspable instant rather than measuring a continuous experience. The song of the crickets is felt by the speaker to be an ancient ritual ('Antiquest felt at noon'), older than any human religion, which only emphasises the transience – the momentariness – of any individual's existence within the ancient cyclical repetition that is Nature. But as with Ives' mysterious and inaccessible beings 'Who Know, See and Hear Nothing', the use of the adjective 'Druidic' signifies for Dickinson not so much an ancient era of human existence but something beyond human experience that can only be hinted at.

Crucially, however, the 'Druidic Difference', though prompted by external realities, is located more in the perception of the speaker, in her internal reality, than in observation of the natural world. Hence it can operate when there is no empirical difference to point to ('No furrow on the Glow'). Katie Peterson argues otherwise:

> Though 'Further in Summer than the Birds –' is isomorphic in structure to Dickinson's more studied poems of aftermath, its conclusion is quite different. What is changed is not a self. No one here finds 'internal Difference / where the Meanings, are' as they might in another poem of

seasonal shift, 'There's a certain Slant of light' (F320). What is changed is a state of nature: 'a Druidic Difference / Enhances Nature now.' It is as if Nature herself becomes the Emersonian Sayer and Namer.[19]

Peterson is right to point out the way the structure of the metaphor operates, but I would contend that this becoming is still a projection of the poetic voice – as Dickinson argues in another poem concerned with animal sound:

> The "Tune is in the Tree –"
> The Skeptic – showeth me –
> "No Sir! In Thee!"[20]

Helen Vendler might, I think, agree – she argues that the poem moves from an elegy to an enhancing:

> The positive verb 'enhance' (derived from the Latin *inaltare*, 'to raise', 'to exalt'), which looks back via its prefix to her earlier sad verb 'enlarge', 'corrects' (without erasing) the poet's first interpretation of the Crickets' ceremonial as one of pathos, her melancholy perception that Loneliness enlarges as the season turns. Now, precisely because she has intuited the almost-invisible approach of Autumn, she sees the 'Glow' more keenly, hears the 'unobtrusive' sound of the Crickets more intently.[21]

This connection of enlargement with enhancement is suggestive: in the notes to her *works for flute*, Houben describes Berlioz as 'one of the first to radically expand ['erweiterten' in the German] the listening space by his reference to 'nearly nothing' ('presque rien')'.[22] Just as the tight focus and circumscribed form of much of Dickinson's poetry enlarges her meaning, Houben, as we shall see, attempts to bring about expansion by means of reduction.

Ives the Emersonian

Ives would also have agreed that the 'Tune' is 'In Thee!'. He writes in the prologue to *Essays Before a Sonata* that:

> as we are trying to consider music made and heard by human beings (and not by birds or angels), it seems difficult to suppose that even subconscious images can be separated from some human experience; there must be something behind subconsciousness to produce consciousness, and so on.[23]

Ralph Waldo Emerson's idealism informed much in the attitudes of both Dickinson and Ives towards nature: 'For nature is not always tricked in holiday attire, but the same scene which yesterday breathed perfume and glittered as for the frolic of nymphs is overspread with melancholy to-day. Nature always wears the colors of the spirit.'[24] In the 'Emerson' section of his *Essays*, Ives indicates something of his attitude to nature's relationship to questions of part and whole (which is another way of asking questions about boundedness):

> Logic may possibly require that unity means something ascending in self-evident relation to the parts and to the whole, with no ellipsis in the ascent. But reason may permit, even demand, an ellipsis, and genius may not need the self-evident parts. In fact, these parts may be the "blind-spots" in the progress of unity. They may be filled with little but repetition. "Nature loves analogy and hates repetition." Botany reveals evolution, not permanence. An apparent confusion, if lived with long enough, may become orderly. Emerson was not writing for lazy minds, though one of the keenest of his academic friends said that, he (Emerson) could not explain many of his own pages. But why should he! He explained them when he discovered them, the moment before he spoke or wrote them. A rare experience of a moment at daybreak, when something in nature seems to reveal all consciousness, cannot be explained at noon. Yet it is a part of the day's unity. At evening, nature is absorbed by another experience. She dislikes to explain as much as to repeat. It is conceivable that what is unified form to the author or composer may of necessity be formless to his audience. A home run will cause more unity in the grandstand than in the season's batting average. If a composer [in MS: poet] once starts to compromise, his work will begin to drag on *him*.
>
> Before the end is reached, his inspiration has all gone up in sounds pleasing to his audience, ugly to him – sacrificed for the first acoustic – an opaque clarity – a picture painted for its hanging. Easy unity, like easy virtue, is easier to describe when judged from its lapses than from its constancy. When the infidel admits God is great, he means only: "I am lazy – it is easier to talk than live." Ruskin also says: "Suppose I like the finite curves best, who shall say which of us is right? No one. It is simply a question of experience." You may not be able to experience a symphony, even after twenty performances. Initial coherence today may be dullness tomorrow, probably because formal or outward unity depends so much on repetition, sequences, antitheses, paragraphs, with inductions and summaries.[25]

There is too much in this passage to unpack fully here, but I want to highlight the way that Ives conceives of a whole without neat internal subdivisions, where ellipsis may be necessary. Though expressed in more muscular language, Ives's account of a momentary glimpse of consciousness in nature resonates with Dickinson's poem (and his revision suggests that such concerns apply to the poet as much as to the composer). But, crucially, Ives does not separate out these moments as bounded instances of truth that we grasp, if we are lucky, amidst an otherwise disordered and meaningless existence. On the contrary, both the 'moment at daybreak' and its forgetting at noon seem to be 'part of the day's unity'. Unity does not, for Ives, require consistency. The obviously coherent may lead only to 'dullness tomorrow'; we should be suspicious of 'easy unity'. His account of 'outward unity' implies the existence of a more profound 'inner unity'. The emphasis on ellipses at the beginning of this passage suggest that such a unity would be one that could accommodate gaps or lacunae. The existence of a boundary at one level does not imply being able to give a full account of the internal topography. Being able to grasp *inconsistent* wholes seems, perhaps, to be a measure of ones ability to accept reality, or to live fully. Ives does not accept a dichotomy between rationality and intuition, and his insistence that nature 'loves analogy and hates repetition' has its echoes in Houben's attitude to the richness and individuality of sounds, as we shall see below.

Organs and sounds

No organ is heard in *The Unanswered Question*, but the instrument was Ives' instrument, just as it is Houben's. As a young man he worked as a church organist – though of course he gave up this form of employment to work in insurance. J. Peter Burkholder has argued that Ives's experience of the instrument influenced many of his compositions, including *The Unanswered Question*.[26] Here is another, much earlier, poem of Dickinson's, (once set to music by Copland):

> I've heard an Organ talk, sometimes –
> In a Cathedral Aisle,
> And understood no word it said –
> Yet held my breath, the while –
>
> And risen up – and gone away,
> A more Bernardine Girl –
> Yet – knew not what was done to me
> In that old Chapel Aisle.[27]

Note that the poem *doesn't* say that the music is more profound than words – it clearly says that that the organ is communicating (actually, that it is talking) but that the speaker doesn't understand it. And yet she is spellbound during its sounding ('held my breath') and leaves transformed without knowing how. Breath seems central to Houben's view of the organ, just as the disappearance of sound is to her conception of the piano.[28] The organ – like the lung – causes the movement of air. Much of what we hear while listening to *druids and questions* d[6.1]b, d[6.2]b, d[6.3]b is the movement of air, at different volumes, with different degrees of darkness and lightness and different textures. In addition to this we hear high whistles (with just once, at 32'48", the merest hint of melody, as a high C# falls a fifth to an F#), low rumbles and gentle mechanical iterations.

A great deal of Houben's music, in common with the work of the other Wandelweiser composers, demonstrates the variety and richness contained in even the simplest sounds. Some of her other pieces investigate this via continuity of sound and long passages of apparent changelessness. An example of this is her double CD of organ music, *dazwischen/immer anders*. These two pieces explore ideas that continue to be of importance in *druids and questions*: the ideas of *betweenness* ('dazwischen'), and of *ceaseless change* ('immer anders'). The latter resonates directly with the Dickinson poem: change is present in the unchanging, not merely in the sense that nothing is ever unchanging (just as nothing is ever silent) but also that the unchanging thing presents, veiled, its own destruction. The word 'luftstrom' (or 'luftströme'),[29] meaning airflow, or current of air, appears in the notes to both pieces on the earlier organ CDs: though it is not spelt out, this implies a connection to breath and hence life, and its eventual end (if the airways are stopped for too long, life also stops). Whereas for Charles Olson, in his poem 'The Kingfishers', 'what does not change is the will to change', here it is more that what does not change is the fact of change, whether we will it or no. Similarly, in Dickinson's work even 'Repose' (of death?) is, it seems, typified by 'Difference', and in *The Unanswered Question* the question remains even at the end of the piece in the absence of the struggle to answer it (an absence which is apparently only temporary – 'the strife is over for a moment', says the foreword).

The strings in *The Unanswered Question* are the most direct musical analogue in Ives' composition to the organ sounds of *druids and questions*. They have movement but no direction (in the sense of telos: we do not perceive a strongly linear harmonic journey, more a gentle shifting among simple harmonies) – but neither (largely because of the tempo) do we experience circularity or repetition. They also exhibit a constant shimmering, a gentle vibration – which contrasts with a very different texture in the woodwinds (which begin seemingly compatible with the strings but quickly exacerbate their shimmerings into more agitated and eventually painful oscillations). Similar, too, is the way that that Ives's score stipulates that the strings should, 'if possible', be placed off-stage – audible but not visible, just like Dickinson's crickets and like the organist in Houben's piece; as an electroacoustic composition it is intended to be listened to on CD, probably at home, rather than in a live environment where the performer is visible (indeed, given the layerings of sound involved, it would probably be impossible to present the piece live without a space containing multiple organs!).

druids and questions is, then, electroacoustic music, but it is not, I would argue, acousmatic music.[30] As I have indicated, it could never have the public performance that the Ives needs – and so listening to it is more akin to reading a poem, a rather private experience. But it is by no means concerned with making the listener forget the origins of the sounds or encouraging them to listen to the music as consisting only of sounds 'in themselves'.[31] On the contrary, it deliberately unsettles our confident division of sound into categories – acoustic, electronic, etc. We may mistake recorded wind sounds or electronic white noise for the hiss of the organ, as I did initially. The piece does not, however, go to any real lengths to hide the origins of the sounds that it consists of, and so we remain aware that they are produced in particular ways, though in the absence of more specific clues we may find ourselves wondering exactly what those ways are.

These associations are not schematically representative, as in the Ives, but are more materially based, either caused by actual similarities in the means of their production (air movement created by pressure differentials; pitch generated by the movement of air over apertures of various dimensions), or by psychoacoustic phenomena (the similarity of white noise to certain natural sonic events). The sounds are, in fact, immensely evocative. As Richard Pinnell observes:

> If you listen for a long time, and let your mind wander, as I have tonight, it is possible to forget the origin of the recordings and begin to hear distant trains rushing through tunnels, air conditioning units, even different instruments instead.[32]

The piece is not a tone poem, but the range of references is large. At times it seems we could be listening to the crackling of a small fire, or even to the buzz of insects – crickets, perhaps. Inspired, presumably, by Charles Dickens' 1845 novella *The Cricket on the Hearth*, Dickinson herself underlined the connection between the sounds of crickets and of fires. Describing a fire indoors during winter in a letter of 1851 to her brother Austin, she wrote of 'winter mornings when the cold *without* only adds to the warm *within*, and the more it snows and the harder it blows, brighter the fires blaze, and chirps more merrily the "cricket on the hearth".'[33]

Ernest Sandeen believes that in 'Further in Summer than the Birds', 'the cricket song is presented under a figure [that of 'a minor Nation' celebrating Mass] which does nothing to describe the sound itself'.[34] The poem focusses our attention, he argues, neither on the concrete nor the phenomenological details of the sound, 'not on the song, but on the poet's reaction to it'.[35] Jeffrey L. Duncan agrees that there is a lack of empiricism in Dickinson's poetry: 'Her hummingbird is remarkably abstract. Sometimes, moreover, as in the case of the crickets, she sounds out *an* idea of the thing. In her words we see the primacy of concept.'[36] This is, I think, broadly correct, in that the poem does not attempt to *describe* the crickets' song. It is, however, possible to hear an evocation of the song in the poem's phonetic material. The first half of the poem is full of sibilance: in seven of the first eight lines the final phonemes are sibilant sounds that imply a hiss continuing beyond the horizon of the line and could, perhaps, be heard to evoke the buzz of the cricket.[37]

druids and questions

Formally, *druids and questions* consists of a series of sounds and silences. Their nature and the structures in which they are deployed challenge our perception of the distinctions (which is to say the boundaries) between sounds produced in different ways. Relationships of size and scale are also brought into question: both sounds and silences can be heard as microcosms in themselves (tiny worlds with rich internal detail) or as part of various macrocosms (via the associations conjured by their varying means of production, or the different temporal textures evoked by the composition's rhythmic strategies). It is possible to redraw the boundaries of the piece via different strategies of listening: do we consider each sound as a bounded object, or only as an incomplete segment of the piece as a whole? Recalling Ives's insistence on ellipsis, can we be sure there is a coherent way to structure the piece from part to whole, from the smallest element to the largest? The similarities between the materials used to construct the piece could be seen as part of a strategy to destabilise any such security of structural architecture.

The sounds are of three types: recorded organ sounds (none of which are repeated), an electroacoustically produced wind sound, and electronic white noise. Sometimes the sounds are a single recording (though very frequently with a number of distinct sounds contained within it); more often, different recordings overlap one another. Tricks are played with our perception, and what seems similar may turn out to be different, or indeed vice versa. 'So – what do you hear?' asks Houben. 'Always organ sounds which differ (no thing in nature is similar, every cloud, every wave is different), and always the same sound (in a quasi "mechanic" way), which differs in changing contexts!'[38] Even silence itself can differ: 'There are two different kinds of silences in *druids and questions*: The silence as a kind of "passepartout", as a kind of frame around the organ sounds. . . . And then there is the silence which may be heard as really nothing: the "lack" on the tape.'[39] These different layers echo the deliberate layering of Ives's composition, as Houben explains: 'As Ives uses different levels (trumpet, strings, flutes. . .) *druids and questions* uses different levels: organ sounds (organ breathing) – white noise – breathing as an artificial sound – silence of the room – silence as a lack. . .'[40]

The wind and other airy sounds that make up *druids and questions* are quiet and largely serene; they come and go frequently, gently presenting a rich array of difference within apparent sameness.[41] But they are not without other emotional notes. Brian Olewnick notes a 'blending of calm and subsurface agitation' in the music, and the presence of a 'breathing sequence, not regular but also not panicky' together with an 'unease beneath'.[42] This 'breathing sequence', the basic formal scheme of the piece, consists of blocks – usually around two to three minutes in length – consisting of alternations of relatively short sounds and comparable lengths of silence, themselves alternating with slightly longer blocks of continuous sound, constructed from multiple sounds. There is a productive juxtaposition of non-measured regularity with mathematically exact timings. Houben explained the structure of the piece to me in her May 1st email: 'The organ-sound appears and disappears as a kind of breath: not measured exactly, but regular: on and off, on and off, on and off. . .' The other sounds appear at more regular intervals: the electroacoustic wind for thirty seconds every two minutes (2'00" to 2'30", 4'30" to 5'00", 7'00" to 7'30" etc) and the white noise for three minutes every three minutes (3'00" to 6'00", 9'00" to 12'00" etc). This cycle repeats every 30 minutes, so we are presented with two full cycles over the composition's one hour duration. Houben further notes that 'you hear, as a fourth "voice", the silence between all these sounds: it's really nothing – only empty time without any sound. It is the background behind all the other sounds as well.' [43] The resulting time structure gives the impression that it could go on forever.

The electronic and electroacoustic sounds are very stable and continuous. In the case of the organ sounds, while they all have their own inner energy and vibratory texture, they tend not otherwise to alter much except at the beginning and end. For example, a pitch may join the sound of air shortly after the latter begins, or a whistle may glissando down slightly before ceasing. There are many little narratives of coming into being or of dying, but a (relative) consistency during the majority of the sounds' 'lifetime'. The sounds are also clearly distributed across the stereo image, giving a distinct impression of right, middle and left. This contributes to a sense of 'betweenness' that resonates with the earlier piece *dazwischen*, but it also does something rather different. For the majority of the piece, the emphasis is on the right and centre of the stereo picture, making the listener most aware of the lefthand space only as an emptiness. Only just before the end of the piece, it seems to me – in its final three minutes – are sounds fully and equally present simultaneously on the left, right and centre. Thus at the very end of the piece there is the merest, gentlest hint of some teleological process at work in the music, some evidence of an alteration that will not allow the situation to continue indefinitely.

Ending and Concluding

I have attempted to trace some of the formal and thematic links between Dickinson's poem, Ives' composition, and the Houben composition that asks us to consider them together. In the final analysis, I would suggest that it is in their treatment of time that these three works have the most resonance with one another. All three works hover between different senses of time: a continual present (a field of simultaneity) coexists with perpetual change. It is only in time that things change, and only through change that things can be at all: there is a dialectic between alteration and persistence. In all three works there is more belief in the eternally creative constancy of change than there is pessimism about the prospects of inexorable decline and inescapable dissolution which thermodynamics teaches us must be the eventual destination of everything.

The French philosopher Michel Serres argues that, as real as the prospect of dissolution is, it is also by means of thermodynamics that noise distinguishes itself from information, that boundaries can be drawn and individuals stand out against the fields they occupy. These processes of distinction – which encompass all processes of perception and reaction – are going on constantly at every level of reality, binding them together even as they distinguish them from one another:

> There is only one type of knowledge and it is always linked to an observer, an observer submerged in a system or in its proximity. And this observer is structured exactly like what he observes. His position changes only the relationship between noise and information, but he himself never effaces these two stable presences. . . Nothing distinguishes me ontologically from a crystal, a plant, an animal, or the order of the world; we are drifting together toward the noise and the black depths of the universe, and our diverse systemic complexions are flowing up the entropic stream, toward the solar origin, itself adrift.[44]

Universal degradation springs from the same thermodynamic mechanisms as any existence that could be recognised as such, which is to say any act of perception or response to any 'Difference' whatsoever in any kind of field. To wish for escape from dissolution would be idle, because it is only by means of the processes which necessitate dissolution that wishing is possible at all. These particular works by Dickinson, Ives and Houben are fully compatible with such an understanding. All, in their different ways, confront wildly disjunctive phenomena with one another: extremes of scale, of time, of resemblance, of origin. These confrontations interrogate the nature of different kinds of boundaries. Is everything ultimately contained in a kind of unitary field, or are there, of necessity, empty spaces? Do these empty spaces demarcate separate fields or is it in the nature of the whole not to be fully and consistently ordered throughout?

Houben, Ives, and Dickinson all, in these works, insist on the importance of the observer and their relationship to the fields they inhabit, but they are also united in resisting solipsism or a radical perspectivalism. The questions may be relative to the questioner, but truth is not merely a chimaera. The fact that the quest may be interminable is not to be seen as an indication of its futility. The ultimate end is still a long way off, and there is more than enough wonder here in the present moment. That is why the last moments of all these works are provisional and fragile: they are endings rather than conclusions. The field of enquiry is still wide open, and the question remains.

Notes

1. Houben, Eva-Maria, *druids and questions* (Wandelweiser, 2011). Many thanks indeed to Eva-Maria Houben and also to Patrick Farmer, Janet Lash, Kate Lash and the editors for their comments on earlier versions of this essay.
2. I should confess here that in my first listenings to the piece I took all the sounds to be generated by the organ.
3. The poem in question begins 'Further in Summer than the Birds'. I quote it in full later in this essay. It is of course no simple matter to decide which text of a Dickinson poem to consider (Franklin's variorum edition includes five full versions, plus various alternative readings for particular words). (There are also some editorial controversies surrounding the score to *The Unanswered Question*.) Franklin has clearly stated the critical paradox: 'Critically, we say that a work of art is not commensurate with its author's intentions, yet the basic text is recovered, edited, and printed on the basis of authorial intention (so that the critic can then go to work with the theory that it is not commensurate with those intentions)' (R.W. Franklin, *The Editing of Emily Dickinson: A Reconsideration*. Madison, Milwaukee, and London: The University of Wisconsin Press, 1967, pp. 138–9). I bear this paradox in mind but nonetheless have decided to focus on an 'Aristotelian approach to criticism', where 'the union of form and content constitutes the particular poem, upon which the critic exercises his interest without reference to the archetypal intentions of an author', rather than a 'Platonic approach to editing', wherein 'the author's final intention is like a Platonic archetype, unchanging, complete, and perfect in its own way, against which any one of its appearances in print can be corrected' (Franklin, *Editing*, pp. 141–2), though I do briefly consider some additional stanzas in a later footnote.
   In fact, Simon Jarvis suggests a way out of this binary. Susan Howe's objections to Thomas H. Johnson's editing of Dickinson (see for example http://www.writing.upenn.edu/library/Howe/index.html, last accessed 17 February 2015), have been themselves objected to by Walter Benn Michaels ('Once we treat the poem as a drawing, "we can no longer", Michaels argues, "have any principled interest in Dickinson at all".'). Jarvis responds with the suggestion that 'care' might be an alternative to the stark binary of 'intention' versus 'accident': '[t]he blank between a

stanza or the blank at the end of the line is surely, precisely, an example of something which a poet might very well care about without it being easy to say that it is the textual repository of a "meaning" which the author "intended"' (Simon Jarvis, 'What Does Art Know', in *Aesthetics and the Work of Art*, ed. Peter de Bolla and Stefan H. Uhlig, Houndmills: Palgrave Macmillan, 2009, pp. 57–70, p. 67. The quotation and para-phrase from Michaels is on p. 57, referring to Walter Benn Michaels, *The Shape of the Signifier: 1967 to the End of History*, Princeton: Princeton University Press, 2004, p. 5).

Houben is by no means the only Wandelweiser composer to have been inspired by Dickinson – Antoine Beuger and Michael Pisaro are two others who have written works directly inspired by her poetry. Beuger's *landscapes of absence (3)* (2001–2) is particularly notable in this regard, in that it evokes 'a "Dickinson-world" . . . comparable to a late summer meadow with its specific overall sound, in which the individual occurrences are contained' (Beuger, interviewed by James Saunders in *The Ashgate Research Companion to Experimental Music*, Farnham and Burlington, Ashgate: 2009, pp. 231–41, p. 239).

4. Taylor, Cecil, liner notes to *Unit Structures* (Blue Note, 1966 [1987]).
5. Richard Feynman, *The Feynman Lectures on Physics, Vol. II*, chapter one, section two (1970). Available online at http://www.feynmanlec-tures.caltech.edu/II_01.html#Ch1-S2 (accessed 21 October 2015). See also Ernan McMullin, 'The Origins of the Field Concept in Physics', *Physics in Perspective* 4 (2002), pp. 13–39.
6. 'First, some simplicities that a man learns, if he works in OPEN, or what can also be called COMPOSITION BY FIELD, as opposed to inherited line, stanza, over-all form, what is the 'old' base of the non-projective.' Charles Olson, 'Projective Verse', in Ralph Maud, ed., *A Charles Olson Reader* (Manchester: Carcanet, 2005), pp. 39–49, p. 41.
7. Berger, John, "Field", [1971], as reprinted in the current book, p. 32.
8. Patrick Farmer and Sarah Hughes' editorial to *Wolf Notes* issue 5 veers a little too close to such an attempt for my liking: 'If Field is the contour of our activity where do we situate ourselves, what is this situation in which we find ourselves and how do we relate to that which surrounds us?' (Farmer, Patrick and Sarah Hughes, 'Editorial' in *Wolf Notes*, issue 5 (March 2013), p. 4. Available from https://wolfnotes.wordpress.com/wolf-notes/ (last accessed 15 January 2015)). I do not think I under-stand what it would mean for 'Field' to be 'the contour of our activ-ity'. We would do well to remember the metaphysical caveat expressed by the Scottish theologian D.M. MacKinnon, in his *The Problem of Metaphysics*. Referring to 'those notions we find ourselves using in dis-course concerning every sort of subject-matter, such notions as thing and property, existence, truth, etc', he warns that their very pervasive-ness means that 'we are betrayed by their injudicious employment to seek substances corresponding to the substantives we use, and have

to discipline ourselves against this fallacy. . . .' (MacKinnon, Donald Mackenzie, *The Problem of Metaphysics* (Cambridge: Cambridge University Press, 1974), p. 12). If this warning is appropriate for genuinely philosophically pervasive notions (thing and property, existence, truth), then it applies *a fortiori* to those words or concepts which are merely common.

9. The composer who encompasses both tendencies in his work at different times – influenced by Ives and, in turn, a primary influence on Houben – is of course John Cage.

10. Ives, Charles, 'Foreword' to the score of *The Unanswered Question* (New York and Hamburg: Southern Music Publishing Co. Inc./Peer Musikverlag G.M.B.H., 1953), p. 2.

11. This is made clear by an earlier version of the poem, which does not have the concluding couplet quoted by Houben, but does include the lines 'Beauty – is Nature's Fact – // But Witness for Her Land – / And Witness for Her Sea – / The Cricket is Her utmost / Of Elegy, to Me –' This version also includes the following stanzas:

> 'Tis Audiblest, at Dusk –
> When Day's attempt is done –
> And Nature nothing waits to do
> But terminate in Tune
>
> Nor difference it knows
> Of Cadence, or of Pause –
> But simultaneous as Same –
> The Service emphacize –
>
> Nor know I when it cease –
> At Candles, it is here –
> When Sunrise is – that it is not –
> Than this, I know no more

(*The Poems of Emily Dickinson: Variorum Edition*, ed. R.W. Franklin, Cambridge, MA and London, The Belknap Press of Harvard University Press: 1998, p. 832) This resonates with Houben's interest in the disappearance of sound, perhaps epitomised by her writing for piano. In the notes to her 2010 double CD of solo piano music (*works for piano*,) she writes: 'the sound of the piano decays. / it cannot be sustained. I let it loose time and again. / it appears by disappearing; starting to disappear just after the attack. / in disappearing it begins to live, to change. / the piano: an instrument, that allows me to hear how many ways sound can disappear. / there seems to be no end to disappearance. / I can hear, how listening becomes the awareness of fading sound.'

12. *The Poems of Emily Dickinson: Reading Edition*, ed. R.W. Franklin. Cambridge, MA and London, The Belknap Press of Harvard University Press: 1999 [hereafter *Poems*], # 895.

13. Dickinson, Emily. *Selected Letters*, ed. Thomas H. Johnson. Cambridge, MA and London: The Belknap Press of Harvard University Press: 1986, p. 8.

14. The 1844 edition of Webster's *American Dictionary of the English Language* that Dickinson used does not include a pejorative definition: see the Emily Dickinson Lexicon at http://edl.byu.edu/ (last accessed 6 February 2013).

15. Benjamin Goluboff has argued that 'during the years of her most important work, Roman Catholicism was at the center of a pervasive cultural discourse with which Dickinson was certainly conversant'. See Goluboff, '"If Madonna Be": Emily Dickinson and Roman Catholicism', *New England Quarterly*, Vol. 73, No. 3 (September 2000), pp. 355–85, p. 355.

16. That is to say that a sacrament both signifies God's grace and brings about beneficial consequences for its recipient.

17. Further underlining its importance, 'grace' is also the only word besides 'the', 'a' and 'no' to appear more than once in the poem.

18. We must remember Dickinson's suspicion of rigid religious organisation when we consider her deployment of this language. She wrote in 1859: 'Mr S. preached in our church last Sabbath upon "predestination," but I do not respect "doctrines," and did not listen to him, so I can neither praise, nor blame.' (*Selected Letters*, p. 149). It is however intriguing to discover that for the leading Scottish Reformer John Knox the concepts of ordinance and grace were crucially linked, and in a way that, like Dickinson's poem, confronts what changes with what does not change: 'John Knox never wearied of affirming the immutability of God. He ever remains the same God, true and faithful to his "joyful promise" to Adam that seed of the woman would break down the serpent's head. This took the form of an *ordinance of grace* in which God provided a way within the history of mankind for deliverance and redemption. It is indeed upon the ordinance of grace that the whole order of creation depends, for it remains the same in the midst of man's sin, and in spite of it, the ordinance of grace assumed the character of the promise.' (Torrence, Thomas. *Scottish Theology from John Knox to John McLeod Campbell*. Edinburgh: T & T Clark: 1996, p. 8)

19. Peterson, Katie. 'Surround Sound: Dickinson's Self and the Hearable'. *The Emily Dickinson Journal*. 14.2 (2005), pp. 76–88, p. 76.

20. *Poems*, # 402.

21. Vendler, Helen. *Dickinson: Selected Poems and Commentaries*. Cambridge, Mass. and London: The Belknap Press of Harvard University Press: 2012, p. 366.

Vendler's turn of phrase is suggestive of connections with Houben's interests: her reference to the 'almost-invisible' is reminiscent of the 'kaum hörbar' ('scarcely audible') in the score to the third of Webern's *Fünf Stücke für Orchester* op. 10, which is cited in Houben's lecture *Presence – Silence – Disappearance. Some thoughts on the perception of "nearly nothing"* (delivered in 2010 at the *i and e* festival in Dublin, and available at http://www.wandelweiser.de/houben/presence.html [last accessed 29 October 2012]).

22. Houben presumably means here to allude to Luc Ferrari's influential 1970 composition with field recordings, *Presque Rien No. 1: Le Lever du jour au bord de la mer.*

23. Ives, Charles. *Essays Before a Sonata and Other Writings.* London: Calder and Boyars, 1969, p. 7.

24. Emerson, 'Nature', in *Nature and Selected Esssays* (London: Penguin 2003), pp. 35–82, p. 39.

25. Ives, *Essays*: 22-3. A related quotation, from Emerson's 'Beauty', is to be found in the notes to the *Essays*, on p. 244: 'For although the works of nature are innumerable and all different, the result or the expression of them all is similar and single. Nature is a sea of forms radically alike and even unique. A leaf, a sunbeam, a landscape, the ocean, make an analagous impression on the mind.'

26. Burkholder, J. Peter. 'The Organist in Ives,' *Journal of the American Musicological Society* 55 (2002), pp. 255–310, esp. p. 276.

27. *Poems*, # 211. Goluboff sees this poem as another piece of evidence for Dickinson's ambivalent interest in Catholicism: 'Like "I heard a Fly buzz-when I died" or "After great pain, a formal feeling comes," the poem gives utterance to a speaker who has arrived on the far side of some irrevocable crossing and looks backward to establish the precise moment of going over. The Bernardine girl speaks not from the aftermath of death or grief; hers is then the aftermath of translation into the 'devouring interior' of Romanism or, to use the nativist rhetoric of the Springfield Republican, the aftermath of infection by the Catholic "contagion"' (Goluboff, 'If Madonna Be', p. 384).

28. Jeffrey L. Duncan argues that breath for Dickinson engaged in a dialectic of the finite and infinite, the mortal and immortal: '"Are you too deeply occupied to say if my Verse is alive?" she specifically asked Colonel Higginson. "Should you think it breathed . . . I should feel quick gratitude—." She assumed that if it breathed it would lack "the power to die," that if, and only if, it had the mortal life of the flesh would it have the immortal life of the ideal, both at the same time, moreover, in the same form, in the very same breath, as it were. All creation is in the finite, a living proof that the finite is a condition, not an absolute' (Duncan, Jeffrey L. "Joining Together/Putting Asunder: An Essay on Emily Dickinson's Poetry", *The Missouri Review*, Volume 4, Number 2, Winter 1980–81, pp. 111–29, p. 122).

29. Normal German practice would be to capitalise the initial letters of these nouns, but in keeping with Houben's preference – shared with many of the other Wandelweiser composers – for the lower case, I retain her orthography.

30. 'Acousmatic' was a term employed by Pierre Schaeffer, referring to Pythagoras' practice of lecturing from behind a screen, to denote a situation of 'reduced listening', where one focuses on the characteristics of the sounds themselves, without enquiring into their origins or resemblances.

31. Seth Kim-Cohen rightly insists that to argue that '[s]ound alone, signifies itself' is to claim that sound can somehow sidestep representation, but that this 'amounts to the same unsustainable premise upon which the phenomenological construction is balanced. It maintains that self-presence takes place in the *Augenblick*, the blink of an eye', whereas in fact '[s]ound-in-itself is just as inconceivable as self-presence; the *Ohrenblick* is just as impossible as the *Augenblick*' (Kim-Cohen, Seth. *In the Blink of an Ear*. New York and London: Continuum, 2009, p. 259). I am, however, also sympathetic to Christoph Cox's rejoinder that Kim-Cohen's attempt 'to bring sound art discourse within the neo-Kantian conceptual purview of contemporary cultural theory' remains circumscribed by 'the presuppositions of textualism and discursivity, affirming a distinction between phenomena and noumena rendered as the distinction between language and the extra-linguistic, culture and nature, text and matter' (Cox, Christoph. 'Beyond Representation and Signification: Toward a Sonic Materialism', *Journal of Visual Culture*, 10:2 (August 2011), pp. 145–61, p. 147–8).

32. *The Watchful Ear* blog, 26th December 2011. Available at http://www.thewatchfulear.com/?p=6438 (last accessed 6 February 2013).

33. Dickinson, *Selected Letters*, p. 70.

34. Sandeen, Ernest. 'Delight Deferred by Retrospect: Emily Dickinson's Late-Summer Poems', *New England Quarterly*, Vol. 40, No. 4 (December 1967), pp. 483–500, p. 496.

35. Ibid.

36. Duncan, 'Joining Together', p. 117. For Duncan this primacy is reflected in the structure of her metaphors, which are permeated with the effecting and effacing of 'Difference': 'In the language of her poems, that is, she depicts the divisions that language causes— between subject and object, for instance, the empirical and the ideal, life and death—and the identifications it simultaneously effects, of subject with object, the empirical with the ideal, death with life. This process of dividing/uniting, uniting/dividing constitutes a fundamental pattern of Dickinson's poetry and accounts for much of its peculiar power, for the way it often has of lifting and dropping us at the same time' (p. 114).

37. The one exception to this is the fifth line, whose final monosyllable does at least begin with a sibilant, emerging without hiatus from the

preceding word, and concluding a particularly sustained chain of sibilant sounds: 'ordinance is seen'.
38. Houben, personal email, 1 May 2012.
39. Houben, personal email, 4 May 2012.
40. Ibid.
41. In reference to accusations of political quietism or escapist pastoralism within Wandelweiser music (which I would contest, while acknowledging that not all the music or each of its enthusiasts always escape such traps), it is interesting that for Emerson the cricket symbolised the musician's tendency to escapism: 'How partial, like mutilated eunuchs, the musical artists appear to me in society! Politics, bankruptcy, famine, war – nothing concerns them but a scraping on a catgut or tooting on a bass French horn. The crickets in the grass chirp their national song at all hours, quite heedless who conquers, Federals or rebels, in the war, and so do these' (from Emerson's journal for September 1862, quoted in David Wooldridge, *Charles Ives: A Portrait*. London: Faber & Faber, 1975, p. 171). Such musicians were precisely those for whom Ives had no time, of course. Accusations of political indifference on Dickinson's part may be more just: see Domhnall Mitchell, 'Emily Dickinson and Class', in Emily Martin, ed., *The Cambridge Companion to Emily Dickinson* (Cambridge: Cambridge University Press, 2002), pp. 191–214.
42. *Just Outside* blog, 29 January 2012. Available at http://olewnick.blogspot.co.uk/2012/01/eva-maria-houben-druids-and-questions.html (last accessed 6 February 2013).
43. This formulation emphasises the digital silence of the CD rather than Cage's idea that all silences are filled with sound. In the domestic situation which is likely to account for the vast majority of experiences of this music, I think that both ideas can be present: played on a stereo system in a space with significant ambient sound, one might be more aware of the interpenetration of the sounds of the CD with those of the environent (Houben's silence as 'passepartout'); listening on noise-cancelling headphones, the spaces in the music might really seem like 'empty time', like a 'lack'. Manfred Werder's *ein(e) ausführende(r) seiten 218–226* (Edition Wandelweiser Records, 2006), in which silence is interrupted intermittently by a brief and near-silent electronic tone, similarly explores the relationship between playback and listening environment.
44. Serres, Michael. 'The Origin of Language: Biology, Information Theory, & Thermodynamics' (translated by Mark Anderson), in *Hermes: Literature, Science, Philosophy*, ed. Josué V. Harari and David F. Bell (Baltimore & London: The Johns Hopkins University Press, 1982), pp. 71– 83, p. 83.

Chapter 7

Field Recording as Writing: John Berger, Peter Gizzi and Juliana Spahr

Redell Olsen

What secret is at stake when one truly listens, that is, when one tries to capture or surprise the sonority rather than the message? What secret is yielded – hence also made public – when we listen to a voice, an instrument, or a sound just for itself?

Jean-Luc Nancy, *Listening*[1]

I. Berger's 'Field'

The implicit problem and the potential of Jean-Luc Nancy's call to 'capture or surprise' the 'sound just for itself' resonate together in Berger's 1971 essay 'Field'. The apparently fixed boundaries between auditor and field, between past and present apprehensions, become disturbed. Berger's essay stages the perceptual agency of encounter, the event *of* environment not as backdrop but as participatory exploration. What Berger records in writing is the field as *itself* in proprioceptive fusion with the listener and, by extension, the reader. Listening, seeing, reading and writing are presented as near-simultaneous manifestations of this reciprocal meeting between context and perceiver.

Berger's essay shares obvious affinities with the work of a number of sound artists for whom the specific locality is an integral element of the recording.[2] This environmental encounter opens correspondences with the concerns of two contemporary poets whose work engages with both literal and conceptual 'fields' in terms of the physical, social, cultural, political and linguistic environments that we inhabit. Peter Gizzi and Juliana Spahr have, in different ways, approached the field recording as writing through a series of explorative associations of subjectivity and attention involving an attunement of the senses through listening, seeing and remembering.

The resulting poems proliferate the temporality of the field recording beyond a single duration in a continuous present.

Berger's essay opens with a conception of environment that finds expression in relation to a domestic and even subjective landscape of memory. His experience of the field is as much about a return to a series of past sensory impressions as it is to a locatable present encounter. There is a 'shelf of a field', the walls are 'papered with blue sky', and there is also a 'curtain of printed trees'.[3] This field is the space of earliest identity formation and it is at once visual, linguistic and sonic: a lullaby of landscape where 'repeated lines of words and music are the paths' (p. 31). However, as the essay progresses he moves towards an understanding of landscape that suggests both an exterior and interior terrain and resists definition as any one contained moment: 'The visible extension of the field in space displaces awareness of your own lived time' (p. 35).

In the 1970s the relationship between field recording and landscape was highlighted by R. Murray Schafer's term 'soundmark'. The word, coined by Schafer, 'is derived from landmark and refers to a community sound which is unique or possesses qualities which make it specifically regarded or noticed by the people in that community'.[4] Schafer also asserts a series of 'keynote sounds' for any environment which are 'those created by its geography and climate: water, wind, forests, plains, birds, insects and animals' (p. 10). Although the examples given here point to forests and plains, Schafer's terms often enact a blurring of the relationship between pastoral and urban landscapes, for example in relation to the event mapping of two blocks of a city (p. 131) or the sonography of fog horns, church bells, telephones and motorcycles (p. 137). The soundscape of a community is as definably marked as the topology of its geographical features, which its inhabitants respond to as part of their ongoing relationship to that landscape as if it were a language (p. 10). According to Schafer, if one wishes to make a sound recording of this 'language', the best approach is to figure it as a map of a space that is encountered from a select and heightened vantage point: 'The best way to appreciate a field situation is to get above it. The medieval cartographer did this by climbing the highest hill . . .' (p. 131). This is not dissimilar to Berger's desire for: 'A field on a hillside, seen either from above like a tabletop, or from below when the incline of the hill appears to tilt the field towards you – like music on a music stand (Berger, pp. 32–3).

Schafer cites a range of 'classifications' possible in the field of listening that are expansive in their remit: acoustic, psychoacoustic, semiotic, aesthetic effects (Schafer, p. 133). At the same time, Schafer admits the difficulty of splitting a soundscape into such categories. It is the potential for the descriptive markers of the auditory classification that are most consistently developed by him to establish a mode of sonography that he admits is necessarily formulaic. It is a method that relies on the 'observer' to catalogue and quantify sonic events in relation to observations such as the estimated distance of the sound from the observer, the estimated intensity of the original sound and so forth, and to translate these notations into graphic forms of notation. He is aware of the limitations of this approach: 'If soundscape study is to develop as an interdiscipline, it will have to discover the missing interfaces and unite hitherto isolated studies in a bold new synergy' (p. 134). While this seems potentially generative of new forms of interdisciplinary sonography, Schafer is dismissive of the possibility that a soundwalk could be apprehended in any other form than the sonic: 'The first rule must always be: if you can't hear it, be suspicious' (p. 132). The purpose of Schafer's approach to notation seems to be 'to offer a few hints which the ear can then follow up in its own way' but he also remarks that 'no silent projection of a landscape can ever be adequate' (p. 132). This warning, as well as Schafer's quantative approach to notation, suggests that there is little point in pursuing the possibilities of a writing, particularly of a poetic writing of the field recording as a possible methodology as part of his mapping process.

By contrast, Pauline Oliveros's practices and pedagogies of 'deep listening' encourage a participatory relationship that oscillates between what she terms 'focal' and 'global' modes of attention to sound, modes of attention that do not seem to be exclusive to any medium or genre of recording and could also include writing as one of their many approaches.[5] From a related perspective, Hildegard Westerkamp's account of her practice of 'disruptive listening' presents recording as a mode of practice that is not media specific: 'Soundwalks, just like listening itself, need to be DONE. Out of that doing comes an entirely new experiential knowledge'.[6] Here, walking and listening are activities that might manifest their integral relationship in a number of potential media and are not carried out from a point of hierarchical detachment.

However, this new experiential knowledge might not always be comfortable. In Westerkamp's 2015 keynote address at the International Symposium on Electronic Art, she described the experience of attending a yoga retreat that was in close proximity to a construction site, the noise of which could be heard in the room where the yogis were practising. For Westerkamp, this elicited an important question that can be related not just to what the practice of field recording should include or exclude but also to the importance of maintaining attention, not in spite of but rather because of the proximity to these apparently disruptive and uncomfortable sonic events:

> No doubt we all have had to grapple with discomfort when exposed to disturbing soundscapes or unsettling inner chatter. At such times, do we decide whether we open our listening *further* to the reality of that discomfort and try to affect changes – which is what I would call the disruptive nature of listening – or do we try to ignore it and psychologically shut it out – which is when the sound itself is in danger of disrupting our lives, stressing us, precisely because we are trying to shut out something that our ears and bodies are still receiving, still perceiving. (n.p.)

The 'disruptive nature of listening', then, is a mode of attention to sound and to the act of listening that involves a renegotiation of the usual filtering devices that we (mostly) unconsciously rely on in our daily lives. This is not the same as saying that our listening is disrupted (although it may well be) but that we are engaged in a *practice* of 'disruptive listening' during which time unwanted sounds become productive additions to our listening rather than impediments to the hearing or to the recording. By extension, a writing that might emerge from such a mode of disruptive listening could involve an attention to what Nancy refers to as the 'sound just for itself', or even what Barthes elsewhere refers to as the 'grain of the voice' ('le grain de la voix').[7]

The 'sound itself' in all its material and bodily possibilities is an important concern for Westerkamp, who acknowledges that part of the power of the 'disruptive nature of listening' is to embrace the experience of the disturbing aspects of the soundscape as an attempt to listen 'further to the reality' that surrounds us. The aim is not to shut out these aspects, which would result in a counterproductive mode of exclusion, but rather to engage in than the *practice* of disruptive listening.

For the writer of field recordings, the place and temporality of record need not be unitary and fixed. For Berger, the immediate field of attention is expanded from the proximate perceptual field to associative fields that are opened still further by the introduction of the possibility of 'contingencies overlapping' during the unforeseen period of attention produced in his account by an enforced wait at a level crossing. This is a space and time that allows him to register the birds in the sky, which might otherwise have gone unnoticed.

Despite this expansion and overlap of contexts there is simultaneously, according to Berger, an 'exact fit' between the area of the field and the time of the event in which perceptual, temporal and topographic boundaries converge (p. 32).

More literally, Berger designates the features of his ideal field: a 'grass field' with a 'minimum of order' (p. 32), a 'continental field' which apparently aligns 'the field' with the French tradition of painting *en plein air*, an innovation that brought the artist out of the studio and into immediate contact with his environment. Berger, however, resists any such easy analogy with painting as one doomed to create a 'cultural context' that 'can only refer back' to an experience rather than precede it (p. 33). As this suggests, Berger's focus is angled towards the conditions of the perceptual event in futurity rather than towards the production of an art object that responds to and is therefore dependent on the traditions of a particular genre. From Berger's point of view, this would serve to cast the expectations of the field on the part of writer and reader back towards existing modes of form and reception.

Berger's essay resolutely invokes a European field but it interestingly anticipates and shares a number of affinities with Rosalind Krauss's influential 1979 essay 'Sculpture in the Expanded Field', in which she theorises American Land Art of the 1970s. As Krauss states, '. . . sculpture is no longer the privileged middle term between two things that it isn't. Sculpture is rather not only one term on the periphery of a field in which there are other, differently structured possibilities'.[8] Within these terms field recording is a related 'differently structured' possibility that has entered the field of art practices. As Eve Meltzer points out, Krauss 'embraced the view that the meaning of all objects including artworks is not substantial but relational in nature, determined not only by characteristics that are essential to them, but rather derived of their interplay with other objects in a field structured by differences'.[9] For Berger, this interplay between distinct phenomena is inherent in the attention to the noise and movement of the blackbirds in relation to the adjacent railway: 'Blackbirds hide in the grass and rise up from it. Their coming and going remains quite unaffected by the trains' (Berger, p. 32).

As the essay cuts across and through a number of different fields, Berger draws attention to the possibility that there are other structures of consciousness at work within and across the so-called ideal field. The field of preverbal memory, for example, provokes a different encounter than that of his imposed span of attention at the level crossing. Similarly, the field described does not have the same features as either the *ideal* field detailed or of the photographic image of the field that serves as an illustration to the essay. Furthermore, the examples that Berger gives are themselves placed in relation to one another. Like Krauss, who 'stare[s] at the pit in the earth and think[s] that we both do and don't know what sculpture is' (Krauss, p. 33), Berger's sudden perceptual awareness that he is included in the noticing of the event in the field is a transformative moment in which boundaries of art shift and are redefined away from traditional modes of visual practice. For Berger, this recognition orientates him in a different direction from the histories of painting and theatre and towards the writing of the experience of the field as event. In many ways, this move is a redefinition of the field of landscape painting into the expanded field of writing.

However, Berger's conceptions of 'field' are very different from either those of Krauss or, from a literary perspective, Charles Olson's ideas of FIELD COMPOSITION as set out in his 'Projective Verse' manifesto.[10] The understanding of 'field' for both Krauss and Olson relates to the experience of open prairies, plains and even the deserts of an American rather than a French or British landscape in which the fields are often bounded by hedges or fences in ways that create an entirely different sense of scale that emerges from a very different social and economic history. Berger hopes for a grass field that 'must be an area with boundaries which are visible – though not necessarily regular; it cannot be an unbounded segment of nature' (p. 32) and it must not be 'hedged on all sides' so as not to restrict the number of 'exits or entrances' (p. 33). By contrast, space is conceived by Olson in terms that are quite at odds from those of Berger's 'field'. Even before the 'Projective Verse' manifesto of 1950, Olson had announced: 'I take SPACE to be the central fact to man born in America, from Folsom Cave to now. I spell it large because it comes large here. Large without mercy'.[11]

In this regard the conceptual parameters and the partially bounded field of Berger's 'ideal' suggest more striking similarities with Fluxus event making and some of the playful strategies of writers featured in the Situationist International than an Olsonian field poetics. In 1958 Gilles Ivain described how it was important for people to 'drift' out of their usual environments in order to free themselves from their habitual social and political constraints.[12] And in 1959 Guy Debord asserted that: '. . . the minimum programme of unitary urbanism is to extend our present field of play to every kind of building we can wish for. The complexity of the field we had in mind would be roughly equivalent to that of an ancient city'.[13] This determination is echoed, with more of a focus on the individual, by Berger's writing of his transformative perceptual encounter with the field. However, the Situationists and, to a certain extent, the Fluxus artists were predominantly concerned with the *détournement* of the encounter in relation to social, urban and, in the case of the Fluxus, artistic environments. Perhaps a more apposite point of comparison is the score 'Open Field' by Pauline Oliveros from 1980 (the year after Krauss's essay and nine years after Berger's 'Field'), in which Oliveros makes evident the same hazing of the distinctions between art and life that were contemporaneously of interest to Berger and Krauss:

Open Field

When a sight sound, movement, or place attracts your attention during your daily life, consider that moment an 'art experience'. Find a way to record an impression of this momentary 'art experience' using any appropriate means or media. Share these experiences with each other and make them available to others.[14]

The fragility of the speech marks within the score around the phrase 'art experience' suggests a blurring of boundaries between art and life but ultimately upholds the distinction by its parenthetical nature. Nevertheless, her approach to the recording of that experience in 'any appropriate means or media' extends the possibility of considering an approach to field recording as writing. The score falls somewhat short of Berger's assertion that: 'The field that you are standing before appears to have the same proportions as your own life' (p. 35). However, the directive to 'find a way to record an impression' has the effect of removing the need for a musician or sound artist even to make use of sonic forms in their practice. All forms of recording are appropriate and this includes written forms. What is stressed is the production and replication – that is how to make them (these recordings in whatever media) available to others. The productive recording of experience and its dissemination is foregrounded in a way that draws attention to the collective enterprise and potential for exchange in the mode of field recording.

For Berger, the field is both a material and an abstract entity. His writing tenders an evocation of a landscape that is at once linguistically and sonically produced. It is at once out of time and a constitutive feature of the space and time of the event: of the here and now. The entanglement of association is productive for Berger as part of a sonic event. For example, 'the noise of the hen', although it remains unseen, produces 'an event' (p. 31). Such sonic events also have the potential to exist simultaneously in different time frames and different life stages: 'Remember what it was like to be sung to sleep' (p. 31).

The apprehension of this temporal aspect of the field is also one of activity and of production. In his distinction between work and text, Roland Barthes referred to the text as a 'methodological field'.[15] By contrast, the work is necessarily fragmentary as it is only ever 'the imaginary tail' of the text, a text that 'is experienced only in an activity, in a production'[16] and presumably also in its reception.[17] In this sense the work is only the residue of the activity that took place in the 'methodological field', but a residue that may traverse many different works, disciplinary fields, times and places.

2. Gizzi's 'Field Recordings'

The poems in Peter Gizzi's *Archeophonics* engage in a series of physical and metaphorical explorations into the archaeology of sounds, both of public language and private utterance, and many of them explore the soundings of emotional and cultural memory in relation to the self of the poet and of poetry. In 'Field Recordings' the 'methodological field' of this textual mode of field recording is evident as both a conceptual and directive parameter.

Field Recordings

For today's tourist, orientation is impossible
RIMBAUD

LANGUOR

The old language
is the old language,
with its lance and greaves,
broken shields
and hammered vowels;
a stairway ascending
into a mirror – see it
climb the old helix,
beneath a scarred
and chipped northerly sky,
rotunda blue.

Sing genetic cloud forms
mirroring syntax
in reflection, and what
would you have?

Paving stones, rhetoric,
the coping of bridges,
leanings, what
is taken from *res*?
To reconstruct? To re-
cognize the categories
have failed? That
the index was a lyre.

The lists have grown
lonely, far from home,
houses of worship,
roofs, toy stores, names,
historical furniture,
descriptions of architecture,
patina in a fanfare city.

I have eaten the air
of that city.[18]

As in Berger's essay, the boundaries between the conceptual, associative and actual field are periodically fused, disconnected and
reconnected in a rhythmical exploration of our habitual practices
of encounter and attention in relation to memory and the natural
world. However, for the writer set on recording the field, one of
the most obvious fields in which to 'observe the event' (p. 34) is
language itself.

Gizzi's epigraph is taken from John Ashbery's 2011 translation
of Arthur Rimbaud's *Illuminations* (1886), 'For today's tourist, orientation is impossible'.[19] The significance of this as a coordinate is
important: Rimbaud is not quoted in the original by Gizzi but at
least one remove via the translation by another contemporary poet
of an older generation. This invokes the field of a particular grain
of voice: that of French nineteenth-century poetic experimentation as filtered through the American New York School of poetry.
In other words, it is through the history of the field in terms of ownership and use that Gizzi is demarcating the field of his poem, this
linguistic and poetic language no more natural, arbitrary or without
history than a hedge in a field.

In 'Field Recordings', as this epigraph suggests, Gizzi is taking a sounding of the line of history and metamorphosis that connects the American poetic idiom with that of Rimbaud. If the poet is here a tourist, then he is a tourist in the field of language. His methodological field or activity is to align himself in relation to the various possible ways of listening to and through the various fields of language-making that constitute the landscape around him. His approach to the writing of record (and of recording) aligns with aspects that Roland Barthes emphasised when he described the importance of the act of listening as 'taking soundings'.[20] Barthes's assertion of 'soundings' places the act of listening alongside that of any other mode of recording that materialises the substance of sound – either graphically or sonically in creative action. Gizzi is sounding the field of language and of poetic tradition in ways that take in listening as a mode of being attentive to the immediate and the historical context of poetic language, but also as a field that can be redefined according to the lyric 'orientation' of the poet and the awkwardness of 'self'-expression that this tradition encodes by way of its very history as a lyric practice. Barthes's description of a 'modern' listening that might include 'the implicit, the indirect, the supplementary, the delayed' and 'all forms of polysemy'[21] captures a similar tension to that which the field recorder, in whatever media, encounters:

> ... such listening is supposed to develop in an inter-subjective space where 'I am listening' also means 'listen to me'; what it seizes upon-in order to transform and restore to the endless interplay of transference-is a general 'signifying' no longer conceivable without the determination of the unconscious.[22]

How to be open to the possibility of Barthes's inter-subjective space and avoid the confessional lyric pitfall where 'I am listening' *only means* 'listen to me' is an anxiety that afflicts work made and read in the poetic lyric tradition, as much as it does that of the post-Cagean sound artist and her audience. Gillian White affirms shame and embarrassment as one of lyric poetry's pervasive contemporary features precisely in response to such anxieties.[23] Schafer's warning to those intent on the sonic mapping of environments – 'if you can't hear it, be suspicious'[24] – parallels the anxiety of the lyric poet in relation to song: if you can't hear it (as song) be suspicious, and if you can, be careful that you are expressing more than 'listen to me'.

Gizzi successfully addresses these thorny issues by writing a poem that is somewhat distanced – even suspicious – of its own materials, its own field of poetic language. The poem is not content with the 'sound just for itself' of language but attentive to the histories and contexts of production that have led to the specific shape of the experience in language.

Gizzi's first title in the 'Field Recordings' sequence is LANGUOR, a word that clearly resonates with just such linguistic disquiet. The potential homographic slip from 'languor' to language plays on the ambiguity of this unfamiliar word. In addition, this particular page setting, with LANGUOR in block capitals beneath the title of the sequence, is also reminiscent of Frank O'Hara's visual 'sounding' of Mike Goldberg's SARDINES in 'Why I am Not a Painter'.[25] In that poem a visual fragment of language perhaps derived from the packaging on a sardine tin is all but obliterated in Goldberg's painting, only to surface as the highlighted capitals SARDINES in O'Hara's poem, where it stands as both word and image of itself. The block capitals draw attention to the materiality of the word and also to its other contextual fields of origin and reference on the packaging of a tin and in a painting.

Gizzi's poem is also a sounding of the disorienting relationship to the experience of grief and of mourning, states in which feelings are both intuitively and culturally shaped. The long traditions associated with the ritualised sounding of a poetics of grief are inhabited with a certain sense of their necessary and ongoing reality and relevance but also as forms of expression as citation which themselves give rise to the very particular sounds of grief in poetry and in everyday life and death.

'Languor' is a word that was has etymological origins in French and Latin. It was first used in English c.1300 and evokes both mourning and lament. This means that it brings with it the expectation of specific sounds that might be engendered from specific forms and genres of poetic discourse, such as the elegy and the ode, but also specific sounds of the language of the body in grief: crying, wailing. Other sonic expectations are carried with it in a series of self-cancelling, or at least overlapping semantic fields, which are often tense in their contradictions. The word connotes weariness, lethargy, drowsiness and lack of energy but also pleasurable relaxation. Each of these states would seem to encourage listening to different forms of quietness. Languor can also be suggestive of longing, illness and even disease. The cry of loss, the sigh of desire for the one that is absent, and also the moan of the body in pain and physical suffering are all sounded in it.

Conversely, it can also be used of the attitude of a person who is of a nonchalant or dispassionate nature; this is a stance that is associated with another mode of quiet, even of sulking. Moreover, the word does not necessarily have to refer to a person. It can also be used in reference to an abstract or immaterial thing that shows slackness, dullness and stagnation. Finally, it is also a condition of the atmosphere and the weather: languor is a heaviness of the air, an oppressive stillness that draws attention to the absence of life and motion.[26]

In short, this title introduces a field of historical and material properties that the poet is sounding out in his poem: as the poem becomes a listening and recording device, in and through the languor/language of poetic utterance. In this context, the irony with which the opening lines, 'The old language / is the old language,' resound, alerts us to the oscillating quality of the overlapping fields of reference, which are never resolved into a single plane of meaning. The medievalism of 'lance and greaves, / broken shields' highlights the sense that it is the language which has the power to hurt with its 'lance' but also is afflicted and in mourning. The 'greaves' suggest the damage to the definition of the lyric subject and indeed the language of the poem. The 'hammered vowels' evoke the making of poetry and the making of the weapons of war – whether this is war between selves, countries or even between poetic traditions is left openly indeterminate. This sonic emphasis also relates to the way in which singers are trained to place stress on their root vowels. In Gizzi's poem the hammered vowels ascend 'into a mirror', apparently to confront the possibility of self-reflection but perhaps also as a reference to John Ashbery's 'Self-Portrait in a Convex Mirror' (1975). It is a meeting with the self as constructed lyric 'I'.

The shape of the 'old helix' suggests at once a spiral staircase, the spiral of grief, the ascent of a scale in music, the double helix of DNA or even the coiled outer shape of the ear ready to listen to the song of 'genetic cloud forms'. These, like the 'chipped Northerly sky', are potentially not natural at all but second-order representations borrowed from other fields: biological, architectural, artistic, digital and computational. The question 'what / is taken from *res*?' shimmers with both the Latin word *res* – the particularity of a thing or matter – and the more contemporary acronym for an English-based renewable energy company which trades under the acronym res and specialises in wind technologies. This double sounding seems an appropriate one, given the final lines of the poem: 'I have eaten the air / of that city'. What, where and how to identify the *res* of existence is raised as a possible question – one that is linked to the sounding of the very material of language. This, in turn, is analogous to the workings of invisible wind-generated renewable energies. All of these are sounded in relation to the invisible technology of the poem: 'That / the index was a lyre'. Here, poetic language is both the index (instrument) of the expression of thought and feeling in poetry. It is also the liar, in the sense that it is the very *res* that is shimmering and scintillates across meaning, across pre-existing fields of reference. Its indices do not allow for the authentic expression of grief, of longing, of spirituality – only its traversal through already existing sonic fields of poetic diction. The languor of the poet belongs also to a poetic language that is heavy with atmosphere, like Keats's negative capability, full of the potential to be transformed into a poetics of energy. 'A poem is energy' Charles Olson wrote 'transferred from where the poet got it . . . by way of the poem itself to, all the way over to, the reader'[27] and this implies a singular channel of energy. What a transfer of sound as energy might be like as it is found already reverberating across existing multiple linguistic and cultural contexts is what resonates throughout Gizzi's 'Field Recordings', where the sound is always figured as more than 'just for itself' alone, cast as it is in relation to what poetic, cultural and social conditions are sounded through and by it.

3. Spahr's Park as Field Recording

> When one fled past, a maniac maid,
> And her name was Hope, she said.

Juliana Spahr borrows this epigraph from Shelley's 'The Mask of Anarchy', which was originally written in 1819 after the notorious Peterloo Massacre in Manchester, for her collection *That Winter the Wolf Came* (2015).[28] Spahr's poem was written in response to the Occupy Oakland movement of 2012–13. The effect of the epigraph is to partially and playfully frame her poems as the writing of the 'maniac maid' called 'Hope'. The poems explore the mania and the hope of the conditions of their production, with Spahr as a participant and recorder of the demonstrations and particular fields of protest of the Occupy movement.

'Transitory, Momentary' records the occupation of a park that is doomed to 'headquarter an oil company' (p. 13). The poem alludes to the fragility and destruction of the environment at the hands of global corporations. The syntax of the poem is constructed as a series of 'low wavering lines' (p. 11). Contextual references emerge apparently disparately at first, and as the poem progresses in successive and circular return, to form closer and closer conceptual *fields* that overlap and extend the physical dimensions of the actual park under threat. Observations on Brent geese, the price of crude oil, a song overheard in a bar in Oakland and the occupation of the field by protestors (who include the poet and her son), move from stark juxtaposition towards the gradual evocation of a heightened sense of an interlinked entanglement between things, persons and ideas across fields. The syntactic patterning of the poem and its lyric sounding runs counter to the apparent bleak futility of the epigraph, a momentary record of the fleeting sense of hope that the engagement in the political protest and its poetics might bring. Spahr's sounding through juxtaposition can be read as a necessary recontextualisation of ideological (and often suppressed) noise into a poetics of writing as field recording.

As if in an extension of Cage's famous 4'33", it is not only that all environmental sounds might be heard as music but that all such 'soundings' might be part of the lyric poem. As Berger writes, in 'that field' of actual and remembered perceptual association: 'I could listen to all sounds, all music' (p. 31). Spahr's writing records the synchronicity of sensing as conceptual, associative and physical in relation to both the immediate environment and also its unseen personal and ideological markers: even and perhaps especially the price of crude oil. All sounds are music but the resonance of the immediate environment is not the only field of listening to be accessed in multiple soundings through multiple temporal and associative frames. As in Westerkamp's analysis of the potentially productive effect of the noisy yoga studio on its participants, the process leaves open the possibility that this may not be an especially comfortable encounter.

In Spahr's 'Transitory, Momentary', these temporal and associative frames have very material implications. As if in a rewriting of Olsonian poetics, the central fact of this SPACE, its ownership and future use are contested by the mother and child among the community of protestors. The specificity of the actual field, its current and past use, and the importance of its geographical and spatial features as a potential future resource for others to appropriate are all too clearly articulated in the description of the removal of the protestors by the police: 'They know what they are doing. It is their third time clearing the park and they will clear it many more times and then they will win and a building will be built there where there once was the park' (Spahr, pp. 11–12).

Although the context is very different, there are a number of connections to be made here to that part of Berger's essay in which he records how he is 'obliged to wait' at the level crossing: 'It is as though these minutes fill a certain area of time which exactly fits the spatial area of the field. Time and space conjoin' (p. 32). The caesura in the title of Spahr's poem 'Transitory, Momentary' enacts a similar spatial and temporal suspension as Berger's imposed wait. It is this momentary suspension that opens up the possibility of other modes of attention to the contemporary and therefore other modes of recording practice that have the potential to come about through an uninvited suspension in direction, this even though Spahr's experience is somewhat at odds with Berger's own more leisurely wait before a very different and apparently uncontested field.

In her poem 'Brent Crude' (the subsequent poem in this collection) the time and space of the poem are marked by the relationship of the time of writing to the price of Brent Crude Oil. Brent is at once a geographical marker (a river), the name of a goose and also the name of a global oil corporation. In 'Transitory Momentary', observations of the behaviour of the Brent geese as they migrate from Europe to Canada are introduced alongside observations on the oil company's naming of their Scottish oil fields after the names of water birds: 'in alphabetical order: Auk, Brent Cormorant, Dunlin, Eider, Fulmar and so on' (p. 13). Nature and the natural world are threatened physically and co-opted metaphorically: 'Brent is also an acronym for the Jurassic Brent formation that makes up the Brent oilfield, for Broom, Rannoch, Etive, Ness, and Tarbet' (p. 13). Spahr's poem suggests a relationship between the co-option of the language of birds and of landscape by the oil industry, in ways that seem familiar, romantic, natural even, and traditional poetic discourse in relation to nature. Her poem draws attention to the way in which the lexicon of the so-called natural world is actually an index for the very forces that threaten to destroy it. On the other hand, the 'new gasses' do not yet have a name and this makes it more difficult for the protesters to record the events of the field with any certainty. The dispersed indeterminacy of Spahr's poem is the chosen mode of record that attempts to recover this event: the physical, political and ineffable tracings of exploitation of what Olson so confidently termed SPACE. The poem presents the reader with a visual and sonic recording of this field:

> While a formation of police clear the far side of the park of the debris of its occupation, another formation of police on the other side shoot the new gasses, the ones we do no yet know by name, into another part of the park where people are clustered. This camera has sound and every few seconds there is a pop. It is unevenly steady. The song is just about

two people who are not near each other, who have probably chosen not to be near each other any more. (pp. 13–14)

This field recording in writing is attentive to the territorial claims on the field. And this emerges as a series of very particular sounds in relation to the force being used by the police to clear the field. Placed in relation to these sounds of the occupation (the 'pops' that unbalance the camera), the writing of sound and song are repeatedly invoked, often as if these were only details of slight significance and signification: 'I want to give you this song sung in a bar in Oakland one night during the ongoing oil wars' (p. 12) writes Spahr. The apparently off-hand comment belies the significance of the phrase as an assertion of a geographical, political and temporal marker, one that both distinguishes the poem that we are reading from the song in her memory and merges with it. Overheard by chance, this poem is also that song. It is a song of loss that can be applied to many different local and universal contexts:

> In this song, as is true of many songs, it is unclear why the singer has lost something, maybe someone. In this time, the time of the oil wars, there are many reasons that singers give for being so lost. Often they feel lost because of love. Sometimes they are lost because of drugs. Sometimes they have lost their country and in their heart it feels as if they have lost something big. And then sometimes they are lost just because they are in Bakersfield. Really though they are lost because in this time song holds loss. And this time is a time of loss. (Spahr, p. 12)

If there is loss, then there is also an accrual and a redistribution of these found soundings. The spatial and 'methodological field' of Spahr's poem incorporates a number of paratactical devices as the basis for its structures. In an apparent act of reappropriation, 'Transitory, Momentary' shares some metaphorical similarities with the stuff at the centre of this contested field. The complex blending of the poem, which takes place at the level of the whole rather than at the level of the sentence, bears comparison with the blended nature of oil itself: 'It contains approximately 0.37% of sulphur, classifying it as sweet crude, yet not as sweet as West Texas Intermediate' (p. 13), writes Spahr in a line that could be reads a comment on the poem's own apparent sweetness, with its ostensible references to birds, the pastoral, childhood and lost love.

Like Gizzi's 'Field Recordings', Spahr's 'Transitory, Momentary' establishes a metaphorical relation between song, poetry and poetics.

The fact that this is a song overheard in a bar appears to divert the poem's affinities from the classical lyric tradition but in its persistence it continues to draw attention to the connection rather than delegitimise it. Spahr articulates the poetics of the poem through an implied similarity to the bar singer's song of loss, which turns around a series of refrains. In Spahr's poem these refrains mark a return to various fields of connected exploration: oil, song/poetics and political action. However, it is the affect of the song that gives rise to one of the most important markers of Spahr's poem: that of feeling in relation to the political action, which is itself, 'transitory, momentary'. It is the epiphanic nature of song which captures the poet's own intense reaction to the singer songwriter's song. It is recognition of this intensity of feeling for song that renews the poet's belief in art:

> It is just an observation, a small observation that sometimes art can hold the oil wars and all that they mean and might yet mean within. Just as sometimes there are seven stanzas in a song. And just as sometimes there is a refrain between each stanza. And just as often this sort of song tells a certain story, one about having something and then losing it. (p. 11)

The sound of the song is in direct contrast to the powerful recording of the near-silent action performed by the protestors:

> All pass bricks, one by one, down the line so as to make a pile. They are silent for the most part, silent enough that it is possible to hear the bricks make a clink as they fall. The pile gets bigger and bigger. It is waist high. Then chest high. Some get out of the line and climb on the pile, hold both their hands in the air because they know now is transitory, momentary triumph and it should be felt. (p. 14)

4. Shimmering Fields

It is this felt listening towards the recording in writing which is so important to Berger, Spahr and Gizzi, and that marks a shape for the space of attention for their poetics of the field recording. Each engages in a mode of associative poetic song. In the case of Spahr and Gizzi the effect is to make us suspicious of the complicity of language in the making of such a sweet record, an effect found in Spahr's poem through her suspicion of this transfer of affect from the name of the bird to an oilrig. As Gizzi puts it, it is important to understand 'That / the index was a lyre', a clause which enacts an ongoing sense of commitment but also suspicion towards the field of language that begins to attune us to the necessary – if anxious and disruptive sound-ings – of a poetics of environmental listening as writing. Writing the recording proposes this listening as near simultaneous to the writing of the record in careful attention to the variable surfaces of linguistic use, buried relational contexts and lost songs, as Barthes puts it: 'the very dispersion, the shimmering of signifiers, ceaselessly restored to a listening which ceaselessly produces new ones from them without ever arresting their meaning . . .'.[29]

What these works demonstrate is a writing of the field recording that is itself a mode of attention, an attentively angled methodology of textual practice that reverberates with a poetics of sonority – not 'sound just for itself' but an environmental, political and social encounter between the writer and the world around them.

Notes

1. Jean-Luc Nancy, *Listening*, trans. Charlotte Mendall (New York: Fordham University Press, 2007). 'Un des aspects de ma question sera donc: de quel secret s'agit-il lorsqu'on écoute proprement, c'est-à-dire lorsqu'on s'efforce de capter ou de surprendre la sonorité plutôt que le message? Quel secret se livre – donc aussi se rend public – lorsque nous écoutons pour eux-mêmes une voix, un instrument ou un bruit?' Jean-Luc Nancy, *A l'écoute* (Paris: Galilée, 2002), p. 17.
2. In this mode, Bernie Krause's environmental soundscapes have in recent years offered an increasingly terrifying record of the shrinking field of ani-mal habitats. His field recordings confront the listener directly with the evidence of the destruction of the natural environment (see Bernie Krause, *Winds across the Tundra*, CD (Wild Sanctuary Communications, 2002)).
3. John Berger, 'Field', p. 31. All references to 'Field' are to the essay as reprinted in this book, with page numbers given in the text.
4. R. Murray Schafer, *The Soundscape: Our Sonic Environment and the Tuning of the World* (New York: Knopf, 1977), p. 10.
5. Pauline Oliveros, *Deep Listening: A Composer's Sound Practice* (New York: iUniverse, 2005), p. 13.
6. Hildegard Westerkamp, 'The Disruptive Nature of Listening', Keynote Address International Symposium on Electronic Art, Vancouver, BC, 18 August 2015. Available at http://www.sfu.ca/~westerka/writings%20page/articles%20pages/disruptive.html (last accessed 21 September 2016).
7. Roland Barthes, *Image, Music, Text* [1978], trans. Stephen Heath (London: Fontana Press, 1993), p. 179.

8. Rosalind Krauss, 'Sculpture in the Expanded Field', *October* 8 (Spring 1979): 30–44, p. 38.

9. Eve Meltzer, *Systems We Have Loved: Conceptual Art, Affect, and the Antihumanist Turn* (Chicago: Chicago University Press, 2013), p. 120.

10. Charles Olson, 'Projective Verse', manifesto [1950], in *Collected Prose*, ed. Donald Allen and Benjamin Friedlander (Oakland: University of California Press, 1997), pp. 239–49.

11. Charles Olson, 'Call Me Ishmael' [1947], in *Collected Prose*, p. 17.

12. 'The main thing people would do would be *to drift around all the time*. Changing landscapes from one hour to the next would end with complete removal from one's habitual surroundings'. Gilles Ivain, 'Formula for a New City' in *Leaving the 20ᵗʰ Century: The Incomplete Work of the Situationist International*, ed. Christopher Gray (London: Rebel Press, 1988), p. 17.

13. Guy Debord, 'Traffic', in Gray (ed.), *Leaving the 20ᵗʰ Century*, p. 19.

14. Oliveros, *Deep Listening*, p. 46.

15. 'Le Texte, lui est un champ méthodologique'. Roland Barthes, 'De l'œuvre au texte', in Barthes, *L'Obvie et l'obtus: Essais crtiques III* (Paris: Seuil, 1982), p. 73; English translation: 'From Work to Text' in *The Rustle of Language*, trans. Russell Howard (Oxford: Blackwell, 1986), p. 57.

16. Barthes, 'From Work to Text', p. 58.

17. '. . . c'est l'œuvre qui est le queue imaginaire du Texte. Ou encore: le Texte ne s'éprouve que dans un travail, une production'. Barthes, 'De l'œuvre au texte', p. 73.

18. Peter Gizzi, *Archeophonics* (Middletown, CT: Wesleyan University Press, 2016), pp. 15–16.

19. Arthur Rimbaud, *Illuminations* [1886], trans. John Ashbery (New York: W. W. Norton & Co., 2011).

20. 'Mais aussi, l'écoute, c'est ce qui sonde'. Roland Barthes, 'Ecoute' in *L'Obvie et l'obtus*, p. 222. English translation: 'Listening' in *The Responsibility of Forms: Critical Essays on Music, Art, and Representation*, trans. Richard Howard (Berkeley: University of California Press, 1991), p. 250.

21. Barthes, 'Listening', p. 258.

22. Ibid., p. 246.

23. Gillian White, *Lyric Shame: The 'Lyric' Subject of Contemporary American Poetry* (Harvard: Harvard University Press, 2014).

24. Schafer, 'The Soundscape', p. 132.

25. Frank O'Hara, *The Collected Poems of Frank O'Hara*, ed. Donald Allen (University of California Press, 1995), p. 261.

26. 'Langour', *Oxford English Dictionary* (Oxford: Oxford University Press).

27. Olson, 'Projective Verse', p. 240.

28. Juliana Spahr, *That Winter the Wolf Came* (Berkeley: Commune Editions, 2015). All subsequent references to this collection are given in the text.

29. Barthes, 'Listening', p. 259. Barthes, 'Ecoute', p. 229. 'En troisième lieu, ce qui est écouté ici et la (principalement dans le champ de l'art, dont la fonction est souvent utopiste), ce n'est pas la venue d'un signifié, objet d'une reconnaissance ou d'un déchiffrement, c'est la dispersion même, le miroitement des signifiants, sans cesse remis dans la course d'une écoute qui en produit sans cesse des nouveaux, sans jamais arrêter le sens: ce phénomène de miroitement s'appelle la significance (distinct de la signification) . . .'.

Part Three

The Field in Practice

Bittern space, a siskin

Patrick Farmer

Bittern space, a siskin.

Between 2013 and 2015 I published three short books concerned with sound, listening, and...

ry i bark was written in Mooste, Estonia; *wild horses think of nothing else the sea*, whilst walking the welsh coast; and *Yew Grotesque*, as I walked in and around Grizedale Forest in Cumbria. I consider the three books to be a species of triangle, a series of de-centred perspectives that behave in waveforms.

Each book acts like a knot of the other in a spawn of its own accords.

ry i bark is something of an outside, akin to a heard poem; *wild horses...* is more of an internal artefact, a slow mapping of fluctuating expanse; *Yew Grotesque*, the third publication, holds up a mirror to their echoes.

Composition spins like a wheel of place, sending and receiving signals in a fog of form and content.

Bittern space, a siskin is an attempt to transform parts of these books into relations of audition, to extract elements of sound from them in the guise of listening's multiplicitous qualities and the myriad modalities of writing. This is a process that can perhaps be likened to carpentry, planing the lines framed by the dimensions of the page, picking shavings up off the floor, endlessly arranging them into trivial giants.

Writing about the writing of sound and listening can relate as the concurrent creation and destruction of perspective and memory. *Bittern space...* is not an attempt to make less legible meanings of sounds legible. Likewise, it does not seek to make them even less legible than they seem to be. It follows that it is not an attempt to clarify what I think I mean, in a singular sense, when I attempt to write listening. I have no desire to fold a concrete relation between sound and text. I am not even sure that listening can be written.

The reflections of the texts herein correspond to processes of speculative listening and remain, as far as possible, incredulous to the origins and destinations of reception.

try i bark sounds as if it is subliminally afraid of the edges that exist at the ends of its many cracks. Such edges are not only those of the page, the ostensible presence of a frame, but the edges of words, sentences, sounds, the very heart of it, the resonant frequency of a place lost among a contingency of indefinite revolutions. The book projects this in an abstract and meaningless sense, which is to say, it did not plan on such encounters.

wild horses... takes this elsewhere by pointing at its own faults, attempting to form shells of edges, erecting downward statues to reach and record the elements that are themselves texts between land and sea.

Yew Grotesque is a loving of such wayward places, diving into them as if it were a cormorant. It is a book of adoration, moving through its various speculative auditions under the dappled echoes of birds and querulous reflections of mirrors. It laps up water from the footprints of close words.

Writing sound and listening. Moving in place as phonemes and meaning intertwine. Can place be raised from the buoyant vessels of oxymoroni imagination? Flattening any number of opposites onto the surface of the page that is a lichen in the oscillating ruins of thought. Can it be heard in the imperious concern for equilibrium, in a writing that attempts to oppose from one moment to the next, any degree of variation?

As I write, do I double up with listening's exigency? Does a reader push an emergence, vivipararity, out of the seeming stillness of the line just as vibration, echo, is thrown out of the cochlea? Perhaps this imagined coupling is a gesture to the ongoing sensibility of relation and equivalence like a brain calling to language, or time rattling a skull; the beauty of bookends, an imposition rather than a beginning. Can we identify with our own listening, or is such recognition the fleeting desire of unidentifiable difference? Is to write about sound and listening to encounter an endless palinode?

This commentary imagines that it exists among the tense edges of three books. Amorphous strata. Liminal place. Sounds can be pulled in as well as pushed through. The more I listen (the more I write about listening) the more it edges.

Holding open the void, Grey hands it to himself. The room is a series of boxes within boxes, each one trying to depart and move into the other. He is the cold–standing–waiting–figure between them all. On his back in the dark, stiff limbs, his eyes break the balance, coming to rest on the ceiling to which the night before he had pinned the conference schedule.

o

Sound moves in with the silence. The prefigured boxes become rooms in a projected flow of close images. Looking across the mirror and up to the words forming words, Grey reads slowly, becoming slower as he moves down the list, pausing between names to hear the pause that becomes longer between the words that break.

From *Yew Grotesque*

On his back in the dark
A parasite in the single sentence of an ear, hectocotylus, a madness of arms
seals the ostiole, denying light and air. From inside rises sound as a voice
growing taller over a wall constantly converging into a dent. One sculpture
a hand survives the descent. The wall is bent in its yellow and the hand calls
from the underneath the fumitory.

On the ceiling to which the night before he had pinned the conference schedu
In quick succession a plaster hand and a note of empty images with regards
to the in-exactness of the cast pour over the wall. The note is hand-typed
and evenly-spaced, its occasional mistakes jut out like a bright work of
inexact personalities. It is a fandango that arrives without warning, still in it
existence without sense. The typography denotes (it is simply so) a collapse
that was premeditated, beating over the wall and landing like spring. An
arch was replaced with the muffled sound of laughter as the hand came to
ground. Not a crack on its surface. On closer inspection, the ungraspable
refractions of precipitation and condensation along the many manipulated
joins and narrows leave internal speech repeating something along the line -
we propose to disintegrate as we please. The sounds in their descent are tho
that keep up the mind, a sadness on another side of a wall, red swells on a
seagull's hook, sending things into masks and boxes as the bird lands on the
reassurance of its clench. The force of the fall turned sound over.

A projected flow of close images
Slow creatures and the smoke of the earth. Letters planted close together
and competing for yeast water. The grammar of space requires unlimited
thickness, cold bodies wanting to blow on the thin face of the mould.
Between concords of issue and reception. To write is to be struck in the ear,
shown in the face.

To hear the pause that becomes longer between the words that break
Bending the personality the more we listen in. Words break on our ears
as wood does under an axe. If we choose to listen we feed, hear degrees in
fields of collapsing dissimilitude, knee-high and deep attractions, overgrov
grasshoppers. Passive we, hear metamorphoses of signals, rush stridulating
crowds of listening forever.

denouement, for want of nothing else, not everything
anything, the negation of other or else–

              hands willingly place the virtues of not thinking in writing

else, anything than the other else remembers the other in spite this all else
anything, causes prevalence

not, anything else–
motacilla alba flings in and out, point to pointing spontaneous, displaying always unknown motion

From *try i*   *bark*

nouement

u know its name, the banks
laden with day, like the name,
u feel it out, with your hand:
ba.'   Paul Celan, *Tabernacle Window.*

e plaster hand and the *alba* are sacrificial anodes, one is the other, passing
er and parting at dawn – a time and a mark of quiet feet–they search for the
er with hidden ears. Catch my short sight in your wing, your spine, your
sent pinnae, says. Your feathers cannot undo my knotted nature.

rcing the hand, myopia, silent words convulse the spine of rash and
ick decisions, projections bend and bruise the source for lack of place
d a contrasting explanation. This listening is not straight and not clear,
e distinction that is burdened by orientation is a transluscent opening
closing. Nets can be deployed if we desire to know which way we listen.
lationships are a celebration of perplexity, every thought reaches infinite
undaries. Where might the struggle take? The growing echo of an inner
ice reads from the closing of books.

hands willingly place the virtues of not thinking in writing
The resolve of the hand as a writing hand found in mud. The approach of
a perspective compared to which ours had lost all interest. A patient hand.
Now it is here. We ask ourselves if it should be called a hand at all. The net
lines would connote a thing, as is expected, watched and treated from many
angles at once. This thing receives from numerous perspectives and tensions
though it fell from only one. How many angles is it possible to conceive at
once? Perhaps it is best to consider this object and our understanding of it
in light of its actions. It could not see over the wall, yet it was determined to
exist. The protruding speckle of colour wished for its own vantage point. It
is not so much a thing as a place, a place that opens up temporal emissions
from which to compose. All of this happens in silence. 'I'm going to write
now, as my hand moves.'

Motacilla alba flings in and out
The hand and the *alba* wish to be the same – though both are by definition
plural – it is a combusatable ash grey, it is an underside flecked with yellow,
like an eel. Interpreting the dimorphism by washing in the imagination of
the other. This is the case, says, without words. It carries a folding bird in
the beak as the sky moves muscles as an unfolding. How might we speak, or
think of only the one thing, it evades our finality, and laughs at the captivity
of our jocular and disparate minds. How is this it, says, and what do we
do, if it is not? What does the heart tell us about the ear? One always in
need of more than the other can give. Are we children trying to catch our
condensing breath? Speaking in front of an obscured reflection we feel in
the voice that an l is missing from the ear. Is it possible you do not exist?
says. That would be cause for great sorrow, if we were nothing of life, says,
emerging from several equivalences into a place where projections converge
Who would opposites be, if that were so? Looking out of the nothing over
hear. Words lost in words with an invisible heart.

The hand now resides on a desk by an open window, its keeper,
unidentifiable shade, professes a fondness for it that exceeds any feelings
extended toward the hands of others. The writing hand is no longer clean,
but it is the only possibility.

Limitless–Transparent–Skin

ry i   bark is part of a strange
nd intermediary attention paid to
he pervading and evasive natures
f sensation and sensibility, the
hings one does not attend to whilst
evertheless attending. It was written
s part of a residency at MOKS in
stonia, and is a seeming product
f removal, by which I mean the
bstracted state in which I wrote.
Virginia Woolf has called this, 'non-
eing', a sort of becoming that is
ot lived consciously, an inability
o recall aspects and events of place
mongst particulars that re-arrange
ersonality, the furrow and cause of
rojections, a time that unidentifies.

vents wipe lines of walking like a
ockerel that competes with its echo.
vents want to respond but cannot
ecause environment absorbs the
ext.

My readings of *try i   bark* are part
of an immanent understanding post-
ublication. Predicated on the things
hat happen when one is not paying
ttention, an unpredictable scattering
of the binary, an inability to recognise
oneself after writing.

try i   bark smells of the arboreal
heat of an Estonian July. Myriad
horse-flies and tics maintain a tense
situation.

Wool is felt in its abundance as a
material that in its composition
and touch serves to push the writer
outward away from the empirical
form of the sentences and toward the
unimagined reader.

The abstraction of wool as the
pulsating cortices of the book
connotes scattered pockets of density
and void. There is an understated
proximity that enables the reader to
pick through the pages as wished.
Muffled scree of neurological material,
akin to holding palms of wool over
pinnae. Lateral paths of association
and dimensionality.

Trailing this inverse topography can
enable words to be experienced in
ways that numb the ostensibly formal
nature of their publication.

The materiality of wool is a restless
map of invisible form, a microcosmic
literary and environmental pattern
that shows up in the atmosphere
of a poem. Clumps of floccus lay
still under the light-ice of clouds
that shine over somnolent lids like
teleconnectic effects over curvilinear
filaments.

Many poets and scholars tend to the life and noise underneath words. Barbara Guest writes of the 'invisible architecture' that can support a poem, constantly being re-built in light of the imagination. Charles Baudelaire also conceived of many analogous structures, though perhaps the most apt here is the life of the Thyrsus, a staff, or straight line, of giant fennel covered in ivy, a correspondent arabesque of wild and tamed metric, a supposed time, a light that is a loss of memory.

In his prose poem, 'Thyrsus', Baudelaire uses its potentially contentious image as a way of further amplifying the blurred boundaries of poetry and prose, considering the essential nature of both as co-extensions of each other, a dualism both itenerant and established, like its mythological wielder, Dionysus. In detailing their intertwined lives and the oft-reciprocal and extended nature of duality as a fluid system, pulsating like a limitless station of meaning and depiction, Baudelaire points at the singular beams defined by their differences in the omni-structural symmetry of *Paris Spleen*:

'Who would dare to decide whether the flowers and tendrils were made for the stick, or whether the stick is only present for revealing the beauty of the flowers and tendrils?'

This is a clear and impish enjoymen of equivalent measure as the poe traces dry fingers over the edge of the line, creating a residue c indistinguishable cause and effect.

As the Thyrsus rattles the know becomes the found.

Like writing and reading we liste for the inherent gaps of perspectiv in words as if they were part of relationship that connotes a continua reapplication of balance that itsel accounts for, and often demands, th existence of these contradictions and antinomies.

Words posture like marks betweei the crawling tendrils and smoke o arabesques. Patterns are like a lake o migratory birds, corresponding and inaudible lights, the polytropic nature of language that cluster among vector of energy underneath walking line that change in accordance to the lif of the reader.

Such synergy enables a constan ejection of fragrance and colour into the world, promoting readings o renewal.

An atmosphere of these three book articulates an injection of writing into writing, an extension, or even a performance, where one has no idea any one is present.

Eyes closed to the marram of foundation. Sweet inflection unawares the tuneless relationship between wind and sand. Pushes sag into a compressed sand. Basking a ways forward sag games for our own interpretation, and of course have an explanation. Sit and wish for the ears of sand. To be deafened, sucked up into the vents of gulls, eggs vanish miles out to sea plastic. Hearing borders and lights up to a threshold heard in always for the first time in speechless words always hovering, squawking. What is there left of hearing to hear? And why must I ask I continually ask. Is **that how in light of thoughtless stretches, sea. Mr. grubby preens a series of cadence? Shells and falling forests in their science vested implications move forth physical composition to statistic, to contradict (every tree) (writing) the same event write**

From *wild horses...*

Eyes close to the marram of foundation
One of the etymological lives of Down is that of a shortened Old English form of dune. Dunes and marram grass are scattered throughout *wild horses...*, they are its ground, or down-ness, part of the low element of the pages that are sunk full of decomposing shells, infinitesimal plastic nodes, and algae. We might imagine the continuous structure of marram as analogous to the myriad networks that move across various sections of the books, linking tropes and sounds by way of accumulation, metabolism, echo, repetition, and cut. Stacked words and sounds. Clearing place so we might speculate language in terms of listening and listening in terms of language. In such ephemeral frames we might focus on making strange the qualities of listening and their plurivalent states, readings that span the sediment and invisible tiers of the texts. We might listen out for that which shimmers, only to disappear at the foot of it, allowing it to enter us and stack.

The tuneless relationship between wind and sand
wild horses... is a residue of the walk that is itself a remembrance of
topographical and phantom things. What is down there in the sound of the
word dune? A sound that absorbs its own messages. Under the dunes where
there is no air, a sinew of life, no path, and darkness, there is potential of
collapse. The sound of a word barely begins to scratch out its own contours
or resounding variousness before it disappears. The image of a dune denotes
a rising structure, but of course there are the inevitable opposites and accords
prevalent in all words. The roots of marram grow in all directions in order
that the dune may keep its particular ground. Marram is a word whose
movement is found in its sound, heard over wild distances. Such sounds, the
spectrums of condition and often unknown possibility from its two syllables,
belong to the history of gnawing animals and the upkeep of vegetation,
mineral, and colour. Marram holds the book together and yet opens it out
beyond the senses or its history into a bottomless nature. It is the metric, the
palimpsestic prints left in the dunes by animals matted by wind. It binds the
book in transience, vocabulary, and structure.

Sit and wish for the ears of sand
The Aeolian nature of the dunes I encountered on my walk (Ynyslas
in Ceredigion is one of the last Aeolian dune structures left in the UK)
provided an ample bed into which vocabulary dug as I slept, creating ample
resonances around which the physicality of sand and its forms poured
through the text.

What is there left of hearing to hear?
Can sound act as a medium in which the imagination moves, vibrating it
as a type of transient matter? Sound moves in waves, thus so might the
imagination, into, through, and removing things. Talk of the in-between is an
abstraction, gifted, both from the imagination and reality. Sounds of words or
things that make no sound can still make a sound in the imagination, often
acting as a pretext for poetry, where noise can move in and out of elastic
geography. It is here that the sound of the voice crawls out of words and
into the sea. To speak of it the reader swims into the production of fluttering
marks, flowing from the current of the outside that the poet is occasionally
allowed to swim against.

I've often attempted to re-write pages from *wild horses...*, focussing on the
exfoliation, suggestibility, and illegibility of phonemes, extracting myriad
sounds out of the words in order that they may form a slopped roof of their
own composites.

The Book of Good Noise

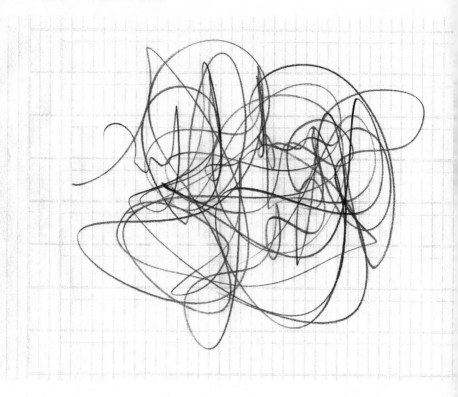

Fetch Lime for Horses

e writing of *wild horses...* reflects
apposition to nature. Looking out
d listening to sea, it attempts to fold
o vantages of place. The surface
1 be calm, it can be monstorous, a
dable thing that can be listened to,
ding sound there in the stillness.
derneath the poem, in the things
d the stuff, the fierceness and the
nstancy of life, we go back there,
ain and again, returning, resorting,
uilding, rethinking, to the fury of
e on the surface.

I began to write and walk *wild*
rses... my awareness of the plural
iverse of water in William Carlos
illiams's epic poem of place,
terson – published between 1946
d 1958 in five parts, with Williams
orking on a sixth as he passed
'ay – was paramount in my attempt
focus on the life all around me as
valked.

location walked through was one
ng or another thing, everything felt
e it was taking apart in concentric
d close motion.

resolute life of creative tension,
at of permanent attentiveness, will
urn and project as much 'positive'
'negative'. Birds both reveal
d absorb the sky. As I tried to
ange such perspectives, I returned
Williams:

ly two leading forces were trying
know life and trying to find a
hnique of verse.'

My preoccupation with *Paterson*
resides in Williams' practise of
listening to others, and of finding his
listening in things, to strangers on a
bus as much as waterfalls. Initially I
was more concerned with the latter,
being as that was where I saw myself,
as a listener of and to things, but
slowly the construct expanded to
focus on relationships, that is to say,
not only literal relationships, but the
distance accorded to liminality.

How much does one need listen to
oneself in order to begin to listen to
anything other? A syrinx of breath in
taxa, expanding negative affirmation.

As Williams wrote *Paterson* he lived
and listened in the webs of the other
Paterson, working to hear a language
that spoke to the dissimilarities of
of human life. By quartering the
subliminal maw,   silence crashes
about the metropolis. The noise of
the Passaic falls, wherein the mass of
Paterson begins, reflects in its spew the
white noise of speech, the difficulty
in listening to the energy that exists
behind relentless appearence.   The
Passaic River mirrors the course of
Williams' life as he searches for his
language, walking the firm banks of
decomposition.

The Passaic is matter from which
the inhabitants of Paterson tacitly
draw their history. The water of the
falls, the constant energy of life and
imagination, rolls up over the lavish
absence of osseous labyrinths.

Dominating the folds of *wild horses...* is an attempted treatment of sound as that which is always already there, in scant need of decoration or company.

Sound plays every relation in *wild horses...* it is its own company, and yet I feel it can only be heard on the quietest of its surfaces.

In these surroundings text attempts to suture itself to the tissue of innumerable centers of convulsive environment in order to transform through its being into any number of other sounds, images, and things.

The multiple relations of sounds inherent in the book and in the mind of the reader can create zones of speculation. Motion between listening and its textual representations, resonating slabs, little stars.

The mud of listening and the silt poetry are often conjunct in th ability to obscure perspective. List relative orientation of inside a outside lost to the tumult of a mi unable to separate itself, relentle seperate, mute utter distinctic Inner and outer surfaces of the pa shadow the reciprocal network tl runs through the lines. An impressi that they are all there is.

I found that Oswald Egger's Roc of Rumour: Tunings, pulls a simi measure out of reading, like feeli for omni-intuitions underneath exposure of neurons to the soun of words. Egger's room is a text tl arranges thermodynamic sequenc of transformation, a place whe vestibular ataxia swallows a reflection.

'nothing vanishes, nothing remai nothing follows'

Projecting onto this entropic triad attempt to render listening into object, encounter discord sealing a stacking, think, 'nothing vanishes'. we are convinced of a truth of so oft thinking new thoughts, trembli instants, and not just listening ourselves formerly listening, it is ea to forget about that which is alrea there, a hue of between, 'nothi remains'. As we listen we assemI reminders toward things alrea known, writing like we are learnir trying to discover what lies behir listening, 'nothing follows'.

gain

motacilla alba reminds me   initially
                means backwards of forwards inside of down *hirundo rustica*
searches for its self corners
                        hearing reflection of looking
small

                a fly behind a pane of glass

                                From *try i   bark*

ı fly behind a pane of glass
 realise now that this refers to the end sequence of Luis Buñuel's last film,
That Obscure Object of Desire. To the hive of symbolic embroidery (interlaced
ıgures in a modern arcade soon to be reduced to rubble, fixing and
ınravelling on the surface of a torn mantilla) amidst ambiguously reflexive
 positions of fantasy. The height of many realities condensed to a speck. The
ıeed to master objects and the need of objects. After I had been fortunate
o see her through a pane of glass, the only thing I wanted in my life, was to
eel that great pleasure again. The walled space of increasing interiority. Our
ives were exacted on a variety of scales. Her was a moment of flux found in
contempt, inaudible words that heard in themselves other languages, their
own steady differences. Witnessed in the grimace of a face and the soft
ubbing of hands, listening was a mirror of the human world, an incessant
echo of spurious appearances. Pleasure took the place of a pane of glass, and
remained unavailable.

reminds me
We are always saying more than we can say, hearing more than we can hear,
drawing things apart to feel the differences as the heart quickens – we try
with varying results–to bring this to a close. Each of us wants to live like the
other, familiarity disappears between us in a burg of spoken solitude.

means backwards of forwards

When we were five we ran away with our sister, through fields, we have understandably forgotten that we found anxiety to be slowly amputating our escape. We came to halt some miles down the road from our mother's house, resting inside a small stone building, hot grey, once used for housing sheep. Not long after we had unpacked our books and board games a part of the roof, a slab that was already hanging upside down like a crop of feeding birds dislocated, letting in more light than we could understand. A coppery glow absorbed the smell of grease and lanolin, and so we abandoned ourselves back into the humidity. Our memory of this event is silent, slow landing is the sound we have given to both the hand and the slab, being as we heard neither. To smile as if for the first time, Walt, is the sound of it. Vibrations harden like glass inside each other. We had with us a tiny pouch, filled with poppy seeds, on which we would suck and be quiet.

small

One moment few–
grated saffron over black radish is beautiful.
Mango leaves dandelion broom–
precipitates of colour, unrecognisable sunlight dappled by
things and place combine
low citrus gape yell a bronze siskin in the sound charcoal–
History, dust. From the bear of sulphur and stone seam
familiar.

hearing a reflection of looking

To see something other than a language in our language, in that world where our hand rested on your body and we adored it. Where your body welcomed recognised and loved that hand, a consciousness aware of being nothing but a series of unfathomable depths. A limit disappears and swallows the visible waves of a frisson. It is down among the distances that we search for our knotted tongues. In a sinking valley.

searches for its self corners

The existence of indivisible molecules and atoms in the air of escape. The beds we make. The conceit that things have an underside as well as an underneath, an above as well as an equivalent.

what is it to write now.
after everything.
felt–
sat
in similarity.
hearing
all the which is not
seen and also
heard, already gone. noticed in bone.
white trees fly, succumb to nesting as *ardea cinerea* in themselves

ghosts of a landscape reduce the skin to lakes.
stone experienced space.
columbia livica domestica lies over water and no trace.
holes in *nuphar* bring light to dark below.
check my leg for *lasius niger*, please–
an old man wanders between fields and field.

insects on the lakes surface are not holes on the lakes surface

From *try i   bark*

What is it to write now

The full stop lasted two weeks and then removed it. That time, a landscape took the place of a body. We grew listening out of the moment.

ghosts of a landscape reduce the skin to lakes

This might imply the untying of a scene, worn hands dropping objects into their immediate return before turning back to the absence. Spreading out is an understanding predicated after the scene of untying, coiling, recoiling.

heard, already gone. noticed in bone

A sense of wish fulfillment, the knots in the ear, an image of tinnitus in sound, the stacking of blood, hiss as they push past the gaps in the knot. I still find this strange, as if I were projecting a desperate character of escape, revealing the desire to be rid of a certain tread within my physiology. I read this now, early signs of future concerns; the negation and affirmation of listening's qualities in text, a total immersion in listening off the page, creating delineations where there need be none, but there must. Opening and closing the mouth to words, crawling around in a tattered teleology.

white trees fly
The book spreads out like a forest full of teeth, a deathless lustre of mouth wood. We might hear black ants circling fast filaments in concentric measure. Gold, I want you under yellow, with such bright moss you might hunch your shoulders, and I guess to the sound of us. Yours, siskin.

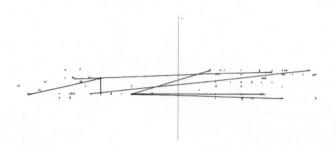

Eidolon / Ideal – one.
Ideal objects appear in sound, to disappear like yellowhammers among courgette flowers. What these phantoms make us think or believe is a chance time of life–how or what we want to hear–inhales us. Listening does not promise, it is itself an *Eidolon*. The world reflection seen in the shades of a mind sowing itself.

Eidolon / Idle – one.
Alba is a number of lines, the lines are direction, direction is energy. The network takes form as a boundary series of yellow stones imperceptible from the ground. Neither the flammable human face nor the deepest ears can rediscover the mirror or echo for which they are searching. Enclosed in the open work that lures us irretrievably towards a sulphur labyrinth, a smell wraps along the yew walls like taught wires pounding against the poles of docked boats, the outline of one shifting to the outline of the other. Gaps in the invisible smoke of the lines claim to evoke emotions we have not hitherto experienced. Thermal walls of greenish yellow on which ideal shadows extinguish the bright space. Unable to hear the slow advance of deconstruction, the conjugation of things with daylight creates beams of transparent yellow, intention folds into affect.

A still movement hinges back to the edge of the water. Black mustard, wolf flowers, sea purslane. We cannot tell from where we are listening, sound is both amplified and subdued along footsteps that extend the perplexity. We cannot listen for lack of privacy.

e remnants of potential sound
countered when we stop reading
different places to the ones felt
we close our mouths. They are
ces that take place from each
her. This is part of the balance of
derstanding between the books,
ding to find betweens that are
mselves surfaces between.

e interrelationships of reading and
aking take form in *wild horses*... as
des of interconnected physical and
ebral resonance. The text vibrates
o its occasion, more distant than
ternal reality. A complex of molar
d molecular difference.

e formation of words and sentences
the mouth and the mind express
rges of meaning beyond and yet
ide everyday meaning, inducing
air of correlation, some matter
issue and return between text and
nd.

e three books span their distances
one book and the geography
t stretches over the writing is
ipiently subsumed below the ink.
ese knotted perceptions come
o the world as if all such things
re occasions not only themselves
t of other occasions – flickering
o resonance, cumulation, and
agination – rolling up into and out
the sea.

The corresponding life of these books
can be imagined as a series of surfaces
in which no one layer transcends
another, where each side of their
surfaces may become a mirror for the
other. It follows that not all activity
need take place in the seeming silence
of a metaphysical reading, the secret
storerooms of thought and language
from which things are seemingly
extracted. It can happen everywhere.

The smallest vats, molecular
grapheme, magnetism of wave,
allusion, enjambment, displacement
of phoneme, caterwaul the paragraph
to condensation, the low frequency
of libraries.

Words can manifest as auras of
a loud bend, as light sources that
obscure outlines. Intertwined in their
concerns, beginning and end move
through imperceptible words and
slip into reflections that burst over
malformed intersections of chance
encounters.

Edges are a pretext for vertiginous
leaps that span anxious chords.
Textures of the quavering ground.
Pieces on an incipient shattering
hand. All of this talk of edges and
bends should not take away from
the surface of the text itself. Taken
together they can form any number
of potentials where the roaming of
interstices becomes a way of reading.

Yew Grotesque provides the third line in the 'triangle' made up of *try i   bark* and *wild horses think of nothing else the sea*. All three (a number of which I am only now beginning to realise the importance) offer a direct and indirect textual correspondence with the experience, concept, and abstraction of listening. The relationships between these publications are typified in the words of Jack Spicer, a poet who felt that his own works 'echo and re-echo against each other', creating resonances that are unable to 'live alone anymore than we can'.

The undertow of the initial publications, located amongst the knots and fluctuating dichotomies of the external and internal, hears its reflection in *Yew Grotesque*, a book stacked full of short sentences and stubborn negations, leaning toward the condition of a possibility. *Yew Grotesque* is a desire to inhabit and reinvent the many divergent angles and qualities of listening unearthed during the writing of the previous two books, it feeds into its own decay.

The triangle between the books not one of Euclidean space. It is r distinct until its sattelites realise th are not alone, finding their cen of gravity among the intimacy voices. The books learn somethi of themselves from each other the place that constructs the sign corresponding between them. Th inhabit an architecture that enab the sounds of the words to mo through the intersections of t medians they appear to be.

If a reading of the triangle can be li listening to a crowd of voices, do that mean the singular points, t books that are themselves differenc are unstable? That they shimmer? listening stable? Does it affirmativ increase uncertainty through t purposeful action of never qu knowing? Pulling things that we apart together.

From *try i   bark*

f

-tracing to re-marking these movements to patterns made and seen in
narkable foraging. The aim is one of deaf representation. The pattern on
e page now makes more sound than the bird that skimmed over the dry
ound. Making the marks left more of a dent on the auditory environment
experienced by bodies, stacking copies in front of the loss. Not to fill but
hide. Many of the letters, giving into the lip, echo under the words that
ce roof. Various memories blocking out the light, a silver birch protrudes
om a conflation of events framed by no singular activity. Two ears protrude
om the skull. *alba* is signal, tracing pathways, transparent.

rtrude Stein writes: 'some one who was living was almost always
tening'. My listening caught sight of the bird at that time, but it made no
und that I could hear, caught up in between absence that suggests sound,
tate that compels me. I am drawn to depict such listening modes as these,
oments of no sound. So what has listening? Full as always of suggestions
sound and memory. Gertrude Stein continues to write: 'some one who
s loving was almost always listening'. My love of birds causes me to listen,
ve is so often a pretext for listening. Listening caught my attention, the
iet skittering of the bird is so often a pretext for writing. Gertrude Stein
ntinues: 'one who was loving was almost always listening'. That one who
s loving was telling about being one then listening. Across the diversity
these truncated words over there is a story that makes up its own sound
ainst its own wishes.

```
d      u s        t            g        r        o un              d
   ed t           o                              du      s      t      gro
                                und
   l          i        n      d      e       r
   d                  u                                s
t
   t              o          dus
   t              gr      ou                      n                      d
```

From *try i   bark*

dus
Is this page an attempt to depict the relationship that exists between the
writer and the already written about? The filter dawns over the senses,
the sounds exhaust the mind, dictate what is put down on the page. The
gaps, the shadows of possibilities, are blobs that forage among the patterns to
create possible routes and find possible sounds. The writer did not move for
the duration yet made more sound than the bird that only moved. It is easy
to imagine the sound, hiss of muscle and wave of beak, opening and closing
on whatever food source or mistake drew the bird in and out. Silent motion
is cause for listening. When one listens to that which makes no sound one
is really listening. The page retains the possibility of making no sound (the
marks eject their phonemes) yet sound always exists on the page, someplace.
As one enters the page it is a recognition of this. I am still recognising what I
heard not what I am hearing, evenly hovering over the skrim of the bird that
got caught up in my attention to the point that I was able to empty it onto
the page, from and onto 'a world of stones'. The letters are over an appearan
that I did not actually have the means of hearing, over an appearance that
did not actually have the means of resounding, which is only sensible,
considering the wide variety of predators in the area.

The writer's sensibility turns a lack of sound in this reality around in the
mind fluttering, attempting to exfoliate the foot into a suggestibility of
distances and potentials.

ɔ

ʾhe double spread that colludes with the erratic residue of the fleeting bird
ɪnfolds the information within its structure. There is no obvious way to
ɛad a field of distended and isolated words, only rarely does the reader find
ɔmething perceptible, and even then, all that it may entail could be a simple
ɪnd lone preposition that in its plurality may well note a relationship between
ʰe mucus of subject and object. The movement and shock of recognition can
ɪury itself deep within a structure, shunting other elements in and out of
ɪerceptive range as it descends and is buried. There is at least one cohesive
ɛntence spread out among the white space – I tend to think of it as a map of
ʰe territory of the book – language combines the landmarks, faint traceries of
ʋords underneath the surface, graphemes roam into multiple connotations
ɪnd flocks of digression.

ʜint at patterns propelled from this small bird and the environment that it
ɛmporarily made me forget. Its voicing seems like the sound on the page
ɔuld be both cause and effect, a result of the perpetual process of landing
ɪnd taking off, the creature, foraging as best it can in the dry earth, creates
ʳoss-hatching relations between the mind and the senses.

    r o u n   *d*

ʌs children, we read *The Floating World*, over and over, from which a
ʋagtail is propelled out of clouds so that it might unearth a geography from
ʰe pre-existent quagmire of mud and silt. Material abounds, constant shift,
ɡranting itself to new perspectives. Today we read tell of Dada the spider,
ɛnt by Amma to set Ogo's chaos in order, 'a cone turning opposite a cone',
ʳtructure from below accident.

```
paper              nautilus
inside             her
| |                open
open               open
```

From *wild horses...*

paper

To imagine a neurological movement of listening could be to conceive of listening as a new mirror or neuron of itself, where everything among sounds a 'reflection once removed'. The bruise and ornament of gossamer shells rise perpetually to surfaces. Great flat tints, a fluid life, repels its centre.

nautilus

'Argo is an object with no other cause than its name, with no other identity than its form' – this is to draw one's own geometry–'for authorities whose hopes / are shaped by mercenaries...'

In 2014 we stayed in a small stone cottage in Trawsfyndd, white caps riddled the mountains and a wind of wet fog encircled wax in the air. Returning from our daily walk around Trawsfynydd lake and away from Basil Spence's power station, a face of no uncertain sound, we slowly placed our feet onto the pristine ice and into a fast scuffle. A resounding pendulum arc caused us to turn, seeing, to our surprise, as we felt nothing, a thing clad from head to toe in a dirt of black material. Its eyes were masked by calcium buoyancy, its mouth detached, dimorphic appendage, a protruding web of respiration. Diving shells compose in fettered light.

In 1965 Liverpool County Council presented a bill to parliament (bypassing the individuals it was to crack in half) in order that they might funnel their increasing urge and need for water (a direct consequence in speed) through the valley of Capel Celyn, a hamlet in Snowdonia. Quaker cemetary, post office, school, clutches of buildings. Funneled ichor in calm above. Seventy slabs of stone fixed into a submerged ground, pushing their quarry into the relentless. A reservoir now covers softening homes in scatter. The underside of a new surface remakes a 'thin glass shell' over the invisible.

open

Devising 'true' and immutable form for the underneath of a poem is no doubt as fruitless as attempting to create an unshakeable hierachy of listening as an qualitative act. Such fleuron and invisible tailpieces need not relate to any universal degree of their own correspondence, held in place like concrete statues that desire to choose between seemingly fixed alternatives. We think of such rippling spaces as impossible labyrinths lit by flowers / roads and headaches raised up to the sound of glittering rubble / fluid psychologica systems traced through bifurcations of a corresponding gaze / 'a street opening and closing'...

Wool—Sea—Glass

Works Cited

arthes, Roland, *Roland Barthes by Roland Barthes* (New York: Hill & Wang, 2010).
audelaire, Charles, *Paris Spleen* (New York: New Directions, 1970).
—— , *The Flowers of Evil* (Oxford: Oxford University Press, 2008).
ergson, Henri, *Creative Evolution: An Alternate Explanation for Darwin's Mechanism of Evolution* (CreateSpace Independent Publishing Platform, 2014).
uñuel, Luis (dir.), *That Obscure Object of Desire* (Studio Canal, 2012).
elan, Paul, *Collected Poems* (London: Penguin, 1996).
ervantes, Miguel de, *Don Quixote* (London: Penguin, 2003).
ixous, Hélène, *Reading with Clarice Lispector* (Mineapolis: University of Minnesota Press, 1990).
reeley, Robert, *Form of Women* (Scaly Mountain, NC: Jargon Books, 1959).
uvier, Georges, *The Animal Kingdom, Arranged in Conformity with Its Organisation* (London: Forgotten Books, 2012).
avenport, Guy, *Da Vinci's Bicycle* (New York: New Directions, 1997).
oolittle, Hilda ('H.D.'), *Helen in Egypt* (New York: New Directions, 1974).
gger, Oswald, *Room of Rumour: Tunings* (Los Angeles: Green Integer, 2004).
orrest-Thomson, Veronica, *Collected Poems* (Shearsman, 2008).
uest, Barbara, *The Collected Poems* (Middletown, CT: Wesleyan University Press, 2008).
owe, Susan, *Spontaneous Particulars: The Telepathy of Archives* (New York: New Directions, 2014).
eats, John, *Selected Letters* (London: Penguin, 2014).
ispector, Clarice, *Agua Viva* (New York: New Directions, 2012).
Mallarmé, Stéphane, *Mallarmé in Prose* (New York: New Directions, 2001).
Moore, Marianne, *Complete Poems* (New York: Penguin 1994).
Olson, Charles, *Maximus Poems* (Berkeley: University of California Press, 1992).
ester, Holly, *go to reception and ask for Sara in red felt tip* (London: Book Works, 2015).
picer, Jack, *My Vocabulary Did This to Me* (Middletown, CT: Wesleyan University Press, 2010).
tein, Gertrude Ada, *A Stein Reader*, ed. Ulla E. Dydo (Evanston: Northwestern University Press, 1993).
tevens, Wallace, *Collected Poetry and Prose* (New York: Library of America, 1997).
Villiams, William Carlos, *Kora in Hell* (New York: New Directions, 1971.
—— , *Paterson* (New York: New Directions, 1995).
Voolf, Virginia, *Moments of Being: Autobiographical Writings* (London: Pimlico, 2002).

Chapter 9

Disquiet*

Lisa Robertson

The agora in time became an indiscriminate container. . . . The fourth century Greek poet Eubolus observed that: 'You will find everything sold together in the same place at Athens: figs, witnesses to summonses, bunches of grapes, turnips, pears, apples, givers of evidence, roses, medlars, porridge, honeycombs, chick-peas, law suits . . . allotment machines, irises, lamps, water clocks, laws, indictments.'

Lewis Mumford, *The City in History*

On ne parle pas seulement de ce qu'on sait, comme pour en faire étalage, – mais aussi de ce qu'on ne sait pas, pour le savoir.

Maurice Merleau-Ponty, *Le Visible et l'invisible*

Callings and Market Stalls

d[9.1]b

I wanted the present to be an ideal library. Infinity, plenum, chaos, dust. I wanted it to be an agora – total availability of the entire thick history of linguistic conviviality and the potential to be completely lost in the strangeness of the civic description.

Duration's artefacts are indiscriminate: the present is disquiet. In the city, law will not be separated out from food; clocks will turn against medlars; irises will be in with lamps. Thus the difficulty.

The present is the encompassing element; in the city more so. I'll define city as a peopled-through sensing. Sometimes I think that the entire history of perceiving is encoded in a city. It's encoded in noise, in shelter, in cloth, in the baths, in stray animals. Noise gives the listener duration as an artefact.

---

* This essay is accompanied by field recordings made at the sites of Atget's documentary photographs of Paris. These are indicated in the following way – d[9.1]b – and are available on the publisher's website at: https://edinburghuniversitypress.com/book-writing-the-field-recording-hb.html [click on the 'resources' tab].

What I am calling noise is the multiply-layered sonic indeterminacy that is the average, fluctuating milieu of dailiness. Here noise does not necessarily pertain to amplitude and intensity, although it might. Using the word 'noise' I want to obliquely approach the irregular and constant fabric of sounding that fluctuates through any given and situated present. Noise is and is not composed; the listener can isolate within its environment individual sounds of various origins, identifiable or not, but no intention or unity structures their overall combination even though that combination has been conditioned by various natural and social factors. Noise is the unwilled surplus produced by the temporal indetermination of conditions and practices in co-movement. Noise has an inchoate shape as weather does – we may measure it, but its movements extend beyond any identifiable cause. Noise exceeds its own identity. It is the extreme of difference. Noise is the non-knowledge of meaning, the by-product of economies.

I like to walk in the city and prefer to be lost. As Rousseau did in certain of his promenades, I'd like to dissolve into the diffuse perceiving of a multiplicity. It is a pleasure to submit to arbitrary directives, to let something outside of one's person determine a route and a mode. So I have, in my walks in Paris, deferred to Rousseau, taking his *Reveries of a Solitary Walker* as my Baedeker, crossing the entire city eastwards, from La Bourse to Menilmontant, or I have followed the ancient industrial Bièvre river, covered over since Haussmann's activities, south-east as far as the outer 13th arrondissement, pausing to listen at drainage grates for its underground movement.

Having walked with Rousseau and an absent river, I decided to follow Eugène Atget. As Rousseau had botanised as he walked, carrying with him his volume of Linnaeus and gathering fragile herbs in his pockets. I would move through the city with my small volume of Atget's photographs and my digital recorder, collecting my own specimens. I wanted to pay simple homage to the combined humbleness and ambition of the photographer of old Paris by visiting the contemporary sites of his photographs with my recording apparatus. I decided to systematically make short recordings of the sound that pulsed through the sites I located. His exposures, I read, were typically counted to 30 seconds; for my sound exposures I imitated him. I would walk, I would listen and I would count. I began because I wanted to make a constraint-based description of the present, using as the terms of my constraint these historical photographs and an idea I had of their maker. I inadvertently embarked on a study of noise. This is its prosody.

Transport

d[9.2]b

Unlike Atget, I did not rise at dawn to make my civic documents. Right away, I parted from my model. This could be how I discovered the luxury of noise. So, although I began my excursions intending to mimic and shadow what I imagined were Atget's own intentions and routes, in my own 30-second exposures what I found was a plenum of movement. I habitually ventured out in early afternoon, in the full economy of day, so I would never hear a clarity; the sound would not become an image. No figure would emerge. The city became random soundfield, and was not a figure either, not separate from field. Listening enmeshed me. I walked within duration. I felt the extreme fragility of time in tandem with the inexperience of my attention. It was like this: an archive of sounding.

When I began my recording walks what I knew of Atget was that he had been a failed actor and painter. In the middle of his life, in the 1890s, he came to Paris and set up as a photographer. He decided to photograph picturesque corners and architectural and decorative details of the city, and he gathered an archive of photographic documents he would offer for sale to editors, painters, architects, builders, illustrators, cabinetmakers, set decorators, and other artists and artisans. The enterprise was successful as a business. A heritage sensibility was institutionally founding itself in Paris, as the excavations for the new Métro began and buildings were razed. Recalling the loss of neighbourhoods and buildings to Haussmann's rationalisation of the city, museum and library archivists sought to document an already mythologised vision of an old Paris before the old city was further destroyed by modernisation. Atget found in this organised nostalgia a reliable economy. Eventually an album of his documents was purchased by the Musée Carnavalet, and over time he sold several such large manila albums to various museums and archives. The Bibliothèque nationale became his steady customer. In these photographic albums he organised, captioned and composed his images by theme – *L'Art dans le vieux Paris, Intérieurs parisiens, La Voiture à Paris, Métiers, Boutiques et étalages de Paris, Enseignes et vieilles boutiques du vieux Paris, Zoniers* and *Fortifications de Paris*. Molly Nesbit discusses these collations at length in her book *Atget's Seven Albums*, describing how Atget persuasively presented his photographs as social concepts – borders, edge conditions, minor economies – in which the margins of the architectural city and of social life were set in critical sequence. The Surrealists, by chance his neighbours in Montparnasse, attempted to annex his work to their aesthetic project in the 1930s; although Atget sold them an image that they used on the cover of *La Révolution surréaliste*, when they wanted to name him and draw him into their project, he would have nothing of it, insisting he was not an artist, that he simply made documents. The young American Bernice Abbott knew him late in his life, and it was Abbott who, after his death, organised and curated the first exhibitions of his work. The only photograph of Atget that I've seen was taken by her: frail yet monumental in the folds of his great, stiff coat, he sits in studio profile. The photographs he took of his own flat and studio show modest, comfortable and intensely ordered rooms filled entirely with books, prints and other tools. He was a great reader of Zola, and he was radically socialist in his politics.

His work could be placed alongside that of his contemporaries, Walter Benjamin and Aby Warburg: like each of them, he undertook a long and methodical indexical labour, returning repeatedly and circularly over decades to his sites and his theme to compile a sprawling catalogue of gestural transience and dust. His attraction was to the minor, the populist, the temporal, the overlooked. Unlike Warburg and Benjamin, he was self-taught and of extremely limited resources. He had his need to make a living, his camera, his glass photographic plates and his discipline. He walked Paris thoroughly. I wanted to follow him. For me the often tedious work of making a systematic record over time, of pausing and moving through the streets in ragged rhythms, of attending to the recording equipment, attempting to shield the microphone from the weather while focusing serially on the most extraneous details of the city, had the effect of loosening self-identity. Wearing my headphone monitors with coiled wire leading to my shoulder bag, microphone in one hand, pocket volume of Atget in the other, I begin to feel like a wandering perceiving organ that belongs to the city, rather than to any autobiography. I find the site, take my stance, press record, begin to count to 30 and I replace myself with the intricate density of the city's noise. I become a plenum, no longer individual. Atget's images led me to the indiscriminate edges of sound.

I arrived at a prosody. The rhythmic opacity of noise or the body or the city fails or exceeds its measure. Listening leans expectantly towards a pattern that is effacing itself – it is the fact of both language acquisition and music. In noise, the listener finds rhythm, and it is discontinuous, effacing its own figuration and count even as it

begins. A lurching, a jarring, a staccato surge, a blockage, a meandering, a too-brief alignment: the prosody of noise parses a discom-
fort that uncovers, in its unstable caesura, the fact of the citizen's
material fragility. The prosody of noise will not banish that fragility
but will accompany it. This arrhythmia, this enjambment, is what
one is – discordant temporality. Enjambment is the counter-semiotic
pause within the rhythmic gesture. It knows that the temporal unit
is sprung on the refusal of the regularization of time, which must
remain situated in the body, *as* the body's specificity, its revolt. The
prosody of noise returns discordance to time. What it shows: temporality as a replete nilling.

Disputations and material ranks, aetherealisation, alarms, numbers,
expropriations, violence, the burning and wresting of commodities – by
this nearness of conversation and conversion, the thickness of the entire
accumulated history of representation is threaded on an incandescent
and erotic duration. Here I use the word 'erotic' as a way of touching
upon the expectant unknowability of an apparently passive poetics of
reception. There is a psychic and physiological pleasure in the choice
of a bodily immersion in the materiality of this uncontrollable outside
that accompanies the time of a tensile listening. One becomes a subject
in the barest sense: a contingent point of coordinated perception of and
response to temporal specificity.

City Walls

d[9.3]b

As the city is not the opposite of the country, noise is not the opposite of silence. Noise interrupts or effaces the binary organisation of
sound as meaningful figure and its supportive field. Nevertheless, the
binary figure/ground analogy remains a dominant trope within European representational tradition, which would include the history of
the Western city's formation and self-identity. Here, the city itself is
a representation – a thick, situated representation of organisations of
social, symbolic and cultural exchange. Raymond Williams describes
and disarticulates the ideological functions of such a representational
dialectic in *The Country and the City*. In an appendix to this book,
he supplies the etymology of the word 'country' as *contra*, meaning
'against' or 'opposite', referring to the 'land spread out over against
the observer'. 'Country' was used in this way, in spatial and perspectival opposition to the word 'city', since the rise of urban capitalism in

the Renaissance, and in its contemporary aesthetic sense – a place of traditional pastoral quietude – since the eighteenth- and nineteenth-century industrialisation of the landscape. As Williams writes:

> The division and opposition of city and country, industry and agriculture, in their modern forms, are the critical culmination of the division and specialization of labour which, though it did not begin with capitalism, was developed under it to an extraordinary and transforming degree. Other forms of the same fundamental division are the separation between mental and manual labour, between administration and operation, between politics and social life. The symptoms of this division can be found at every point in what is now our common life.

In this figure/field dialectic, the country acts as the stable and receptive field of tradition, both in terms of values and of practices, against which the city can appear as active, often modernising, figure. But for Williams, the economic rationalism of the city itself produces, symbolically and economically, the nostalgic concept of the country; each trope depends upon the other's endurance. I am arguing here that the aesthetic, economic and social division between noise and productive, symbolically integrated sound is one more expression of the economic rationalisation of lived sensual space, and that this division does not express the embeddedness of the two concepts, noise and sound, nor their profoundly implicated relationship. Already, the placement of *noise* and *silence* in an accompanying binary relation is misleading: it would be more precise to consider sound and silence as two parts of the same institutional figure of a sonic symbolic. Noise falls outside this positively figured meaning system, troubling and disfiguring its totality. Beyond the notion of intertwining, a third concept intervenes. Again, we hear the disquiet agora.

Decorative Work

d[9.4]b

Noise is a confusion of figure and field. It presents no discernible figure of meaning. It's not silence's opposite, but an outside, mutating term. In a way, it is the double of silence, with this difference: silence's indiscernibility is more often institutionally codified and mystified as value – whether spiritual, punitive or economic. Money, Justice and Gods buy silence. The objects of exchangeability and value can then appear as figure on silence's supporting field, and exchangeability also has its correspondent, communicative sound-objects. From the perspective of these systems of value and meaning, noise belongs to poverty and the failure of value. Noise is pollutant, a sign of the wasteful expenditure of unused energy. Noise is inefficient. Like garbage, it has no meaning at the same time that it signifies an excess of signification; meaning become so dense and continuous that it transforms into field, having previously functioned as figure. In noise, meaning has de-coalesced.

An unknowing expands within noise, but it feels convivial.

Noise suspends itself: a thick and tactile curtain, a temporal fabric composed of tiny sub-cognitive movements that function below the spectrum of recognition and outside the range of rational signification, but not outside of time. Noise is the historicity of non-meaning.

Noise does fold, in Deleuze's and Leibniz's sense. A gathered density of inconspicuous perceptions (as waves to oceans, or crashings to forest), noise is the obscure differential relation within the ordinary, the habitual, the unremarkable auditory plenum. Within noise, the listener might choose to cognitively battle the non-logic of perception, or she could submit to the lack of discernibility. Noise doesn't cohere with the figural self-identity of meaning; it distributes sound as non-identity. This distributive movement is extensive, not intensive, leading the listener outwards to a worldly and abundantly shared incongruity. In noise, the remarkable obscurity of the ordinary becomes medium. Deleuze's baroque fold offers one model for thinking about the proliferative sensual perception of an incipient incoherence, a perceiving that is not dependent on the figure/ground dialectic:

> tiny perceptions are as much the passage from one perception to another as they are components of each perception. They constitute the animal or animated state par excellence: disquiet. These are 'pricklings,' or little foldings that are no less present in pleasure than in pain. The pricklings are the representative of the world in the closed monad. The animal that anxiously looks about, or the soul that watches out, signifies that there exist minute perceptions that are not integrated into the present perception, but also minute perceptions that are not integrated into the preceding one and that nourish the one that comes along ('so it was that!').

In Deleuze's description, perceiving does not halt or rest at the point of figural stability. Perception moves: it *is* movement, where movement observes no distinctions between inside and outside, figure and field.

For waves or vibrations, there are no such binary distinctions. What is non-integrated is nonetheless unfigurably necessary to the movement of changing. The incipient movement of sound is astructural, asystemic, asemiotic. This non-integration of noise into a meaning-laden structure or convention of perception is also what permits noise to bathe the listener in potential, in the very obscure and indiscernible agency of the present as *uncoordinated* disquietude. No privileged point of view can provide a coordinating vantage. The fold of noise is purely external, purely uncertain, and purely present, and it ripples through the listener. Noise is time's excess. It indicates our own bodily opacity.

Interiors

d[9.5]b

In his book *The Soundscape*, the composer and ambient recording pioneer R. Murray Schafer says, 'Hearing and touch meet where the lower frequencies of audible sound pass over to tactile vibrations (at about 20 hertz).' Twenty hertz is below the threshold of hearing, but in the range of vibration sensitivity. Chest cavity, palms and soles are particularly receptive. We listen to infrasound through our feet and our hands. This average and vague receiving, this unstaunched corporal immersion in a bath of sound that is both audible or tactile, is what I would like to frame. Noise constitutes the shared rhythm of the political. We city dwellers constantly bathe in the semantic folds of non-communicating noise, and this is also the polis.

Noise permits the subject's sense of interiority to figure as silence at the same time that it constitutes the outer limits of that interiority in terms of the tactile. This limiting founds and unfounds itself rhythmically, so that we feel time as a sensing.

In the city, I try to think with, rather than against, the ambient vernacular. At first feeling arbitrary, and so destabilised, I could follow the unravelling of meaningful or symbolic sound into noise as a movement outwards. Instead of conceptualising noise as blockage, negativity or detriment, something privative to be banished from the cherished peace of interiority, or from the formal ordering device of figure and ground in Schafer's terms, I'd like to frame noise, present it, articulate the way its sounding reveals also an intimate structure, a micro-surface of folds, and the continuation of these folds into our bodies. The urban experience of being within noise brings the frictive relation of bodies to economies right into perception.

What an economy rejects, we call garbage; what it distributes, we call value. Both are kinds of waste. Pollution-behaviour ritualises economic belief and behavioural systems. Non-contributing environmental traits and corporalities are expunged to a non-ethical outside. Disease, animals, foreigners, garbage, non-conforming sexuality and related border states, once ejected, traditionally emphasise the structural identity of the centre. This has been the most basic gestural trope in the consolidation of authority and identity in the Western city. Sound too has entered this civic figuration trope. The legal categorisation and treatment of some sound as pollution is a recent behaviour which can be traced to new regulatory protocols in the nineteenth-century city, and the advent of noise by-laws: on the one hand, pedlars, hawkers, rag-pickers, street musicians, prostitutes and other wanderers from the centralising capitalist economy were silenced with new civic ordinances. On the other hand, mechanised factory din was confined to labouring class quarters. In the 1960s the vocabulary of ecology entered the soundscape as a privative expression. The concept of noise pollution suggested that the city had a natural balance, a natural sonic state, and this balance would refer nostalgically to a previous stage or era of civic economy. If the 1960s were the beginning of global capital, the sonic 'health' of the Western city would not reflect the movements and dislocations of people and resources, the escalating cycles of consumption and waste, the hoarding of profit. The active sonic traces of this new economy would be cast in terms of pollution, and the identities of Western cities would wishfully gather themselves around the carefully preserved and mythologised artefacts of previous economies. The concept of sound pollution ironically functioned to camouflage the concentration of new capital.

Old Signs

d[9.6]b

R. Murray Schafer's World Soundscape Project (WSP) was a Canadian ambient sound research group that included among its members composers (Schafer himself and Hildegard Westerkamp), poets (Peter Huse, Brian Fawcett) and communications theorists (Barry Truax, also a composer). They began their work in the early 1970s and were based in Vancouver at the then-new Simon Fraser University in Burnaby, British Columbia. The WSP, with their portable recording equipment – at that time reel-to-reel – set out to systematically record, first in the city of Vancouver, then elsewhere, especially in villages and cities of Europe, what they called 'signature sound-objects', place-specific but threatened sound specimens that expressed the uniquely situated sonic traditions of communities. Examples might include echoes, squeaks and other sound qualities transmitted by vernacular stone or wood construction and paving, and the signifying sounds of animals, weather, clocks, bells, hunting horns, postmen's whistles, hand-pumps, millwheels, trams and so forth. The project developed in response to the 1960s' mounting discourse about 'noise pollution' – a soundscape that could be characterised by the globally blanketing and non-specific droning sounds of late capitalism – motors of aeroplanes, cars, air conditioners, lawnmowers and other similarly powered mass-produced tools and vehicles, all to be curtailed with noise by-laws and sound mitigation planning. (Poet Peter Culley refers to the current era as the 'Age of Briggs and Stratton', named for the largest manufacturer of the two-stroke engine). Generally, 'noise pollution' was judged by Schafer to have replaced or endangered local 'high fidelity' *differentiated* sound traditions exhibiting clear figure–ground relations, with a "low fidelity" unending and blanketing drone. Noise pollution destabilises the figure/field structure of the soundscape, where individual sounds specifically signify meanings with heritage identities. The work of the world soundscape recordists was a preservationist and anthropological practice of acoustic ecology (the term is of their own coinage), directing positive listening attention towards remaining desirable hi-fi and often mechanical sounds of the nineteenth century, and preserving these as an archive of lost or endangered figure–ground sound relationships. As acoustic ecologists, they performed an important pedagogical role in a reclamation and articulation of listening as an interpretive and productive socio-aesthetic practice. They insisted on thinking about sound as one component of a broader social, economic and psychological system of affect. My feelings about their work are interestedly ambivalent. They were botanists of the sensorium, intrepidly combing deepest Europe for fugitive samples of a lapsed authenticity to bring home to the New World's universities and studios. I follow then with combined gratitude and disbelief.

The WSP's acoustic ecology can be interpreted as an incipient audio analogy to the professionalisation of city planning. Nostalgia-based urban planning concepts of architectural heritage, inner-city regeneration and neighbourhood preservation responded to the high

Modernist urban rationalism of the 1960s, which had resulted in the emptying of city centres, the parsing of old cities by freeways, and the hygienic clearing of small industry and pre-modern living conditions from urban neighbourhoods. The WSP's acoustic ecology sought to return to and preserve what they sensibly theorised as a more liveable and human-scaled soundscape. For them, the record and preservation of clear figure–ground sonic relationships would contribute to a continuity of tradition-based human meaning, and, by extension, individual psychological health. But the concept of acoustic ecology was a direct expression of late capitalism's division not only of labour but of labourer from consumer. The din and racket of resource extraction and manufacture was sent out to an anarchically polluted and polluting productive beyond – Mexico, China, the oil-rich Subarctic of Canada – while the freely circulating consumer of the North American or European city was to enjoy a healthful, hi-fidelity, noise-free, symbolically authentic soundscape. The old cities of the West, cleansed and preserved, were to harbour 'clean' exchange, not least of which would be the privileged exchange of tourism.

The constituting gesture of the Western city is expulsion. We rid the bounded site of what we next configure as danger, pollutant, threat to the self-identifying community. The efficiency of the expulsing gesture has demonstrated itself: the means of living are what are extracted or wrested from an elsewhere, and brought apparently cleansed into the agora, in order to be exchanged for the stance and insignia of authority. It interests me to record signs of the failure of this hygiene. However thoroughly policed and legislated such a system is, it is never totalised. Migrants slip through borders, illegal or sub-legal economics proliferate, or the central economy suddenly reveals its own illegality. In spite of dominant intentions, movement doesn't stop. The city never becomes a static image of its own nostalgia, because some movement will always be indeterminant. Centrally defined limits and products are misused, transgressed. Border practices take place on a deeply layered and concentrated history of related counter-activity. To be in the city is also to be in the ancient habitus of refusal and resistance. Bodies assert their incalculable drives. Noise is made. It is the present.

I too wanted to make a record of the present. But unlike the WSP, I was not looking for sound objects that distinctly represented and captured figural remnants of heritage lifeways and economic nostalgia. I wanted to represent the city as digressional, not causal; as ephemeral, not monumental; as commodious, not commodity. I wanted a record of the dissolution of exchangeability, propriety and borders I heard acting within noise. I would record what was already there – cacophony. Within its habitus, I feel the extreme fragility of time, in tandem with the inexperience of my attention. Listening extends into non-identity, the danger zone bordering the institutions of meaning's exchangeability. Maybe I could offer some plots of noise as the inconspicuous descriptions of a civic thinking. Such inconspicuousness is the necessary non-separation of perceiving from thinking, of figure from ground, of economies from bodies. What is initially at hand? The present in its complete and necessary sonic density is here the site of all average beginning that goes nowhere, a beginning that stays with itself, that stays with materiality as the proliferative folding of perception into an always unstable environment. But a retreat into the present's inconspicuousness is not asocial; thinking moves in the replete temporality of other thinkers, listening moves among other listeners, continuing on paths others have taken. This is a present also. Disquiet indicates that what is there for thinking will not appear as an object. Listening or thinking moves in the thickness of what has been banished from identity: it moves in noise.

Edge Dwellers

d[9.7]b

The counting stops. The prosody of disquiet will have failed. Within this immodest failure, the world, worldliness, survives, entirely provisional and improvisatory: within and saturated by historicity. Noise is a semantic survival, a living on and amid the potential of an unstaunched corporeality, the affective site of the migration of perception to an outside always in disequilibrium, as economies and identities and bodies are in uncontrollable disequilibrium. Again, noise is a moving survival. It shapes the collective body as replete historical potential, signifying for nothing.

Chapter 10

Hedges

Daniela Cascella

FIELD

Prelude

Standing outside the field by a hedge. Standing days and nights and more. The hedge became the indefinite present frame for the infinite vertical motion connecting the earth beneath the field to the air above it. It felt as if I'd fallen from the sky.

Where To, Hearing What

To a field or a meadow not mine, once more, get there, after a long metaphorical walk in mind, heart, soul, my heart, soul, mind, having walked through that special type of soft rain that bends the leaves and a forest of glass-blades only just so, then they stretch back to where they were, they bend then stretch out again, I'd hear a gentle rattle if I was much closer and smaller, but the way I am now, it's just a shapeless imagined hiss, hiss in the quiet field, or is it a meadow, not mine, then the thunder and roar as I listen and scan layers of past histories all present here and nowhere.

To a field for a promise, having walked past the pine trees that seemed to catch fire as I walked past them, that took on shades and flames of rosy red and orange, past the churches of convention and taste, past the peaks of trees that I can only see now suddenly move like they never did, is that rosy-red and orange hue a sunset, or is it blood.

To a field that could be a field or maybe a meadow, not mine. But to me it is at once field, meadow, and mine so I could go underground, and what is under the ground here matters as I hear matter.

How

If I was to paint it I'd like to be Leonora Carrington, because she could make any space feel enclosed and covered and yet strangely and compellingly other. If I was to write a fiction around the field I'd have to be Herman Melville, to write the field like he writes the sea, his perception so ingrained in oceans that he saw oceans even in fields. But for sounds, for these words as recordings I don't want to be anyone, sounds are not meadows nor rooms, not fields nor oceans, these words holding sounds as recordings that exceed the field, a mine, dense and dark, out of which I extract material other than mine, to point at beyond from within what is close, from the edge of self to the horizon of what surpasses my finitude.

By the hedge I listen, on the frontier where sound sounding clues are no longer enough because instead of sounds I want to write the shapes of life through listening, at the end of a day filled with attempts at dissolving. Careful. The field is gradually becoming a meadow. Careful. It is meadow, mine, down underground to the edge of breath and the edge of dreams. Careful, atonal, unstable.

Will I learn to record the temptations of trespassing?

What

This is a recording of words extracted from archival layers that were before and aside me, a polyphonic arrangement of criss-crossing voices. It starts near a field then fields, goes through hedges and ends on edge, where I find something I didn't know I'd lost. The only way to hold that moment is to make you believe it happened, even if in a mind not mine. So that, presently, you hear the sounds you wanted to hear. Never forgetting the parts in the shade, attended to by silence.

Some History for a Start

One of the earliest documents of the Italian language is the Veronese Riddle: four verses written by a monk in the eighth or ninth century.

Se pareba boves
alba pratalia araba

albo versorio teneba
negro semen seminaba.

In front of him (he) led oxen
white fields (he) ploughed
a white plough (he) held
a black seed (he) sowed.

The oxen are the fingers of the writer, the white fields are the pages, the white plough is the quill and the black seed is the ink. Writing as field seems inherent to the messy origins of my native language. It speaks to me from a past more remote that my lifespan, not always entirely understood but heard, and passed on to me through books and voices. The more I read the conclusion of John Berger's 'Field', positing the field having the same proportions as one's life, the more I am drawn to the edges and hedges that mark such field, to the borders and thorny limits past which my writing can flip over from the proportions of my life to the timescale of a history that might not be inside the field essentially, but creeps in it, can be seen past its edges, ultimately grounds it.

Listening I trespass and reach out. Writing and reading I listen, to encapsulate the otherness of memory and history, to touch and erode the hedges around my field and rewrite them, slightly differently every time. So that I can still move towards the edge towards what is not yet here, or heard, or not quite.

The resulting texts are kept together by loose strings of associations, phrases echoing other phrases cast from words that were before me, recalled from archival layers reaching beyond the finitude of myself. Gestures on the margins marking frayed hedges, drawing disappeared marks on the soil, '. . . these themes gradually became organized into bundles that were more or less separate but juxtaposed in a sequence of chapters constituting something like a number of successive episodes in a whimsical steeplechase I would be obliged to conduct, across hedges, streams, tilled fields, and other features of a most irregular terrain.'[1] Beyond the field and beyond origins, becoming.

Plough: An Echo from the Previous Text

In the field, plough rhymes with now . . .

While in the fields the lonely plough
Enjoys its frozen sabbath now.[2]

. . . in a setting of absence, in winter, bleak, bare.

Plough: A Song Version of the Above Rhyme

That field of corn would never ever see a plough
That field of corn would be deserted now.[3]

. . . without a song.

That is, without the sun, without the 'good' season, beneath the soil, below and beyond the earth, in that chthonic level where James Hillman situates the motions of psyche.

Remembering a Verb

Inselvarsi: in Italian, to place oneself in a wood, where *selva* notably echoes Dante's 'selva oscura', 'dark wood'. Also implying, 'to place oneself into a wood to the point of becoming a wood'.

The Italian poet Giorgio Caproni used this verb to maximum effect in his poem *La preda* (The Prey), where a mythical prey symbolising a Double manifests itself in 'our voice' as it becomes wood and we become wood and prey too, through voice.[4]

An awkwardly sounding verb, coiling presence in, generated by a strong sense of place until place becomes verb and voice.

Reverb

Can there be a verb to make myself into a field? Make myself into a hedge? Become hedge, margin?

A Suspicion

that in the field of discourse, in the field of language where field is a site in the open, it is necessary to search for what is beyond the limits, beyond the written, for what withholds its presence underground, or hides it, silences it, the pressure of the matter from the past cut through the horizon of the future.

A Prompt to Exceed this Text

You could also search for dreams in the underworld[5] and the spell of the sensuous.[6]

Undeveloped Sketch

You could expand around the quote 'What's dead now? Just about everything in this field' from Peter Greenaway's *Drowning by Numbers*: to consider death with nature and field, recording as death and presence, then the residues.[7]

Now This Should Begin

Having been told how many words maximum this text should be, and what it is supposed to be about, I have been lingering on its edges. Paralysed by echoes of tired rhetorics of nothing and non-writing, I do not want to see this page filled with blank then tear it up. I have troubles with field in the same manner as I have troubles with discipline. The all-including stance, the limits, remind me of the struggle at school when I had to study the 'history' of philosophy, the 'history' of art: what terrible dead ends, to be tricked into the reassurance of defined answers of philosophy and art, whereas art and philosophy are first of all in the plural and they are all ever so troubling and unsettling and alive because they hold no answer or definitions. Instead, think of those histories as the recorded sounds of long-gone voices: like ghosts, they are enough and plenty, they exceed their recorded limits, you can be haunted by them for the rest of your life rather than defining them. Transfer this elusive state of mind into writing outside defined fields, that restless state portrayed by Melville in a letter to Nathaniel Hawthorne: 'The

:alm, the coolness, the silent grass-growing mood in which a man
)ught always to compose, – that, I fear, can seldom be mine.'[8] I hear
t in the words of Martin Glaz Serup: 'The view doesn't interest the
ield, it doesn't have a calming effect on it, it had heard it's sup-
)osed to be something special. . . . No, it's not for it. No. All that
;pace, it doesn't seep into the field as calm, the open landscape, it's
,omething you hear others talking about.'[9]

Recording

How much time do I need to record the field if I choose to con-
;ider the falls into rabbit holes, the dry patches and the barren soil?
How much time do I need for a writing-recording that is not direct
irticulation entirely exposed to the light but reaches out for cuts,
)odies, faults, falls, breaths, knots and falters? Is writing as record-
.ng some sort of preparation, a continuum waiting for a shock?
[ohn Ashbery, writing of Thomas Lovell Beddoes's writing: 'The
`ragments don't separate easily from the matrix, and when they do,
;omething is found wanting: they need their rough natural setting
o register fully, even as it partially obscures them.'[10]

Crop Circles

Or (back to the plough) I could think of writing the field as
:rop circles. I find online a reproduction of a woodcut pamphlet
`rom 1678 entitled *The Mowing Devil, or, Strange News out of
Hartford-shire*, representing a devil cutting crop circles in a field:
in interference of otherness in a meadow not mine, not symbolic
)ut diabolic.[11]

Museum

[oseph Cornell, *Museum* (1949): a series of cylinders containing
unspecified trinkets, sealed, that make sounds when shaken, except
)ne with nothing inside, making silence and I hear silence here as an

intermission in the field recordings of a self, a detached self, from the edge of the world. Or is it the sound of boredom?

Magnetic

In search for prompts and clues towards this text I flick through *The Magnetic Fields* (1920) by André Breton and Philippe Soupault and on page 25 I find: 'Look around you. There's nothing left now but the sky and these vast plots that we shall soon end by detesting. We touch those tender stars which filled our dreams with our fingers. Yonder, they told us that there were prodigious valleys: horse-rides forever lost in that Far West as boring as a museum.'[12]

A Recalled Song Echoing the Above, Closing the Circle

I do get bored, I get bored
In the flat field.[13]

Sustain

In Italian the word *campo* is 'field' but it is also 'I live', specifically as in 'I sustain myself'. In a pun generated by assonance, testing out possible beginnings for this text I start chanting to myself in the rhythm of a nonsense rhyme, repeatedly, 'campo in un campo', 'I sustain myself in a field', 'campo in un campo . . .' then as if to mock myself because I cannot find a beginning I start singing, sneering, 'che ne so io di un campo' 'what do I know of a field'. At once the melody becomes very specific; I realise I have precipitated into one of the most clichéd collective aural memories for Italian people, passed on by one generation before mine: it's made of thoughts and words, it is sung by a plaintive voice on a plaintive melody with all the requirements for those upsurging tormented feelings so dear to Italian audiences. Thoughts and words, *Pensieri e parole*, is the title of a song by pop star Lucio Battisti, the best-selling song in Italy in 1971 (the same year Berger's 'Field' was published), where two melodic threads, sung by the same voice, call and respond to each other, interweaving and embodying the dualism of thoughts and words stated in the title.

> Che ne sai tu di un campo di grano
> poesia di un amore profano.

> What do you know of a field of wheat
> poetry of a profane love.

> La paura di esser preso per mano che ne sai.

> The fear of being held by hand, what do you know.

I'll spare you a translation of the whole song. Suffice to say it arrestingly stages, in the climaxing choir, a disturbing play of *Doppelgänger*, or, a pop rendition of Rimbaud's 'je est un autre':

> Davanti a me ci sono io.

> In front of me there is me.[14]

Me in front of me / HEDGES

Breath, Air, Psyche

I must linger some more time on the edge of this text before me and
on its title, to reflect on what it is and what swarms beneath it, what
it hides. Months ago I decided to call it *Hedges*. I chose *Hedges* in the
same way as the 1929–30 journal, edited by Georges Bataille, was
titled *Documents*: because it was to be everything but the promise
of its title. 'Documents of your state of mind,' wrote the publisher
to Bataille, as the journal shifted the axis to the imaginary beyond
any truth attached to an idea of document.[15] Likewise by calling for
hedges I wanted to shift the axis from confined self-as-field to a realm
that trespasses borders, beyond any fixed idea of field-as-self, field-
as-discipline, field-as-contained-identity.

I thought I would call this text *Hedges* and I realise now it is a text
on edge too, always on the verge of starting and always on the verge
of falling/failing. And if it falls off its edges and fails, I shall call it *H*
instead. I become preoccupied with this H, haunting intermittently
on the edge, transforming the abstract marking of edge into something more real, spiky, knotty, leafy, brambly. Is it the H of history,
is it an aspiration, a breath? Is H the undergrowth of this writing,
at the end of the undergrowth of this writing, its spirit? What is
beneath and above the field, beneath and above the soil? In *Dream
and the Underworld* James Hillman writes of a certain symbolic
quality of the space deep underground, at a chthonic level beneath
the soil of generation: it is the space of pneuma, of breath, of psyche.
And in *The Spell of the Sensuous* David Abram reports the belief,
for the Navajo, that the air 'in its capacity to provide awareness,
thought, and speech, has properties that European . . . civilization
has traditionally ascribed to an interior, individual human "mind"
or "psyche" . . . That which we call the "mind" *is not ours* . . . [it is]
a property of the encompassing world.'[16] A loop begins to spin in my
head, encompassing H, aspire, pneuma, breath, underworld, psyche,
adding more sounds as it returns and turns and breathes.

H, breath as the breath of the landscape, echoes the title of
Toshiya Tsunoda's record *O respirar da paisagem*. In the CD liner
notes he writes of boundary lines: '[A boundary] does not constitute
a barrier for the continuity of physical phenomena . . . Space and
perception are linked through vibratory phenomena . . . The frame
actually dissolves in perceptual continuity.'[17] The edge as agent of

dissolution rather than enclosing mark. I listen to Tsunoda's recordings as they outline perceptions of space through acoustic vibrations.
I think of *pointilliste* paintings, where on close inspection the surface
appears to be made of minuscule particles of colour showing how
every different texture is actually made, when rendered as surface,
of the same matter: dots. With sound as it is treated by Tsunoda, an
inverted *pointillisme* seems to take place, eschewing representation
and reduction to a surface and preoccupied instead with dissolving,
through collections of rarefied encounters with places that are there
yet are perceived as vanishing in endless fugues of vibration. Place
breathes out of its horizon, the boundaries of a place coincide with
its vanishing points, as Tsunoda notably pointed out in a text written
with Minoru Sato in *Site of Sound*.[18]

H, breath, is generated within field but marks altitude in Geir
Jenssen's CD *Cho Oyu 8201m. Field Recordings from Tibet*. The
recorded field in this case is definitely not flat, neither does it point
at a vanishing horizon: it is measured as vertical axis, it marks an
exhausting escalation of a peak in the Everest through layered trajectories of listening into psyching: a journey 'extremely demanding
both physically and mentally' where the field is most prominently
made of and heard through the perceptions of agonising, breathless
bodies.[19]

H, breath as pneuma, literally appears in a scene in Andrei
Tarkovsky's *The Mirror*, where we see a man at the edge of a buckwheat field.[20] He moves away, a dog barks from afar then silence,
seconds of silence soon broken by a sudden airwave moving the
buckwheat stems, we can feel its pressure, its force, taking the movement of the scene right back to the front, to another edge.

H, breath, exhales out of a text by Robert Smithson, breathing the
h off the edge of meaning, sounding in front of the recurring question, what do words do in front of art (the field), and the title of the
text is *The Hum* and the body of the text is a hum from the body,
because 'perhaps an uninterrupted hum would be the best description of the art you see:

HMMMMMMMMMMMMMMMMMMMMMMMMMMMMM
MMMM.[21]

H, breath that sounds life from the edges. It marks the sensual matter we are made of and through, in other words: psyche. A breath, a
respiration necessarily made of rhythms, in as vital as out, the H as
relevant as the edges it cuts through.

H is the breath across these short texts-hedges too, it binds their co-presence even when it's not ploughed into the soil, not written down, but is allowed to exist through them: where life blends into writing, when recording the field dissolves but the spark of the encounter stays. Something has happened, it whispers, it may not be relevant but it happened.

H, breath of difference and contrasts of passing time. It does not need to be explained, it is: like the Zen master who would speak out some poetry and then stay silent.

Intermission with Whispered Instructions

About the field (presently but not quite audible)
About the field (broadening your horizons)
About the field (flat)
About the field (magnetic, plural)
About the field (looking far out, absent)

From the hedge (modestly)
From the hedge (disappearing)
From the hedge (contemplating innermost quietude)
From the hedge (not stepping out thereof)
From the hedge (irreparably)

On edge (breathing in)
On edge (drawing the missing h)
On edge (drawing a last breath)
On edge (until exhausted)
On edge (breathing out)

Whispering Stalks Ask

'Anyone who has walked through cornfields knows the uncanny experience of being scrutinized and spoken to by whispering stalks.'[22]

Of course I know. As I stand by the hedge I hear a question from the field, 'Who are you?' I'm not a 'writer in translation', I don't fall here or there, accomplished in a form, I cut across forms as I chose to migrate on to another language, that is not mine, on the edge, unqualified. Over from the edge of languages, I gather traces from the past so I can be every now. I make up a hybrid language that is part recounted, part recalled, part written, all stitched together and very patched. Patched, this language of interference, cliché and convention, patched where lopsided angles and out of tune tones come out of juxtapositions rather than one linear unravelling. I think of presence and omissions – the secret sound of these pages, what is not there, the under-layer that stays, what Giorgio Manganelli called 'the subtle noise of prose'.[23] Rabbit holes in the field make its surface rough, uneven, open to slanted lines of understanding that admit singularity and change.

What Dorothy Wrote

'Truant in the open, she saw, closing her eyes to the surrounding twilight, not the features of the scenes whose memory was the power that had drawn her forth to the gently clamorous sounds, but the corner of an unlocated meadow, rain-drenched and so near that she could perceive, as if she were some small field-beast in their midst, a forest of grass-blades, coarse, rank, July grass, the ribs and filaments of each blade clearly visible . . . And now the whole of the unknown field lay clear, hedged and sloping, and she was above it, looking down upon a wide stretch of open country, sunlit, showing here and there a nucleus of remembered beauty.'[24] I hear Dorothy Richardson breathing through these words, so close, so much with me, towards the end of her *Pilgrimage* which becomes mine too, and her alter ego in the book, Miriam, is not even in a field or meadow, she is in fact in a room during her first Quaker meeting, and lets her mind wander, and this coexistence of room and meadow, of a regimented type of silence and a more porous one make her prose so intimately connected, it is so close to the heart, it prompts memories of yet another silence and

another hedge, by heart

Another silence in Giacomo Leopardi's most renowned poem, 'L'infinito' (The Infinite) (1819), where the constrained field of vision marked by a hedge is the possibility of an opening, where a hedge appears as 'always dear' to the poet, as the element 'which takes so large a share of far-flung horizon from my view'. And because of the hedge, he can imagine 'infinite spaces beyond it', so infinite that he is nearly afraid.[25] Yet the sounds he hears of the rustling of the leaves are there with him, and a different type of imagination is at play, triggered by sound. The hedge, the mark, the familiar, allow drowning in boundless thoughts through listening, all held together across time.

Silent

She listened to familiar songs she knew by heart, not because she wanted to belong but longing to hear strangeness again – herself strange again, in them familiar.

> Following the silent hedges
> Needing some other kind of madness.[26]

EDGE

Think

Think of dead ends, rabbit holes as devices to mark the beyond-the-field beneath. Of a desire for walks across fields as sequences of interments and descents: to caves, catacombs, underground tunnels and car parks, empty storerooms.

Think Fall

'I am covered from head to foot, unable to move, a small boy, standing upright; I taste dirt on my lips . . . I have fallen, with my arms pinned to my body, into the empty post-hole, around the edges of which I had a moment before been playing . . . I had wandered . . . discovered the freshly dug holes along the edge of the field, had inspected one after another, skipping over them, leaning into them, dropping pebbles in, and finally, reaching the last and loneliest, farthest from the house, had slipped on the clubfoot, and, as in a burial of a sailor died at sea, had slid beneath the surface and out of sight . . . The desolation and helplessness, the abandonment; the stopping of time, and, in its place, a circular expansion of sensation, a vortex in reverse, limitless in proportion to my physical confinement.'[27]

Think Nocturnal

Something shall be said about a field at night. Or, nothing shall be said, but to be aware of it, the nightly dimension, the obscure parts of writinglistening or listening-into-writing, what is often untold but not unheard, what does not appear in the light but still moves, makes, undoes. Written words as nocturnal cloaks that wrap sounds gone and recalled: cut from the fabric of absence they suggest modes of absence, make themselves felt. Without the night, the darkness, the fall or the accident, little sense would be made of all this.

I long for the nocturnal phosphorescence of the hidden unheard thoughts that will deafen these horizons at dawn.

Poets

I start thinking of things that can be found in a field: a rusty scythe, for example. I smile as I sound the scythe in my mind and quickly move from scythe to site, the scythe I've found on the site of this writing. I think of the overlap between finding and inventing, *invenio* in Latin is 'to come upon', so to invent is not to create anew but to rearrange the rusty scythes/sites of memory, their debris and leftovers. In my memory first, and later on a shelf I find John Ashbery's *Other Traditions*. Weeks ago I'd marked that page where he quotes John Clare, 'I found the poems in the fields / and only wrote them down' and says that 'for him experiencing is the same as telling'.[28] Like a field recording perhaps, like its sameness, its persistence.

A Record

I find myself now, through the telling of invention, on the edge of the field leaning over a hedge, or am I in my head, head, hedge, hedge as head on the cover of Terry Riley's *A Rainbow in Curved Air*, the field here appears low in the overall field of vision of the vinyl cover, there's very little of it at the bottom, a rather insignificant strip of land, above it the head, partly eerie partly reassuring, an odd head radiating rhythms in trance, does it dream of them or do they dream of it, is it a head or a hedge in the shape of a head, it's the terror of not finishing this thought that makes the head look like a hedge, sense the weariness, sense the search for clues, stops, hooks, steady points, hence the hedges, and it's hedges not fences, porous like this music, nor walls, because there is not a solid demarcation, because hedges can be tangled but still not solid, still, not solid, no, this has to do with hedging off a self through a self.[29]

Yet I have to find the most moving answer to the question you have not asked yet.

Divining an Answer

Now look at the marks on pages, not just words as edges. See the underlinings, the corners turned, the marks made while reading. What did I underline into and out of Berger's text, connecting to and interfering with so many others, pulling towards change, cycles, times of the day, decay and metamorphosis? As a site it may be circumscribed but, as I heard in Smithson's hum, it exceeds itself too. To exceed once again the field of my writing I open Breton's *L'Amour fou*, my Italian Einaudi edition, on page 16. I often use this book and *Nadja* as divining props to find clues on where the writing will go next. I am drawn to a mark I made last year, a pale blue rectangle drawn around a paragraph about trapdoors, and at the bottom of the page I read how Breton often used a pack of cards that on the back bore the inscription: 'Mein Feld ist die Welt', 'My field is the world'.[30] In a 'magical-circumstantial' twist, field opens up to what my personal confines cannot hold, but point at, flipping over the edge of the cards, marking the necessity to go beyond the self, like the back of the pack of cards, you turn them and it's another field. The prompt is once more towards hidden motions, less apt to scrutiny, no grips, no hooks, sliding somewhere else, else of me.

No Words

'Into the silence, which was also at times a roar, of my thoughts and questions forever returning to myself to search there for an explanation of my life and its purpose, into this concentrated tiny hub of dense silent noise . . . the difficulty of writing about it'. I am drawn to this difficulty and the way it rubs against the evidence of something being written nonetheless. And for what reason, for what purpose? None, there is no explanation or purpose other than doing it, on the edge, doing nothing, breathing, sitting, staring, listening, reading, reading Jean-Jacques Rousseau's *Confessions* via Roland Barthes preparing a novel he won't write: 'I like to be busy doing nothing, to begin a hundred things and to finish none, to come and go as the whim takes me, to change my plans at every moment, to follow each twist and turn of a fly, to dig up a rock to see what is underneath it . . .'.[31]

Forbidden

Not permitting myself to return there, at the edge of the field I felt the field even if I could not see it. I was listening to your voice and to sounds on headphones and the pressure was strong as the pressure of the idea of the field. For some time I have thought of the field as a nothing and only its edges, hedges marking it, only to wait and to find, invent across them. In the end the answer to the question not asked is: margin.

It's Margin

I looked back at these notes and thought I should say something about the paintings of Agnes Martin as fields and their edges, are they hard, are they soft. I became amused at the realisation that instead of Martin I'd spelled Margin. Agnes Margin, my hand was quicker than my mind, mind the field, mind, field, mine, field, minefield. I meant mine, not mine, mind, not mind, meadow, not mine.

Notes

1. Michel Leiris, *Scratches*, trans. Lydia Davis (Baltimore: The Johns Hopkins University Press, 1997), p. 241.
2. John Clare, 'The Shepherd's Calendar', cited in John Ashbery, *Other Traditions* (Cambridge and London: Harvard University Press, 2001), p. 18.
3. The Supremes, 'Without a Song', *I Hear a Symphony*, LP (Motown, 1966).
4. Giorgio Caproni, 'La preda', *Poesie, 1932–1986* (Milan: Garzanti, 1995), p. 578.
5. James Hillman, *The Dream and the Underworld* (New York: Harper-Collins, 1979).
6. David Abram, *The Spell of the Sensuous* (New York: Vintage Books, 1997).
7. Peter Greenaway (dir.), *Drowning by Numbers* (1988).
8. Cited in Paul Metcalf, 'Genoa' in *Collected Works, Volume 1, 1956–76* (Minneapolis: Coffee House Press, 1996), p. 145.
9. Martin Glaz Serup, *The Field*, trans. Christopher Sand-Iversen (Los Angeles: Les Figues, 2011), p. 95
10. Ashbery, *Other Traditions*, p. 32.
11. http://oldcropcircles.weebly.com/uk-1678-hertfordshire.html (last accessed 3 August 2015).
12. André Breton and Louis Aragon, *The Magnetic Fields*, trans. David Gascoyne (London: Atlas, 1985), p. 25.
13. Bauhaus, 'In the Flat Field', *In the Flat Field*, LP (4AD, 1980).
14. Lucio Battisti, 'Pensieri e parole', *Pensieri e parole*, 7" (Ricordi, 1971).

15. Denis Hollier, 'The Use-Value of the Impossible', *October* 60 (Spring 1992): 4.
16. Abram, *The Spell of the Sensuous*, p. 237.
17. Toshiya Tsunoda, *O respirar da paisagem*, CD (sirr.ecords, 2003).
18. Minoru Sato and Toshiya Tsunoda, 'The Boundary of a Place: Discovering the Vanishing Points' in *Site of Sound: Of Architecture and the Ear*, ed. Brandon LaBelle and Steve Roden (Los Angeles: Errant Bodies Press, 1999), pp. 138–45.
19. Geir Jenssen, *Cho Oyu 8201m. Field Recordings from Tibet*, CD (Ash International, 2006).
20. Andrei Tarkovsky (dir.), *The Mirror* (1975).
21. Robert Smithson, *The Collected Writings*, ed. Jack Flam (London, Berkeley and Los Angeles: University of California Press, 1996), p. 328.
22. Abram, *The Spell of the Sensuous*, p. 130.
23. Giorgio Manganelli, *Il rumore sottile della prosa* (Milan: Adelphi, 1994).
24. Dorothy Richardson, *Pilgrimage* IV (London: Virago, 1979), p. 500.
25. Giacomo Leopardi, 'L'infinito' [1819]. Available at http://www.leopardi.it/canti12.php (last accessed 28 August 2015).
26. Bauhaus, 'Silent Hedges', *The Sky's Gone Out*, LP (Beggars Banquet, 1982).
27. Metcalf, 'Genoa', p. 101.
28. Ashbery, *Other Traditions*, p. 17.
29. Terry Riley, *A Rainbow in Curved Air*, LP (Columbia, 1969).
30. André Breton, *L'Amour fou*, trans. Ferdinando Albertazzi (Turin: Einaudi, 1974), p. 29.
31. Roland Barthes, *The Preparation of the Novel*, trans. Kate Briggs (New York: Columbia University Press, 2011), p. 155.

Chapter 11

Stirrup Notes: Fragments on Listening*

Jonathan Skinner

The stirrup transmits sound vibrations from the hammer and anvil to the oval window, a membrane-covered opening to the inner ear. It is the smallest and lightest named bone in the human body.

d[11.1]b

Auto pulse return lock slides synapse trucks walking along minor key in all sunlight withstands oscillating sync of life at pond morning. Each of every day given over to wasteful activity. Literally washing

---

*Audio recordings accompanying this text can be accessed at https://edinburghuniversitypress.com/book-writing-the-field-recording-hb.html [click on the 'resources' tab]. They are referenced as follows: **d[11.1]b**, **d[11.2]b**, etc. Listening with headphones is best for an immersive experience, though not essential. Many of these recordings are clips, some are edits from extended adventures in listening, and some document sonic events, which range widely in duration. They all reward a complete listen (many hold surprises) but can be sampled more briefly in conjunction with the text.

I also chose these recordings in hearing of their imperfections – hiss, wind sound, microphone handling, spiking, suboptimal equalisation – 'noise' that I have deliberately not filtered or edited out (except as regards any dangerous amplitude levels). This is, for the most part, and barring the compression to mp3 format, raw audio. The 'high fidelity' of 'clean' sound, abstracted from the uneven resonances of reflective and absorbent materials, and filtered from the noise of our instrumentation, is a construct of the modernity within which we have developed our listening (Thompson). While primarily a result of my amateur recording skills, I have retained these imperfections, as they mark some of the boundaries of this kind of listening, boundaries I have also tried to listen through.

Some of the recordings are 'low fidelity'; some are made at higher resolution. Some were made with a Sony minidisc player and inexpensive Sony stereo microphone. Many were made with a Marantz pocket-sized digital recorder, mostly using the built-in stereo mics but sometimes with an Audio-Technica or a Rode external mic. One recording was made with an iPhone, and one recording was made with a Sennheiser shotgun mic and Marantz field recorder.

Like the essay fragments, these sounds can be dipped into and out of. Listened to consecutively, and counting the one longer, 10-minute ('bug safari') recording, they last just under 80 minutes total. The vast majority of clips are less than 3 minutes long. These recordings were made over about 17 years, in a broad range of locations.

one's essence. Necessary redundancy. Spikes emerge from a dog day. White spindrift particular eats the soda. Winged messengers at full daze, throttling the wage scopes, the din submarine echoes.

Infant twister ducks slide the pop along walls, incognito hills and love mountains. If the sun the hills the cars the roads the lakes the cows: underwater ways a swift engine thrill. Groan in the concert hall. Bash clash and why write why produce, an insectoid burrowing activity.

Twist pry pull up kill eat compose and consume. Get comfortable. An unscripted body bloats and wilts. If you knew, you would not push for more cowbell. In the back room at the end of a dark forest a quiet secret human makes music.

d[11.2]b

Since I began recording soundscapes in the field, not only in 'nature' and not always 'outdoors', my instinct to switch on the radio or the hi-fi, or to put on headphones, to listen to pre-recorded material has dwindled. I often go for several days without listening to recordings of any kind, including the recordings I myself have made. Yet I rarely go for several days without pressing record on my digital pocket recorder. This inversion intrigues me. Has the 'recording stance' made me a better listener? And what do the recordings sound?

d[11.3]b

In the weave, the bee loud, list. Sound meshes promise of objects beyond self, of lives other than human. An illusion of *materia primordia*. There is no sound without event. Yet the nothing that is there is time, the space of a walk, the distance to and from a point of attention, a match from frequency to reception. Scale and granularity: the high frequencies are healing, says one recordist. The lower frequencies draw us in and comfort, says another. At one end of the spectrum our nerves are touched, at the other bones and muscles. We mark the sounds with footsteps, with breath we listen.

Some would make this sound fundament. Rooted in the bass, or in the nearing faring here and thereness of the flesh. Others value sound for the way it blows out the paper veil of here and now. There is nostalgia to sound, when it re-presents. Can we get close to the naked ear, listen blindly, or is that beside the point?

Low frequencies are less directional but travel further; high frequencies needle their way towards us, one unobstructed space at a time. On the one hand, we privilege the seeming of visible signs, marks that sow meaning, seed and signal. On the other, we distribute intelligence according to articulate sound, where recognition demands vocalisation, even erased as writing.

Subjects sound, the silent body resists sounding. It may be that the primordial threshold for animate awareness is another body rustling or shifting, and this includes the earth when it shifts and takes on seeming agency: we are on guard, there may be attention, subject, predation. Threat, attack, defence.

d[11.4]b

The mesh sounding cosmos, earth, air, water, fire, the buzz that promises and cuts short all promise. We give in to directionless shifting, mutability that is not change, geology before and after the human. The human listens into noise, sounds it, the entropic environment of acoustics, negating it with a slice of life. A dialectic of high fidelity in the low fi. Intelligence is high and what is low? The sound of trees in a chipper, water falling, fuel combusting, earth and stone tumbling. A coqui frog pierces the fog of sound.

d[11.5]b

Directions for the Ear

'The following forty poems echo forty sounds collected on minidisc between June and October 2000. All forty sounds are included on the accompanying cassette. Each cassette bears a unique spectrogram of one of the sounds. The poems are written between eye and ear, sound and spectrogram.'

Sources and locations of sounds include: Niagara River rapids, Whirlpool State Park, Niagara Falls; Freight train, railyard by Tifft Farm Nature Preserve, South Buffalo; Bug zapper and taxi, Niagara Falls; Lake Erie/wharf pilings, Lighthouse Point Park, Buffalo; Canada Geese, Tifft Farm; Cow, Etretat, Normandy; Bridge traffic, Buckhorn Island State Park, Grand Island; Common Loon, Lake Louisa, Algonquin Provincial Park, Ontario; Wind in poplar, Lighthouse Point Park; Escalator, Leicester Square Tube Station, London; Whirlpools in oar's

vake, Lake Louisa; Leaves underfoot and surprised fawn's bounding
100ves, Tifft Farm; General Mills Elevator, South Buffalo; Rock inlet
)f the Niagara River, Whirlpool State Park; Jet and water lapping,
_ake Louisa.

```
LOON 2.


laughs and lakes and laps

   a twittering wit

      spills his spaghetti

on the fire
```

I[11.6]b

My friend picks me up at the Buffalo airport and takes me to Tifft
Nature Preserve. Looking from the mounds across Route 5 towards
Lake Erie and the sunset, she remarks how, even from the midst of
this preserve, she could not get over the omnipresent sound of traffic.
I am surprised that what nourished and opened up a world of listening and manifold attention is for others a damaged place, 'less' than
sustaining, irritated.

```
JET

flights burn away the night
'a crowd    inside      provisioned'
begins, cease, and then again
lapped and laved by waters
our human thoughts recede
behind sounds of a primal scene
waves sloshing in heads
as we crawl through this world
standing up in our ears
```

We discuss the intolerance for noise that develops with age and its
attendant forms of tinnitus. While some irritation is physiological
some may be psychological. We might pre-empt irritation through
attention. Digital recording became accessible to me in my thirties – I
wonder how my attention might been different were I fifteen years

older at the time. How much of one's annoyance at 'noise' in middle
age has to do with language and the attention towards an encoded
signal, with frustration at losing the semantic triggers of consonants
in the wash of sound? Is the detail of hearing ambient sound similarly impaired, or does listening rather widen with the release from
tracking a signal, from hanging on consonants?

```
POPLAR

what builds is a sudden tense
rush of light off surfaces
leaves gather and lift
even to sea swells
breath alights
does it end
like this
gusting
winded
ghost
```

A 'frontier' sound drew me to these ruined landscapes, an absence of
human voices: vespertine melancholy, wintry fixation on white noise,
vernal emergence. Yet had I not developed my listening transcribing
interviews? I was learning to identify birds, to disentangle warbler song
from the myriad chorus of a spring migration. Noting how faraway
sounds affect the hearing of what is near. I could only begin to write
about the sounds when I learned how to see them.

```
DEER

stealth tracks under cover
of the humming skyway
to step on a leaf
spring that triggers the fawn
energy bounding from detritus

the ears of 'Eternal Delight'
        are perked
```

d[11.7]b

Directions for the Ear compiles forty 'sound objects' – inspired
by Pierre Schaeffer's concept of the *objet sonore* – and a poem for
each sound, a poem that could be read while listening to the sound

(Schaeffer, pp. 132–3). Forty cassette audiotapes contained all the recordings, each in a cassette box labelled with a unique spectrogram of one of the sounds. Forty, nine-line poems were printed on forty small (7 × 11 cm) notecards in Courier font and included in a cassette-sized manila envelope with each cassette.

```
STROKE

lifted upper hand slices
blade toward canoe
forward pull pushes on lower
fulcrum hand's
stopped at hip, shoulders
follow through
upper twists paddle, lower
places throat on
gunwhale and pries away a J
```

Rather than the usual view of frequency plotted vertically with time running horizontally, the '3D surface spectrograms' showed time as a series of 'mountain ranges', nine evenly spaced samples of the recording, whose profiles mapped the frequencies in each sample, height varying with amplitude. Time is mapped by the advance of these ranges across the spectrogram (Figure 11.1).

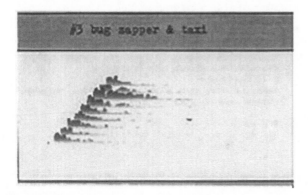

Figure 11.1   Bug zapper and taxi

Thus I was able to generate a manifold 'sound object' whose channels modelled lines of poetry, a 'stanza' with nine lines of varying density. Each 'channel' or range in the image represents a temporal slice of the frequency and amplitude profile of the soundscape. (I had not yet distinguished between ambient and focused sound in my field recording practice.) Amplitude would register prosodically – 'a belch as a sigh' reversing the meter of 'on the breathy main'.

```
BROWSE


pleasant interview's
house of peristalsis
on the breathy main
in the zone of totality
one Norman bee drones
a belch as a sigh
cud patiently transferring
pleasure from cow to sky
milks the grass cliffs
```

d[11.8]b

Lines of poetry did not follow what I heard but what I saw.

```
LONDON


'dogs        must
    be              car-
ried        on
    the             es-
ca-         la-
    tor             at
all         time-
    s'
```

d[11.9]b

The microphone or paddle an Inuit holds to his jaw to listen for seals beneath the ice is an instrument for acousmatic perception, for veiled sound or sound abstracted from its originating cause: the ἀκουσματικοί were probationary pupils of Pythagoras who, so that they might better concentrate on his teachings, were required to sit in silence while listening to their teacher deliver his lecture from behind a screen. Cover the sound to sit still to silence. No neutral discipline. Can we imagine a protest without 'noise' (Attali)?

d[11.10]b

Warblers

Black-and-white Warbler
Mniotilta varia

scrapes on Lima
pointer's down
on insect toes
flicks zebra barks
for juicies, icies
eye sees icy heat
sees large gun-
metal orca cleans
up shady shades

Warblers are field-based poems that follow 'limiting factors' cued to the field experience: 'listen to the bird's song, translating its rhythm and pitches', 'acknowledge that warblers are restless, hard to see, and give you a crick in the neck'. Writing the poems focused listening to learn how ears might pry open a tree in 'birdsong' to reveal specific performances, a world swarming with particulars. One hears warblers before one sees them. Eye follows ear, close listening with purpose, to a confirming blaze of colour.

'Lower limit speech/ upper limit [birdsong]' (Zukofsky, 'A'-12, p. 138)? A sonic horizon that allows 'anybody who does not know Greek to listen and get something out of the poetry of Homer (Zukofsky, 'A Statement for Poetry', p. 20).' Homophonic translations of Latin in Catullus and botany inspire this birdsong. As does the 'meaning inside speaking' that comes from listening for voices inside waterfalls, for the communication of departed spirits: 'include words from poets writing in the North as well as the South – warblers feed on both sides of the border' (Feld, p.132, p. 136). Translation, migration, transmigration.

Pine Warbler
Dendroica pinus

dimly streaked breast
low-contrast wings
yellow promiscuous
too fast for starlight

eddies battered fender
bender may confuse
other probes with loves

meandering time tone
caught in the tree
trunk's sweep of shadows
rapid upslurred trill

l'ovale c'est sa joue
lui monte à la gorge
the wolf in the glass
and looping bark . . .

Between the 'weesa weesa weesa' of the Black-and-white, the 'weeta-weeta-weeta-wit-chew' of the Magnolia, and the 'pleased pleased pleased ta meetcha' of the Chestnut-sided warblers, the poem speaks meaning inside birdsong. I hear 'eye sees icy heat' inside 'weesa weesa weesa'. I see the field marks of decurved bill, long toes and gunmetal-blue backstreaks.

Try pointing your field recorder at a tree in spring migration and recording *a* bird. They get me to listen without pressing record: the poem itself as a recording device.

d[11.11]b

Does the rendering of whale vocalisation into 'ambient' nature music equal the 'rendering' of oil from whale fat? Field recording both connects to and separates from an environment.

d[11.12]b

A Room for Opal: Listening with Julie Patton

Opal Whiteley was a precocious young nature writer who published a best-selling diary in 1920. Whiteley claimed to have written her diary from 1904 to 1905, living with her family and attending school in Walden, a logging community in Oregon's Willamette Valley:

There, in the latter half of her sixth year, Opal began to write a diary, which she kept in a hollow log in the nearby forest. In it she described her home, her animal friends, her cathedral area among the trees, and 'the singing creek where the willows grow.' Using her own phonetic form of spelling, she printed with crayons on pieces of scrap paper a neighbor woman brought her. (Hoff, p. 6)

With her friends, Opal goes on 'explores': 'I like to go in among the rushes where the black birds with red upon their wings do go. I like to touch fingertips with the rushes. I like to listen to the voices that whisper in the swamp' (p. 269). Opal sings to plants, puts her ear close to the rock and listens to the 'lichen folk' who 'talk in gray tones' (p. 194).

Julie Patton brought Opal Whiteley into conversations with a show about sustainability at the Bates College Museum of Art. How can we stop speeding and 'have feels' for the times of others? We decided to focus our listening on an old bird sanctuary at the heart of Lewiston, a mill town on the Androscoggin River: to listen with elders and with children, at the stone walls between generational plots. Our walks through Thorncrag drew a timeline across the retreat of the Laurentian Ice Sheet, right down to the shrinking of the polar ice caps and inundation of coastal cities.

Opal ended her life in London as a ward of the city. 'During the second world war,' her editor Benjamin Hoff notes, 'she was often seen scavenging for books in the rubble of bombed buildings.' She was found living in a flat 'filled from floor to ceiling with wooden boxes holding an estimated total of ten to fifteen thousand books, many of which were said to contain underlined passages and notes in Opal's handwriting' (pp. 65–6). Opal was committed in 1948 to Napsbury Hospital, outside London, where she died in 1992 at the age of 95.

Books serve as pedestals for bird houses, taking flight, casting their profiles on the time line. At one bird house visitors can hear a collaborative performance, at one conversation with elders, at one games with children, and at one Charlie Parker mixed with *Peterson's Guide to Eastern/Central Bird Song*. A desk anchors the installation – with its alphabet blocks and birds' nests, the Enlightenment classroom is an enchanted place in its own right, where natural history and childhood wonder mutually reflect. Also a site of terrible discipline and constraint, its hold has made us poor listeners. The abuse Opal suffers at the hands of adults punctuates her narrative. Such deafness threatens the very life that is not heard: non-hearing that the extinction timeline on the wall, in place of the usual alphabet train, indicts.

With Opal, Patton invites us into their room for 'explores', to stay for more than a few minutes, to 'look looks down upon the mill town', and to get small on one's knees, to begin to listen. Only by making ourselves small can we begin.

d[11.13]b

Loons are tricky: their vocalisations are ambient in a way that requires stereo mics to capture properly. But they can also be distant, which would indeed call for a shotgun. A parabola can isolate a bird in a windy tree, but without the range a shotgun mic has. I got good results just sitting by a lake with a small stereo mic and recorder. The night was still. You can get close to the birds. To almost get knocked from a kayak by a sturgeon jumping for the moon. To put oneself *into* the soundscape.

d[11.14]b

Grus

Once the deer cross the river, the cranes come in to land. On the Platte River, right alongside Interstate 80. Gusts of trumpeting crane music, as hundreds of thousands of sandhills spiral in to roost. A life oriented to migration corridors – species transporting sun-fed biomass around the planet (Leopold, p. 19). Cranes (*Grus*) travel from their wintering grounds on the Gulf Coast, the Southwest and northern Mexico, to summer breeding grounds as far north as the Arctic.

Sandhill cranes (*Grus canadensis*) were once down to twenty-five breeding pairs in Wisconsin when Aldo Leopold conducted his 1929 Midwest US wildlife survey (p. 11). The largest gathering of cranes on earth can be witnessed – about half a million or 80 per cent of world population – along a seventy-mile stretch of the Platte River in Nebraska. While the Platte is 10,000 years old, fossils of a sandhill crane-related species have been found here that date back 10 million years (Bartels). Poet Allison Adelle Hedge Coke invited me to the Crane Trust to witness this gathering.

Crane cultures around the world share the counter-clockwise ceremonial dance ('stamping down the turtle' in Hedge Coke's words) of cranes 'kettling' – as they spiral in great numbers to roost. The sandhill's voice trumpets from an exceptionally long trachea that itself curls in its breast like a French horn. Ojibwa speakers call them 'Echo Maker' (Eisenberg). These great council meetings are social occasions critical to survival. Parents teach adolescents to dance; unsuccessful pairs can switch partners. It is impossible not to hear human speech inside their calling at the enormous Platte River roosts.

Cranes had been around a long time when humans emerged. Humans have reduced the flows of the Platte by as much as 70 per cent – a river that was once 15 miles wide in places (in braided channels) has been narrowed to a fraction. Cranes gather to dance on just 60 miles of river. They dance thanks to preservation of this slender channel of semi-wild water and wetland habitat along the flyway – and thanks to wintering habitat in Mexico. A wolf biologist asks, 'why have we had success with the cranes and not with other species?' Gary Snyder writes: 'in the wetlands, / in the ongoing elder / what you might call, / *really* the real, world (p. 51).'

The Japanese – who revere the crane as their national bird – are also people of the crane flyway. When I first listened to these cranes, the Fukushima nuclear disaster was unfolding, in the wake of the 2011 Tōhoku earthquake and tsunami. In an anthology in the library of the Crane Trust, I found a seventh-century tanka by the Nara-period poet Yamabe no Akahito, written in AD 724 (Jensen, p. 94):

> As the tide flows into Waka Bay
> The cranes, with the lagoons lost in flood
> Go crying towards the reedy shore.

d[11.15]b

Music anthologist and artist Harry Smith in his final years was into recording what he called 'long wave' sounds and claimed there were audible patterns that repeated only every eight to ten hours or so.

The 'naked ear' of the microphone always catches unexpected sounds (Westerkamp, pp. 148–51). It would seem obvious to note that much depends on how and where one is pointing it.

'Core samples' of one, three and five minutes create a standard frame, one easy to work with. Parabolic and shotgun microphones are still no substitute for halving, or even quartering, the distance between oneself and the sound source. Sitting *very* still for a *very* long time – to let the birds come to you. On the other hand, loons multiply the sound. Ambient, inseparable from echo. Thoreau listened for this 'aeolian' quality – also to wood and hermit thrushes (Journal entry for 31 December 1853). From the 'middle' of the lake. Or from the bay on the lake with the best echoes. One is embedded in, if not located *by*, the loon's call.

d[11.16]b

Running, listening, crying, stroking, burning, flowing. Rhythms locked inside of rhythms, overlapping, in and out of sync, a tonal physical mesh. How can we participate in it and critique our participation, at one and the same time? Can we be more rhythmically attuned? Does it really begin with listening, or with running. Eat fishes but first observe their luminescent galleries. Almost two different orders of experience. The colour of the fish leaches out on the deck of the ship, like the poet said. Aesthetics is distance, highly medium-dependent, a neural contact in the oscillators of our brain movie. Proleptic, retrospective, in time not of the present, we are merely the switchboard between delays cast off echoing shimmers in the material strata, resonating interactive emanations triggering overlapping impulses sorted via rhythm and further resonance into signals out of noise. The noise is the rich matrix but without a shaping signal the brain implodes, the social media implodes, the expansion is infinite and dissipates, how to concentrate it back in. If sync is a state of entropy, what is the negentropic resistance. And where?

d[11.17]b

Animal Transcriptions – Listening to Listening

A facility at Cornell University houses the world's largest collection of recordings of animal sounds, the Macaulay Library of Natural Sounds, along with the Bioacoustics Research Program and the Cornell Lab of Ornithology. Many field-recording techniques were pioneered and developed at Cornell. What does a sound lab *sound* like? Can one listen to scientists, engineers, archivists, technicians and their machines the same way one listens to birds and other non-humans? I ask lab staff to discuss the sounds at the heart of their work – sounding their knowledge on archiving, acoustics, field work, gear, communication, looking at sound, music, evolution and conservation.

It turns out that poetry has helped acoustic biologists interpret the animal sounds they study, as with Katy Payne, who has referred the patterns she studies in whale vocalisations to the mnemonic structures of Homeric verse. When we speak of animal 'song', we bring metaphors from the arts of poetry and music into science. I want to know why the Macaulay LNS collects its 'specimens' and how such a collection is thought about within a matrix of philosophical, aesthetic, ethical and political concerns. Staff at the Cornell Bioacoustics Research

Program study spectrograms of ambient African forest recordings for elephant vocalisations but also for the vertical signature of poachers' rifle cracks. On the *Voyager* spacecraft's Golden Disk, whale songs (and other sounds) are carried into space. To 'sound the animal' is to pull on threads and follow 'risky attachments' (Latour, p. 22).

d[11.18]b

Acoustically damped for sound, all the senses exist simultaneously, approaching noise-sound, the new materials, oscillators, turntables, generators, means for amplifying small sounds, 'noise' as metaphor of all that's excluded, lured by extra-musical sounds, interpretation gives way to experimentation, remembering to remember aural memory, the once discrete, static relations among artist, art object and viewer quiver and resound, what the listener hears is not a representation, but the work itself, this failure of sound to construct a distinct category, a painful noise that betrays a disturbing set of emotions, the medium is often not the message.

d[11.19]b

Blackbirds

interpreting   graphs
        who are we to say
    YOU   are ANimal?
mwa'ahahaha   we don't know
        we'll eat you

A European blackbird (*Turdus merula*) sings at the edge of town on a golf course in the English Midlands. I slow the recording down to quarter-speed and generate a spectrogram for each vocalisation (Figure 11.2). The slowed-down spectrograms reveal the distinctive parts, modelling the five to eight lines of each stanza.

like the homeless   who keep losing
            their lawn
                    furniture
        scanning a chunk of thunderstorm
            rifle   shots crack
                    bulge into echoing
            ivory's   market

Figure 11.2   European blackbird

d[11.20]b

Non-pulsed time, sound as an anonymous, non-human and imper-sonal flux, the sound of saliva being sucked out, an instrument of differentiation, music as locus of repetition, as a phenomenon appears, leaves behind noise, aggression, animal heat, the clash of war and lust, battle cries, screams that force themselves from mouths, before the word, an audio file made of sonic grains mim-icking the behaviour of a starling murmuration, data-mining the noise floor, how to get taken up into a big wave, a column of rising air, a prosecution of silence, where ringing in the ears perceived in the absence of external sound soon becomes unbearable, blocks of ice in the gallery, surrounded by microphones.

d[11.21]b

> Bugs can synchronize, frogs can synchronize, even some species of crabs. But few other primates show much interest in dancing to a single beat . . . Versions of this model can explain the mechanism of the human heart, which takes about ten thousand oscillators. (David Rothenberg, *Bug Music*, p. 11)

Pulse, cycle, return. Entrainment: clapping human animals will stick to their beat or join the beat around them.

If rhythm is pitch is time is all of sound the whole physical universe nested vibrations then each monad a locus a centre of vibration an oscillator. Each system vibrates on its own clock, set the day the universe banged open, flinging clocks into space. Interpenetrating, overlapping, clocks clocking clocks. External timekeepers are inter-nal keepers, the inside rules without.

If you stopped your clock you would hear, in the brief moment of afterlife, a thousand clocks ticking inside your own head. Horns sombrely proclaim the end of the world, but it would be much more silent and perfunctory, no fireworks, just the second hand going dead. What advantage does it take to imagine life a vast insectoid chorus of synchronising clocks?

Ships rise above the desert, a dry place sits in memory: how much of that is just an oscillating memory cell, ready to be extinguished or manipulated? In times future we will have technologies to modify and sculpt these 'memories'. Total recall of the life we had wanted to leave, amidst the more chaotic system we ended up living. Noise is promise, the mechanism of the human head, or where it meets the heart.

d[11.22]b

The rubber stamp, 'listen', was the lecture and the walk was the demonstration, noises are the sounds we have learned to ignore, rooms within rooms that impinge their acoustic characteristics upon each other, surfaces thought of as acoustic lenses, home theatre systems buried in rooms built of concrete, a soundscape as simultaneously physical environment and a way of perceiving that environment, reverberation now become just another kind of noise, unnecessary and best eliminated, sensory overload only the beginning.

d[11.23]b

In the polyrhythmic swirls of the entomological soundscape, that was quickly an amphibian soundscape, that was presently an avian soundscape, that had always been a plant-based soundscape, how did the mute sliding, crawling, swinging creatures emerge? Amphibians have a rhythm to their undulations, and maybe primates swinging through branches, mammals loping, striding or running, express a rhythm.

Shaker buzz fills a hall, a night vision arcadian symphony, cascades fall out over lattice of dragonfly wing. Light cons a sun into refracting rainbows through filmic material that is secreted, without hindering the naked radiation. If wave works orchestrate battles, yes, that's easy, what about the sea, perhaps rhythm was sloshed gravitationally in the dance between moon and earth, a cosmic scale replicated microtonally in the insects' shaking song. What does electrification do to all of this, when we burn up the carboniferous to radiate our rock 'n' roll across the planet? It's a loss and it's gain. You can't shake a cicada at it. Eat one.

d[11.24]b

Vibrational Communication

Magicicada septendecim emerge synchronously and in tremendous numbers every seventeen years, to aggregate into chorus centres producing their distinctive 'Pharaoh' calls to attract mates. They sing by vibrating their tymbals, or cartilaginous clickers, into abdominal resonation chambers. (Some derivations trace the name to the Greek κικκοσ, 'membrane' plus αειδω, 'singer', so, literally, 'membrane singer'.) These abdominal Helmholtz resonators also generate energy that travels through cicada bodies to induce strong vibrations in the substrate, what we might call the 'seismic channel' (Bennet-Clark, p. 1682).

I would no longer listen to copy, but to return vibration – turning us towards what lies beneath our feet as well as what rises above our heads. 'Vibrational communication' in the substrate is effected by treehoppers, picked up by inserting a phonograph needle into a leaf stem in a Virginia field (Chadwick). Treehoppers communicate by literally vibrating the plant material on which they are perched: the moaning, churring, tapping, mewing sounds picked up by the scientists' probe are translations for human ears of the vibrations treehoppers feel through legs, thorax and abdomen (Hill, pp. 156–9).

This dual role of sound waves – to communicate but also to echo back and in so doing to sound the substrate, in the submarine sense of 'sounding' – has been exploited by the hydrocarbon industry to map the subsurface lay of its prospects. Integral to seismic prospecting is the percussive generation of controlled seismic energy sources: explosives, air guns, sparker, thumper trucks, seismic vibrator, boomer sources.

A poet in black holds a dying sunflower to the oil company's road sign, a poet travels by car across America sleeping in Walmart parking lots and speaking with the homeless, 70,000-plus kilometres of poetry are written in resistance to the oil company's pipeline and scrolled across our screens, a poet unfurls a core sample from Pablo Neruda's Great Ocean across the congressional representative's office floor, a poet sings her prairie dog translations to the coral reef scientist at the National Center for Atmospheric Research, a poet filling her tank moans at the gas pump, a poet's verse is unpacked in court for a description of how the barricade was constructed, defending the snake mound a poet sings of genocide to the Game Fish & Parks Department, a poet teaches children in Paradox Valley how to think climate change with metaphor, a poem is installed in a zoo facing *into* the gorilla enclosure, a poet fills a city hall with dead leaves, a poet translates the radial syntax of bark beetles, a poet writes an autobiography

of plastic cleaning the shoreline as she walks, a poet composes lines
with the words we throw out: 'It rises and falls through the repercussions of songs of birds' (Johnson).

d[11.25]b

You enter a realm of micro-perceptions, suspended in chemical solu-
tion, the imperceptible perceived, an overwhelming feeling of proximity,
crushing and caressing you at once, the percussive tones of compression waves as holes momentarily closed by waves, defying the natural acoustic mortality of silence, to reactivate the elements and release
the stratifications that problematise the aesthetics and politics of this
audiospatial sensorium, the passage from a kingdom of songbirds to
that of insects, experts in stridulating scratching and scraping.

d[11.26]b

Favourite listening situation must be in a canoe. A stance, against
the current. Being raised in a tradition of active, resistant silence, I
was encouraged to listen early on. Listening is political – especially
when focused with action. But the withholding of one's ear is already
a form of action. You must listen a lot longer than most anyone considers normal.

d[11.27]b

Countersong

With each dying
             person
    a piece of us all
          dies
                        With the construction
                          of mountains, the
                          collision of continents
With the ancient
    sea floors made of skeletons

                        With being driven
                   far inland, worn down and sculpted
                        by ice and wind

        With the decay
            of manufacturing
                        With rapid evolution of ruins
                          a shift . . .

The year 2015 was the greenest in the mountains of Northern New Mexico in well more than a decade, and with the moisture came an abundance of wildflowers, with the wildflowers insects, and with the insects more birds than I remember ever hearing sing in those mountains. I translated the countersong of two hermit thrushes, recorded at dusk just below treeline (Figure 11.3). If you listen closely, you will never note a repetition: 'Always they are either rising or falling to a new strain' (Thoreau, journal entry for 22 June 1851). By visualising the signals and slowing them to half-speed, one is able to discern some of the structure of the vocalisations: the opening keynote (up and down a nearly pentatonic scale) and the diversity and harmonic overlaps of the rising, fluty flourishes that follow each opening note. The Bartókian intricacies of these flourishes are barely visible even here: we are left gazing at the Grand Canyon from 30,000 feet.

The birds fit an astonishing number of notes into their short, vocal flourishes. The Hungarian musicologist and ornithologist Peter Szöke (in his 1969 paper, with W. W. H. Gunn and M. Filip) had to slow the hermit thrush song down thirty-two times to show how a single vocalization, less than 2 seconds in length, may contain 45–100 or more notes, along with 25–50 or more pitch changes, many of them sounded simultaneously (through the two pipes of the bird's syrinx). Szöke was so entranced he dubbed hermit thrush song a 'musical microcosm'.

Throughout the recording, one can hear the dry 'tsik' alarm call of what may be a dark-eyed junco, wondering what on earth I am up to.

Figure 11.3   Hermit thrushes

d[11.28]b

Sound spreads and leaks, like odour, the soft catastrophe of space, a form of detention or agglutination of place, rather than its dispersal into movement, the result of collisions, abrasions, impingements or minglings of objects, objects become events, the divinity of sourceless sounds, an ear prone to damage by an excess of stimulus, involuted, devious, sequestered, esoteric, the room between medium and code, sound and museum, not like a musician.

d[11.29]b

Water, geese, freight, motorcycle, cardinal.

d[11.30]b

'[T]he flowing structures that we can create with microsound do not necessarily resemble the usual angular forms of musical architecture. On the contrary, they tend toward droplike, liquid, or cloudlike structures.' (Curtis Roads, *Microsound*, p. 340)

d[11.31]b

Soundscapes
Cardinal Birds Dictionary
of Sounds Frogs Thrushes Child of
Tree Bobolinks Night Images Gregorian
Chant Coqui Storm Inaugurates Coqui Walks
Rainforest Bears Ravi Shankar Woodcocks Finches
Toads Towhees Four Sounds Common Ground Colony
Dome Open Secrets Ted Enslin Answering Machine Spring
Peepers Dogtown Drums Owls Culleymoss Great Lakes Cities
Olmsted Riverside Emerald Necklace Central Ice Cranes Frogs
Roberson Quiet Cricket Sounds Wolf Talk Bears Millay Occupy
Poetry Library Schism Reading Kyger Radio Drive Winter Solstice
Shifting Stations Sonic Geographies Ice Interviews Driving Sarasota
London Cycling Cornell Catbird Chicago Woodstock Modernist Echo
Reverberate Singing Pebbles Animal Renderings Dawn Chorus Sierras
Porcupines Reno DuBois Home Shack Field Hop Recording Research
Collective Preenactment Abbey Bolinas Iceland Before the Law Memo
Whispering Breakup Cardiff Spring Poetry Blackbird Cicadas Vicuña
Coppice Bard Bugs Polyphony Bells Albion Beatnik Klee Maggie
Symposium Jet Readings Gallery Allotment Hay Wain Concert
Thoronet House Extinctions Marathon Owls Semele Jays
Robins Lectures Galleries Detention Fantasies Church
Gigs Loops Bell Tone Garden Tour Activists Colo-
rado Hermit Thrush Mullen Constraint
Algonquin Translation Confluence
Oars the Maz Freight Yo
La Tengo Ears

d[11.32]b

Does a microphone know how to listen? Practitioners and theorists of field recording, as of compositions based on such recording, increasingly *emphasise the context*, including techniques and cultures of listening, that precede, inscribe, and follow acoustic technologies (Sterner, Thompson, Westerkamp).

How then does one write *about* field recording? If writing is to sound, I want it to sound more than acoustically, to return data on the dimensions of a relation, spatial or otherwise. A microphone is totally deaf, and that is why it hears so well.

d[11.33]b

> Brightness of shifts slides to radiance shuffle
> A raven rattles its coverts, embarked appointments
> Distant contact yelps a loon's nonexistent breakers
> A roar the broken sound envelope's at magnitude
> Voices or mosquitos in tangent the intangible bay
> Bright laps a lip curls infolding the shore in liquids
> High sigh a murmuring near far intemperate overhang
> Paddle on gunwhale hull chops a fumbling moment
> Echo of pebbled loud insuck shimmering in woods
> Peep a contact flecks and chips in flaky habitat
> A hum a distance over under bottom clipped tinnitus
> Infield shakes grasses feathering the sun-baked hill
> A sonic wash of intruding presence overcalls remember
> Direction's crackling ember pits loon to cricket's leg
> Inbreathed cavities outwheeze the beating fore
> Sparks of tingle the fractured shimmer's white noise
> White-crowned sparrows dislodged notes a loose relief
> Stiffer thickets meet a brisk incoming compass slight
> Detonation's offensive horizon apocalypse a note behind
> Monstrous sounds the bodies gas contracts eructs to clear
> Thimble falls a whorl to swirl the nuthatch crow and raven
> The flat earth at bottoming or clips reduce levels to ensphere
> Child's voice carries echoes of its future anterior
> A neck deep human shoots a howl into woods redundance
> Possibility zones answer sharply from earth to island

d[11.34]b

d[]b (SOUNDS)

1.1   'smallest and lightest named bone in the human body': Spring
       Peepers, 54s
       Marantz pocket recorder (unless otherwise indicated, subse-
       quent recordings were also made with this device), Bowdoinham,
       Maine, 2011

1.2   'a quiet secret human makes music': Colectivos, 1m26s
       Sony minidisc recorder and mic, La Paz, Bolivia, 2002

1.3   'what do the recordings sound?': Casino, 4m3s
       Reno, Nevada, 2012

1.4   'Threat, attack, defense': Bobolinks, 3m29s
       Bowdoinham, Maine, 2008

1.5   'A coqui frog pierces the fog of sound': Coqui frogs, 3m2s
       El Yunque, Puerto Rico (with Isabelle Pelissier), 2009

1.6   'spills his spaghetti / on the fire': Loon, 1m23s
       Sony minidisc recorder and mic, Algonquin Provincial Park,
       Ontario, 2000

1.7   'the ears of "Eternal Delight" / are perked': Deer, 33s
       Sony minidisc recorder and mic, Tifft Farm Nature Preserve, Buffalo,
       NY, 2000

1.8   'milks the grass cliffs': Cow, 1m2s
       Sony minidisc recorder and mic, Etretat, Normandy, 2000

1.9   'at/ all time-/ s': Escalator, 26s
       Sony minidisc recorder and mic, London, 2000

1.10   'Can we imagine a protest without "noise"?': Tide ice, 2m57s
       Bowdoinham, Maine, 2011

1.11   'the poem itself as a recording device': Warblers, 3m33s
       Ithaca, NY, 2012

1.12   'both connects to and separates from an environment': Moving
       walkway, 30s
       Sony minidisc recorder and mic, Chicago O'Hare airport, 2002

1.13   'Only by making ourselves small can we begin': Acapella sound-
       scape (edit), 4m54s
       Phippsburg, Maine (Bates College Soundscape workshop),
       2009

1.14   'To put oneself *into* the soundscape': High Sierras (Western mead-
       owlark), 49s
       Marantz field recorder and Sennheiser shotgun mic, Carman
       Valley, California, 2012

1.15   'Go crying towards the reedy shore': Sandhill cranes, 54s
       Wood River, Nebraska (Crane Trust), 2011

1.16   'One is embedded in, if not located *by*, the loon's call': Hermit
       thrushes, 1m45s
       Bowdoinham, Maine, 2008

11.17   'what is the negentropic resistance. And where?': Polyphony
1m21s
Malvern, England (Armonico Consort), 2012

11.18   'to pull on threads and follow "risky attachments"': Katy Payne
1m43s
Ithaca, NY, 2012

11.19   'the medium is often not the message': Hornsey train, 37s
Hornsey, North London, 2015

11.20   'echoing / ivory's market': European blackbird, 1m57s
Leamington Spa, England, 2013

11.21   'blocks of ice in the gallery, surrounded by microphones': Legacy
Wrestling, 4m1s
iPhone 4S, Leamington Spa, England, 2015

11.22   'the mechanism of the human head, or where it meets the heart'
Occupy, 3m30s
Zuccotti Park, Manhattan, 2011

11.23   'sensory overload only the beginning': Gargilesse angelus, 5m12
Gargilesse-Dampierre, France, 2015

11.24   'You can't shake a cicada at it. Eat one': Bug safari (edit), 10m
Annandale-on-Hudson, NY (Bard College), 2013

11.25   'It rises and falls through the repercussions of songs of birds'
Magicicadas, 32s
Annandale-on-Hudson, NY (Bard College), 2013

11.26   'experts in stridulating scratching and scraping': Radio tuning
1m21s
Berkshires, Massachusetts, 2011

11.27   'longer than most anyone considers normal': Canyon wrens
1m23s
Bandelier National Monument (NM), 2015

11.28   'wondering what on earth I am up to': Countersong, 3m6s
Pecos Wilderness (NM), 2015

11.29   'not like a musician': Pebbles, 3m39s
Olin Library Terrace, Cornell University (with Katherine Zelt
ner), 2012

11.30   'Water, geese, freight, motorcycle, cardinal': Train III Cardinal
4m14s
Sony minidisc recorder and mic, Tifft Farm Nature Preserve
Buffalo, NY, 2002

11.31   'liquid, or cloudlike structures': American Woodcock, 3m5s
Bowdoinham, Maine, 2011

11.32   'Yo / La Tengo': Towhee, 37s
Bowdoinham, Maine, 2009

11.33   'why it hears so well': Park ranger, 44s
Marantz pocket recorder, Waterton Park, Alberta (with wildlif
warden Rob Watt), 2011

11.34   'answer sharply from earth to island': Owl, 13s
Bowdoinham, Maine, 2010

Works Cited

Attali, Jacques, *Noise: The Political Economy of Music*, trans. Brian Massumi (Minneapolis: University of Minnesota Press, 1985).

Bartels, Alan J., 'Cranes in Nebraska: The most regal of birds has a long history in the Cornhusker State', *Prairie Fire* (March 2010), http://www.prairiefirenewspaper.com/2010/03/cranes-in-nebraska (last consulted, 15 October 2017)

Bennet-Clark, H. C., 'Tymbal Mechanics and the Control of Song Frequency in the Cicada Cyclochila Australasiae', *The Journal of Experimental Biology* 200 (1997), pp. 1681–94.

Chadwick, Alex, 'The Secret World of Insects', *Radio Expeditions*, NPR/National Geographic Society, 8 Nov. 1999, Radio.

Eisenberg, Cristina, 'Hegira: Voices on the Wind', *Platte Valley Review* (2010).

Feld, Steven, *Sound and Sentiment: Birds, Weeping, Poetics, and Song in Kaluli Expression* (Philadelphia: University of Pennsylvania Press, 1982).

Hill, Peggy S. M., *Vibrational Communication in Animals* (Cambridge, MA: Harvard University Press, 2008).

Hoff, Benjamin, ed., *The Singing Creek Where the Willows Grow: The Mystical Nature Diary of Opal Whiteley* (New York: Penguin, 1994).

Jensen, Pamela J., ed., *Legends of the Crane* (Denver: Sandstones Press, 2000).

Johnson, Ronald, 'Beam 20, Labyrinthus', *ARK* (Chicago: Flood Editions, 2013), p. 51.

Latour, Bruno, *Politics of Nature: How to Bring the Sciences into Democracy*, trans. Catherine Porter (Cambridge, MA: Harvard University Press, 2004).

Leopold, Aldo, *A Sand County Almanac: With Essays on Conservation* (New York: Oxford University Press, 2001).

Roads, Curtis, *Microsound* (Cambridge, MA: MIT Press, 2004).

Rothenberg, David, *Bug Music: How Insects Gave Us Rhythm and Noise* (New York: St. Martin's Press, 2013).

Schaeffer, Pierre, *In Search of a Concrete Music*, trans. Christine North and John Dack (Berkeley, University of California Press, 2012).

Skinner, Jonathan, *Directions for the Ear*, Elevator Box Project, ed. Michael Kelleher (Buffalo: Michael Kelleher, 2000).

—, *Animal Transcriptions: Listening to the Lab of Ornithology*, Sounding Out! Podcast #12, 21 March, 2013, https://soundstudiesblog.com/2013/03/21/skinner-podcast/

—, 'Countersong', *The Goose: A Journal of Arts, Environment, and Culture in Canada*. 14.1 (2015), http://scholars.wlu.ca/thegoose/vol14/iss1/26/

—, 'Blackbird Stanzas', 'Vibrational Communication: Ecopoetics in the Seismic Channel' in *Big Energy Poets: Ecopoetry Thinks Climate Change*, ed. Amy King and Heidi Lynn Staples (Buffalo: BlazeVOX, 2017).

—, *Warblers* (San Francisco: Albion Books, 2010), 3:2.

—, 'A Room for Opal, Room for Time: Listening with Julie Patton', *ON Contemporary Practice* 1 (2008), ed. Michael Cross, Thom Donovan and Kyle Schlesinger, http://on-contemporarypractice.squarespace.com/pdf-archive/

Snyder, Gary, 'Really the Real', *Danger on Peaks* (Washington, DC: Shoemaker Hoard, 2004), pp. 50-51.

Sterne, Jonathan, *The Audible Past: Cultural Origins of Sound Reproduction* (Durham, NC: Duke University Press, 2003).

Szöke, Peter, W. W. H. Gunn and M. Filip, 'The Musical Microcosm of the Hermit Thrush: From Athanasius Kircher's Naive Experiments of Musical Transcription of Bird Voice to Sound Microscopy and the Scientific Musical Representation of Bird Song', *Studia musicologica* XI (1969), pp. 423–48.

Thompson, Emily, *The Soundscapes of Modernity: Architectural Acoustics and the Culture of Listening in America, 1900-1933* (Cambridge, MA: MIT Press, 2002).

Thoreau, Henry David, *The Journal of Henry D. Thoreau*, Vols I–VI, ed. Bradford Torrey and Francis H. Allen (New York: Dover Publications, 1962).

Westerkamp, Hildegard. 'Speaking from Inside the Soundscape' in *The Book of Music and Nature*, ed. David Rothenberg and Marta Ulvaeus (Middletown, CT: Wesleyan University Press, 2001), pp. 143–52

Zukofsky, Louis, 'A'-12, *'A'* (Berkeley: University of California Press, 1978).

—, 'A Statement for Poetry', *Prepositions+: The Collected Critical Essays* (Hanover, NH: Wesleyan University Press, 2000), pp. 19–23.

Notes on Contributors

Stephen Benson is a senior lecturer in the School of Literature, Drama and Creative Writing at the University of East Anglia. He is the author of *Cycles of Influence: Fiction, Folktale, Theory* (Wayne State University Press, 2003) and *Literary Music* (Ashgate, 2006), and the co-editor of *Creative Criticism: An Anthology and Guide* (Edinburgh University Press, 2014). He has published a number of essays on the relation between literature and music.

Daniela Cascella is an Italian writer. She is the author of *Singed. Muted Voice-Transmissions, After the Fire* (Equus Press, 2017), *F.M.R.L. Footnotes, Mirages, Refrains and Leftovers of Writing Sound* (Zero Books, 2015), and *En Abîme: Listening, Reading, Writing. An Archival Fiction* (Zero Books, 2012). She edits Untranslated at *Minor Literature[s]* and has published in international magazines such as the *Los Angeles Review of Books*, *Music and Literature* and *Gorse*. She has taught at a number of institutions in Europe and as an Associate Lecturer on the MA Sound Arts at LCC / University of the Arts London.

Patrick Farmer is co-founder of the online curatorial platform, Compost and Height, co-editor of the new-music journal, *Wolf Notes*, and curator of the Sound I'm Particular lecture series and the Significant Landscapes festival. He has published four books and written compositions for groups such as Apartment House and the Set Ensemble. Festival appearances and residencies include Audiograft (Oxford), The Wulf (Los Angeles), LMC (London), Geiger (Gothenberg), Forestry Commission England (Cumbria) and MOKS (Estonia). His work has appeared on labels such as Another Timbre, nadukeenumono and Winds Measure.

Dominic Lash has studied literature, composition and film at the universities of Oxford, Oxford Brookes, Brunel and Bristol. Among his publications are articles on Derek Bailey in *Perspectives of New Music* and on V.F. Perkins in *Screen*. He is also a musician active in improvised, contemporary and experimental music.

Nicholas Melia is an archivist, musicologist and composer. His research interests include the history and politics of experimental music and sound art, and the interrelation of continental philosophy and art practice. He is currently cataloguing the archives of composers Trevor Wishart and Richard Orton at the Borthwick Institute for Archives, University of York.

Will Montgomery is a senior lecturer at Royal Holloway, University of London. He specialises in modernist and contemporary poetry, with a particular interest in sound. He is the author of a book on Susan Howe (Palgrave, 2010) and the co-editor of an essay collection on Frank O'Hara (Liverpool University Press, 2010). He makes electronic music and works with field recordings, and has released music on the Winds Measure, Cathnor, Entr'acte and nonvisualobjects labels.

Redell Olsen is a poet, performer and critic, and professor in the Department of English at Royal Holloway, University of London. Her publications include *Film Poems* (Les Figues, 2014), *Punk Faun: a Bar Rock Pastel* (subpress, 2012) and *Secure Portable Space* (Reality Street, 2004), along with critical essays on Susan Howe and Frank O'Hara. In 2017 she published two bookworks, *Smock* and *Mox Nox*. She is a former editor of *How2* and in 2013-14 was the Judith E. Wilson Lecturer in Poetry at the University of Cambridge.

Michael Pisaro is a composer and guitarist, a member of the Wandelweiser Composers Ensemble and Co-Chair of Music Composition at the California Institute of the Arts. He has composed over 80 works for a variety of instrumental combinations, with recordings appearing on labels such as Edition Wandelweiser Records, Compost and Height, Another Timbre and Cathnor, and extensively on his own label, Gravity Wave. His work is frequently performed in the U.S. and in Europe. Most of his music of the last several years is published by Edition Wandelweiser.

Lisa Robertson is a poet and essayist. Her publications include *3 Summers* (Coach House Books, 2016), *R's Boat* (University of

California Press, 2010), *The Men* (BookThug, 2006; Enitharmon, 2014), and *The Weather* (New Star Books, 2002), which Robertson wrote during her Judith E. Wilson fellowship at Cambridge University. Her prose works include *Occasional Works and Seven Walks from the Office for Soft Architecture* (Coach House Books, revised edition, 2010), and *Nilling* (BookThug, 2012). Robertson has been the subject of a special issue of *Chicago Review* (2006). In 2017 she was the inaugural recipient of the C.D. Wright Award for Poetry.

Jonathan Skinner is a poet and critic. He was founder and editor of *ecopoetics*, a journal which featured creative-critical intersections between writing and ecology. His work includes *Chip Calls* (Little Red Leaves, 2014), *Birds of Tifft* (BlazeVOX, 2011) and *Warblers* (Albion Books, 2010). He has published essays on Charles Olson, Ronald Johnson, Lorine Niedecker and Bernadette Mayer, and translations of French poetry and garden theory. He is currently associate professor in the Department of English and Comparative Literary Studies at the University of Warwick.

Carol Watts is a critic and poet. Her poetry collections include *Wrack* (2007) and *Occasionals* (2011), both published by Reality Street, and a number of chapbooks, including the *When Blue Light Falls* series (Oystercatcher Press, 2008, 2010, 2012) and *Mother Blake* (Equipage, 2012). While at Birkbeck, University of London, Carol ran the innovative Voiceworks project with colleagues at the Guildhall School of Music and Drama, bringing postgraduate writers together with composers and singers to produce songs annually performed at London's Wigmore Hall. She is currently professor and Head of the School of English at the University of Sussex.

Index

Several of the entries – field; field recording; listening; sound – refer to subjects that appear *passim*.